Chokepoints

T0329706

Chokepoints

Global Private Regulation
on the Internet

Natasha Tusikov

UNIVERSITY OF CALIFORNIA PRESS

University of California Press, one of the most
distinguished university presses in the United States,
enriches lives around the world by advancing scholarship
in the humanities, social sciences, and natural sciences.
Its activities are supported by the UC Press Foundation
and by philanthropic contributions from individuals
and institutions. For more information, visit
www.ucpress.edu.

University of California Press
Oakland, California

Library of Congress Cataloging-in-Publication Data

Names: Tusikov, Natasha, 1974- author.
Title: Chokepoints : global private regulation on the
    Internet / Natasha Tusikov.
Description: Oakland, California : University of
    California Press, [2016] | Includes bibliographical
    references and index.
Identifiers: LCCN 2016023978| ISBN 9780520291218
    (cloth : alk. paper) | ISBN 9780520291225 (pbk. : alk.
    paper)
Subjects: LCSH: Internet governance. | Intellectual
    property. | Privacy, Right of. | Data protection—Law
    and legislation. | Piracy (Copyright)—Prevention. |
    Internet—Censorship. | Internet service providers.
Classification: LCC TK5105.8854 .T877 2016 | DDC
    384.3/3—dc23
LC record available at https://lccn.loc.gov/2016023978

25   24   23   22   21   20   19   18   17   16
10   9   8   7   6   5   4   3   2   1

Contents

Tables

Preface

During my research for this book, in early June 2013, Internet surveillance made headlines globally. Edward Snowden, a security contractor for the prominent U.S. defense contractor Booz Allen Hamilton, leaked highly classified files that revealed global surveillance programs operated by the U.S. National Security Agency and its allies. The Snowden files, as they are known, reveal—among other things—how the NSA's surveillance programs tapped into the U.S. telecommunications network, including the operations of Verizon, Sprint, and AT&T, to track and record phone communications.

Several NSA programs, with the colorful code names of Prism and Muscular, focused on obtaining information from popular U.S.-based Internet companies, particularly Google, Microsoft, and Yahoo. The NSA and its allies, particularly the United Kingdom, targeted these companies because they collect vast amounts of data from everyone who uses their services. The NSA obtained information from these services through secret court orders served to Internet firms from a previously little-known U.S. court—the Foreign Intelligence Surveillance Court—and by covertly hacking into Internet firms' systems (Greenwald 2014). Media coverage of the Snowden files sparked heated public debates around the world regarding government and corporate surveillance and the nature and limits of digital privacy.

NSA-style total surveillance is becoming ubiquitous in the modern world, and not just in national-security circles. "Surveillance is the business model of the Internet," argues leading security analyst Bruce Schneier (Schneier 2013). Former U.S. vice president Al Gore critiqued the intensity of online surveillance in 2013, characterizing the Internet as a "stalker economy where customers become products" (Levine 2014). Given Gore's past extensive involvement in Internet policy making and his vocal support for Internet issues, his criticism is potent.

Internet companies like Google, Microsoft, and Yahoo, along with Facebook and Twitter, provide services that are premised upon the collection and sharing of personal information and upon their users cultivating ever-expanding social and professional networks. These firms provide free search, email, chat and messaging, and social networking services in exchange for amassing, tracking, and monetizing users' data. These troves of personal information are valuable not only to advertisers but also to state security agencies. By siphoning information from these firms, security agencies can track users' digital footprints, including website browsing history, their personal social networks, and location data, as well as the actual content of emails, video calls, and text messages.

The Snowden files expose enmeshed, interdependent relationships between major U.S.-based Internet firms and the U.S. government. Some scholars term this dynamic an "information-industrial complex" (Powers and Jablonski 2015, 47). Internet firms with large, global operations, such as Google, PayPal, eBay, and Yahoo, have developed a considerable capacity to make and enforce rules for their services that can affect hundreds of millions of their users worldwide. The information-industrial complex is partly characterized by mutual interests in extending policies and standards that preference U.S. economic interests and further the country's national security programs over the Internet through U.S. companies' provision of information and communications technologies (Powers and Jablonski 2015). The U.S. government is interested in expanding its surveillance apparatus at the global level to maintain U.S. economic and military hegemony. In turn, large U.S. Internet companies like Google and Microsoft are interested in allying themselves with the U.S. government to further expand and entrench their businesses practices globally.

This book focuses on a parallel but largely unknown dimension of the information-industrial complex. It traces a series of secretly negotiated, handshake deals among small groups of elite corporate actors and government officials in the United States and Europe to counter, not terrorism, but the illicit online trade in counterfeit goods, from clothing and electronics to pharmaceuticals. Although the targets of the surveillance programs revealed by the Snowden files and these anticounterfeiting agreements obviously differ, the programs share several important commonalities in terms of actors involved and, most importantly, the methods they undertake to achieve their objectives. Several of the central actors discussed in the Snowden files—Google, Microsoft, Yahoo, the U.S. government, and the U.K. government—are also key figures in the anticounterfeiting agreements. States and, increasingly, powerful corporations are turning to Internet companies that provide essential services to monitor online behavior and global flows of information. By regulating Google, the idea goes, one "can regulate the Internet" (Kohl 2013, 233). The agreements primarily benefit prominent, multinational intellectual-property owners like Nike, the pharmaceutical firm Pfizer, and the consumer care company Proctor & Gamble.

State-endorsed corporate mass surveillance on the Internet is a principal element of the anticounterfeiting agreements. As part of their duties under the informal agreements, Internet companies monitor how people use and interact with payment and advertising platforms, search engines, and marketplaces, in order to detect suspicious activities. These companies control and block flows of information and also disable websites selling counterfeit goods by withdrawing important commercial and technical services. The impetus for Internet companies' expansive efforts as gatekeepers is coercive pressure from the U.S. and U.K. governments, which is fundamentally changing the companies' regulatory responsibilities and the ways they identify and target problematic behavior.

Consequently, these anticounterfeiting processes, agreements, and methods are important not only in and of themselves but also for what they reveal about the nature of the emerging surveillance society and surveillance state. Who regulates the Internet, and how, are vitally important questions given its centrality to economic, social, and political life. Major Internet firms play principal roles in regulating flows of information on the Internet. They have considerable authority to decide what information people can access, use, and share, what items they can purchase and how, and the personal information users must divulge to Internet firms. Further, these companies also have significant discretion to determine the legality of certain types of content, such as the kinds of images that constitute child pornography or copyright infringement. These regulatory practices, however, have the potential to create surveillance dragnets that target and track millions of law-abiding

Internet users. And, since Internet firms' enforcement occurs outside of legislation or court orders, the firms are essentially unaccountable, and their efforts are largely opaque and prone to error.

My aim in this book is not to analyze the illicit market in counterfeit goods, or to evaluate the effectiveness of corporate regulatory strategies against the online trade in counterfeit goods. Rather, it is to critically trace the creation and operation of a transnational private surveillance and enforcement program that operates largely outside of legislation to control the online market in counterfeit goods. In doing so, the book provides the first scholarly analysis of the little-known enforcement agreements quietly negotiated among small groups of industry and state actors to address the distribution of counterfeit goods on the Internet.

More broadly, the book explores the complex, shifting dynamics between corporate actors and states in relation to setting rules online to control information flows and monitor users' behavior. It asks: What can the anticounterfeiting agreements tell us in general about how corporate and state actors can set and enforce rules and standards on the Internet? In what ways can informal rules govern the way we access and use services, technologies, and applications on the Internet, and in what ways can these rules control global flows of information? Further, what are the consequences for how we understand and use the Internet? In answering these questions, the book argues that powerful states, particularly the United States, play a direct, often coercive role in shaping corporate regulatory efforts on the Internet to serve their strategic interests.

Acknowledgments

I benefited from the generosity and insight of many while working on this project. Thanks must first go to Peter Drahos, Peter Grabosky, and Kathryn Henne at the Australian Nation University for their thoughtful, critical questions and for encouraging me to look at the big picture. Ian Brown at the Oxford Internet Institute at the University of Oxford and James Sheptycki at York University generously gave detailed feedback that strengthened the book's analysis and conclusions. Thanks to the anonymous reviewer of this book, and to Roger Brownsword and an anonymous reviewer who evaluated the manuscript proposal, for their useful critiques that strengthened the book. My sincere gratitude goes to Susan Sell for her generous review of the book. I also thank Sara Bannerman, Mamoun Alazab, and Erin Tolley for their valuable critiques and encouraging words during the final manuscript preparation.

The collegial intellectual environment at the RegNet School of Regulation and Global Governance at the Australian National University was an 'ideal environment in which to undertake the research that became that basis of this book. I enjoyed discussing regulatory theory during RegNet's lovely teas, seminars, and writing groups with John Braithwaite, Val Braithwaite, Kyla Tienhaara, Cynthia Banham, Benjamin Authers, Emma Larking, Russell Brewer, Robyn Holder, Cheryl White, Budi Hernawan, Lennon Chang, Christian Downie, Sekti Widihartanto, and Jeroen van der Heijden. This book is better because of all you.

xiv | Acknowledgments

Thanks to those at the Center for Criminology at the University of Oxford, particularly Ian Loader, for hosting me as a visiting scholar. I spent many wonderful hours in the beautiful Bodleian Library and Radcliffe Camera. The Baldy Center of Law and Social Policy at the State University of New York (SUNY) in Buffalo provided an ideal space in which to finish this book. Thanks to Errol Meidinger at the Baldy Center and members of the SUNY Buffalo Law School for offering constructive feedback on my ideas. Earlier versions of these chapters profited from presentations at McMaster University and Brock University, as well as from conference papers delivered to the International Studies Association and Law and Society Association conferences in Honolulu, Seattle, and New Orleans, as well as the American Society of Criminology conference in Washington, D.C.

Thanks to all the people I interviewed who took the time to share their knowledge and experience with me. I deeply appreciate the kindness you showed me in explaining the fast-moving world of intellectual property regulation on the Internet. I am very appreciative of Maura Roessner and Jack Young at the University of California Press, who ably shepherded me through the publishing process.

To my uncles—Vit and Valdi—for providing a beachside retreat in Mollymook with wine and oysters on the stunning New South Wales coast, my sincere gratitude. Thanks to my parents, Peter and Barbara Tusikov, and my sister, Katrina, for patiently listening to discussions of transnational private regulation and counterfeit goods. I transcribed many of the interviews in the lovely B.C. Okanagan Valley and afterward sampled the local wineries. I also thank Bailey and Charles Murray, lifelong friends, and new friends Tira and Sigmund. Finally, and most importantly, my deep thanks to my partner, Blayne Haggart, for all your support. Your encouragement helped me through the roadblocks and made this book better.

Abbreviations

ACTN	Advisory Committee for Trade Negotiations
ANA	Association of National Advertisers
AOL	America Online (previously known as)
API	application programing interface
BP	British Petroleum
BPI	British Phonographic Industry (or British Recorded Music Industry)
BSA	Business Software Alliance
COICA	Combating Online Infringement and Counterfeits Act
CSIP	Center for Safe Internet Pharmacies
DCMS	Department for Culture, Media and Sport
DMCA	Digital Millennium Copyright Act
DNS	Domain name system
DTSG	Digital Trading Standards Group
EFF	Electronic Frontier Foundation
EU	European Union
FACT	Federation Against Copyright Theft
FCACP	Financial Coalition Against Child Pornography

GATT	General Agreement on Tariffs and Trade
IAB	Interactive Advertising Bureau (U.S.)
IAB	Internet Advertising Bureau (U.K.)
IACC	International Anti-Counterfeiting Coalition
IASH	Internet Advertising Sales House
ICANN	Internet Corporation for Assigned Names and Numbers
INTA	International Trademark Association
IP address	Internet protocol address
IPC	Intellectual Property Committee
IPEC	(Office of the U.S.) Intellectual Property Enforcement Coordinator
IWF	Internet Watch Foundation
LVMH	Louis Vuitton Moët Hennessy
MPA	Motion Picture Association
MPAA	Motion Picture Association of America
NIPRC Center	National Intellectual Property Rights Coordination Center
NSA	National Security Agency
OECD	Organization for Economic Cooperation and Development
OPEN Act	Online Protection and Enforcement of Digital Trade Act
PIPA	Preventing Real Online Threats to Economic Creativity and Theft of Intellectual Property Act, or Protect Intellectual Property Act
PIPCU	Police Intellectual Property Crime Unit
RIAA	Recording Industry Association of America
SOPA	Stop Online Piracy Act
TPP	Trans-Pacific Partnership Agreement
TRIPS	Agreement on Trade-Related Aspects of Intellectual Property Rights
U.K.	United Kingdom
URL	Uniform Resource Locator
U.S.	United States

USTR	Office of the United States Trade Representative
VeRO	Verified Rights Owner Program (eBay)
VPN	virtual private network
WIPO	World Intellectual Property Organization
WTO	World Trade Organization

Secret Handshake Deals

January 18, 2012, has become famous in certain circles as the date of the "Internet blackout," the climax of the world's largest, most dramatic, and—arguably—most effective online protest to date. On January 18, web giants including Google, Wikipedia, Reddit, Tumblr, and Mozilla blacked out some or all of their web pages, as did thousands of smaller websites.

Over the course of several months leading up to that date, a transnational coalition of academics, technologists, civil-society activists, Internet users, and Internet companies came together to oppose Internet censorship and Draconian rules that they said would impede the functioning of the Internet. The protest focused on two intellectual property bills in the United States: the Stop Online Piracy Act (SOPA) in the U.S. House of Representatives and its sister bill in the U.S. Senate, the Preventing Real Online Threats to Economic Creativity and Theft of Intellectual Property Act, or Protect Intellectual Property Act (PIPA). These bills targeted websites (or "sites") globally accused of violating U.S. intellectual property laws, which govern the production and use of creative works like movies and music, as well as the commercial manufacture of goods. Such sites offer unauthorized downloads of copyrighted content, particularly movies music, games, or software, or sell counterfeit goods, which are unauthorized reproductions of trademarked products like those bearing the famous Nike "swoosh."

Protesters had reason to be concerned. SOPA and PIPA would have fundamentally altered online efforts to enforce intellectual property rights. The bills proposed requiring Internet intermediaries, which provide or facilitate Internet services, to police intellectual property rights. These intermediaries would be required to act as regulators with the goal of preventing the distribution of counterfeit or copyright-infringing goods on their platforms. Under the proposed bills, rights holders of intellectual property, like the sporting goods firm Nike, could seek court orders to require online payment providers, such as PayPal and Visa, and digital advertising firms like Google and Yahoo, to target sites distributing copyright-infringing content or counterfeit goods. These Internet firms would have been required to withdraw their services from targeted sites for the purpose of disrupting the sites' operations.

Critics of the bills argued—and not without reason—that they would extend punitive U.S.-style enforcement strategies globally. Under the bills, U.S.-based rights holders could have singled out sites worldwide that they claimed violated their intellectual property rights. Censorship was also a central concern. The bills could have endangered free expression on the Internet if actors inadvertently—or, more worryingly, deliberately—targeted legally operating sites and stifled legitimate speech. Moreover, critics claimed the bills could potentially damage Internet infrastructure through the types of technical enforcement measures proposed. SOPA and PIPA were explicitly designed to favor rights holders, particularly large institutional copyright owners in the movie and music industries, and multinational companies like Nike and Pfizer, at the expense of Internet firms that provide essential online services. Largely absent from SOPA and PIPA was any consideration of Internet users who rely upon the Internet to participate fully in economic, social, and cultural life. In articulating their concerns, SOPA protesters tapped into wider societal anxiety over state and corporate actors' power to determine what kinds of content we can access, share, and use, what we can buy and where, and how we can use Internet services, technologies, and platforms.

Until the Internet blackout, intellectual property was not thought of as a subject that triggered widespread public protests or generated heated debate in the mainstream media. In fact, it was generally considered to be an arcane, commercial matter of interest only to large corporations and lawyers (Haggart 2014). The groundbreaking protest against SOPA and PIPA changed that and transformed intellectual property into a topic of popular conversation. At the zenith of the protest, on January 18, over a hundred thousand web pages went dark in protest and 10 million people signed petitions against the bills. So many people attempted to contact their elected representatives in the United States that the surge in traffic temporarily took down some U.S. senators' web pages (McCullagh 2012). Representative Darrell Issa, a Republican from California and a staunch opponent of the bills, described the protest as an "Internet mutiny" (Franzen 2012). Faced with an unprecedented public outcry over intellectual property bills, the U.S. Congress backed down and withdrew the bills on January 20, 2012. The protest was the first major political defeat for U.S. intellectual property proponents in over thirty years, a monumental achievement of Internet activism, particularly given the strong bipartisan support for the issue in the United States (Sell 2013). Opponents celebrated as the anti-Internet policies appeared dead, at least until the next attempt at legislation.

FROM CONTROVERSIAL BILLS TO HANDSHAKE DEALS

The anti-SOPA uprising and surprising defeat of SOPA and PIPA have been widely reported in academic and mainstream sources. Without doubt they will be the subjects of important studies of online activism and transnational social movements for years to come. What is less well known, however, is that the Internet blackout failed to kill the provisions contained with SOPA and PIPA. While protesters were campaigning against these bills, a small group of U.S. policy makers, rights holders supportive of SOPA and PIPA, and their trade associations were active behind the scenes. In closed-door meetings, they quietly drafted a series of informal, non-legally binding handshake agreements with Internet firms and online payment providers that incorporate some of SOPA's toughest and most controversial provisions, which were opposed by tens of millions of people in the United States and around the world.

The United States is not alone in creating non-legally binding agreements to regulate intellectual property on the Internet. The United States and the United Kingdom are the epicenters of these nonbinding agreements, as each has multiple agreements. Officials from the European Commission also crafted their own agreement. As happened in the United States, small groups of multinational corporations and officials from the U.K. government and European Commission conducted negotiations outside democratic, legislative processes, between 2010 and 2013.

Government policy makers describe these nonbinding agreements as "voluntary, industry-led initiatives" (Espinel 2013). Industry participants refer to them as "best practices." As these "best practices" are identified and determined by industry, however, they do not represent objectively evaluated measures. Negotiations occurred in closed-door meetings with little participation from consumer or civil-society groups, despite the fact that the agreements broadly affect how people can use popular—and indeed, essential—Internet services. Signatories are major U.S.-based Internet companies and payment providers with global operations: PayPal, Visa, and MasterCard, along with Google, Yahoo, Microsoft, and eBay.

One of the agreements' key targets is websites and marketplaces aimed at consumers in the United States and Europe but located elsewhere, especially China. For rights holders, China is of particular concern because it is the primary manufacturer of counterfeit goods that are exported to North America and Europe. Rights holders are also concerned with counterfeit goods sold through the China-based Taobao marketplace, which is the equivalent to eBay in China. U.S. and European rights holders not only want to combat the manufacture of counterfeit goods in China, but they also want to expand sales of legitimate versions of their brands in China's burgeoning e-shopping environment, particularly through key venues like Taobao.

At their core, the informal agreements are intended to push large Internet intermediaries to go beyond what they are required to do by law in the protection of intellectual property rights. Advocates of this position, including the European Commission, approvingly refer to it as a "beyond-compliance" regulatory strategy (European Commission 2013, 5–6).

The puzzle at the heart of this book is why powerful, globally dominant Internet firms and payment providers adopted non-legally binding agreements to police the online market in copyright-infringing and counterfeit goods on behalf of rights holders. At first glance, this type of regulation does not appear to be in intermediaries' material interests. Further, why did these intermediaries agree voluntarily to go beyond what they are required to do by law? The answer is governmental pressure. Despite government officials' use of the terms *voluntary* and *industry-led initiatives,* the agreements are neither voluntary nor wholly private. State actors—the U.S. and U.K. governments, along with the European Commission[1]—threatened the intermediaries with legislation and legal action to compel the companies to adopt non-legally binding enforcement measures. These state actors did so in response to lobbying from prominent rights holders keen to expand the online enforcement of their intellectual property rights.

State pressure was necessary to encourage—and compel—intermediaries to exceed their legal responsibilities. This is because, while the intermediaries did not entirely oppose increased enforcement of intellectual property rights, they did not consider this problem to be primarily their responsibility. In addition, the intermediaries largely resisted rights holders' efforts to revamp their enforcement efforts. Intermediaries' adoption of the nonbinding agreements lessened their risk of being subject to legislation or legal action. However, intermediaries also had another motivation. State actors and intermediaries have some overlapping interests in exerting greater control on the Internet. Intermediaries want not only to expand their markets but also to influence state standard-setting in relation to issues important to them, such as data collection and storage policies and rules regarding privacy of users' personal information.

More broadly, this book explores the growing practice of states designating powerful corporate actors as global regulators to set and enforce rules on the Internet. This regulation increasingly occurs in the absence of any meaningful public or judicial oversight, through non-legally binding arrangements. Such practices raise critical questions of fairness, due process, legitimacy, and the degree to which relying upon private-sector actors to deliver public-policy objectives is good for democracy. Core questions guiding my argument in this book are: what effects may informal corporate regulation have on how we access and use Internet services, applications, and technologies; and what are the associated problems?

New Global Regulators

A valuable and intriguing lens through which to examine the growing practice of informal regulatory practices carried out by corporate actors on the Internet is the regulation of intellectual property. *Regulation* in this context refers to the practice of nonstate organizations, including private companies and nongovernmental associations, setting and enforcing rules, standards, and policies that guide the provision of important Internet services, such as search or payment processing. The online regulation of intellectual property is an important case study because it is a key area of Internet governance, since it involves setting rules that govern the global flow of information and goods.

In terms of intellectual property, the two main areas I study are copyright law and trademark law. Copyright law lays out rules that determine how knowledge, and creative and artistic works like music, films, and books can be accessed, used, and shared, by whom, and with what technologies. Trademark law determines the entities that can lawfully manufacture, distribute, advertise, and sell trademarked products. Counterfeit goods are a form of trademark infringement. On the Internet, regulating trademarks entails making rules that determine how and on what platforms goods are sold, by whom, and in what ways, and how goods can be advertised. Rules governing intellectual property fundamentally affect what content people can access, and how they can access this content and exchange goods and services online.

Responsibility for policing those rules is increasingly falling upon Internet intermediaries that act, sometimes reluctantly, as gatekeepers on behalf of rights holders. Intermediaries are typically for-profit entities that provide important commercial and technical services that enable the effective functioning of the Internet. Some intermediaries, such as search engines or web hosts, facilitate access to or the hosting of information on the Internet. Others, such as social media platforms like Facebook and Twitter, or payment providers like PayPal, enable transactions or interactions among Internet users. Internet intermediaries vary widely in size, scope, and market share. Some intermediaries provide services across multiple sectors. Google, Yahoo, and Microsoft, for example, all operate search engines and digital advertising platforms. Certain intermediaries, such as Visa, MasterCard, and PayPal, can be used in both real-world and online environments. Other intermediaries, like domain registrars, exist solely online.

Large intermediaries like Google, eBay, and PayPal can be thought of as "macrointermediaries" owing to their global platforms, significant market share, and sophisticated enforcement capacities that protect their systems and users from wrongdoing like fraud or spam.[2] Macrointermediaries can set rules that govern hundreds of millions of people who use their services. They are in a powerful position to shape the provision of essential Internet services, such as search and payment processing, by virtue of their ability to monitor their platforms, remove unwanted content, and block suspicious transactions and behavior. Given their regulatory capacity, cooperative macrointermediaries can allow rights holders to police mass populations globally in ways that were previously unattainable, technologically unfeasible, or prohibitively expensive.

Why do rights holders want to work with macrointermediaries? These Internet firms act as chokepoints with the capacity to exert significant control over the access to and use of essential online sectors, including payment, advertising, search, marketplaces, and domain name services that enable users to access websites. People commonly—but mistakenly—understand the Internet to be a relatively ungoverned space, a "Wild West" of loosely connected networks that extend globally. Contributing to this perception are frequent claims by various governments and law enforcement agencies that they struggle to enforce laws on the Internet and are relatively powerless to reach outside their legal jurisdictions to target bad actors. Despite this Wild West stereotype, in many ways the Internet is a highly controlled environment. By withdrawing their services, macrointermediaries can disable sites' capacity to process payments, thereby "choking" sites' revenue streams. These intermediaries can also impede users' ability to locate and access counterfeit goods by controlling search and domain services and restricting the operation of marketplaces, thus creating access barriers. In essence, intermediaries use revenue and access chokepoints to deter unwanted behavior and target inappropriate content.

Given macrointermediaries' market dominance and global reach, they have a significant capacity to set rules governing hundreds of millions of people and determining how global flows of information are handled. Further, as these macrointermediaries police and sanction their users, remove certain types of content from their platforms, or withdraw their services from particular sites, they are shaping public policies in areas as diverse as privacy, data collection and retention, intermediary liability, intellectual property rights, and freedom of expression. As a result, through their roles as regulators, intermediaries are becoming de facto policy makers on an array of complex social issues, including obscenity, intellectual property rights, promotion of terrorism, and child pornography (DeNardis 2014). Internet firms' work as regulators or policy makers, however, may not be readily apparent to or fully understood by the general public. Internet users may not realize how intermediaries have changed rules relating to their services until users are unable to access certain information or use particular features. Intermediaries' global reach and sophisticated enforcement practices make them a valuable enforcement partner for rights holders and for states, as the Snowden files show in regard to the NSA's surveillance programs that siphon information from Google, Yahoo, and Microsoft.

Uncovering the Informal Agreements

This book is the first to map the creation and operation of nonbinding enforcement agreements as they pertain to the online control of counterfeit goods. Informal agreements provide an ideal regulatory solution for actors who favor increased protection for intellectual property rights online. As is discussed in chapter 2, non-legally binding measures enforced by intermediaries enable rights holders and government officials to sidestep failed bills in the United States, stalled legislation in the United Kingdom, and a series of lawsuits between intermediaries and rights holders in the United States and Europe. Away from the public eye, small groups of government and corporate actors had the freedom to negotiate enforcement measures that significantly expanded intermediaries' responsibilities for policing the online trade in counterfeit and copyright-infringing goods. The goal of the nonbinding agreements is compliance-plus enforcement, in which intermediaries exceed their legal responsibilities and undertake regulatory duties in the absence of legislation or court orders.

In this book I discuss eight informal agreements struck among Internet firms, government officials, and rights holders and their trade associations in the United States and the European Union. The agreements lay out broadly worded general principles to guide Internet firms' regulation of websites that distribute counterfeit goods and copyright-infringing content. Within these agreements, intermediaries participate from five Internet sectors: payment providers (e.g., PayPal); search and advertising intermediaries (e.g., Google); marketplaces (e.g., eBay); and domain name registrars (e.g., GoDaddy), which register domain names, the unique names given to sites, such as www.wikipedia.org. Each of these intermediaries acts as a revenue or access chokepoint, which is why rights holders pushed them to adopt the informal agreements. By partnering with the intermediaries, rights holders are able to strengthen their online enforcement of their intellectual property rights.

REGULATING INTELLECTUAL PROPERTY

My goal in this book is to illuminate often-opaque interdependencies between corporate-state regulatory practices on the Internet and the little-known practice of governing through chokepoints. Consequently, it is vital to appraise how these corporate-state regulatory efforts may affect the way we use Internet services and technologies and, more broadly, the online environment as a whole. To understand why prominent industry actors and government officials are devoting significant attention to the illicit trade in counterfeit goods and copyright-infringing content, it is important to first appreciate what intellectual property rights are, as well as why certain companies and governments are keen to strengthen the online protection of copyrights and trademarks.

Intellectual property is an issue of significant economic and political importance. In the modern globalized economy, ownership of intellectual property rights is central to economic dominance. Economic benefits from intellectual property primarily flow to those who own these rights. Individuals and corporations in industrialized countries, particularly the United States but also countries in Europe, own the greatest proportion of intellectual property rights.[3] In the case of trademarks, this means that rights holders in the United States and Europe receive considerable revenue from the manufacture of products, even though the production of those goods increasingly takes place in lower-cost countries, particularly China (Dedrick, Kraemer, and Linden 2009). For example, a 2011 study of Apple's production of iPads reveals that manufacturers in China receive approximately ten dollars per iPad in direct labor wages, which amounts to 1.8 percent of the value of the iPad (Kraemer, Linden, and Dedrick 2011, 4).[4] Apple, in contrast, captures 58 percent of the value from the iPad because it owns the trademarks and patents (the latter refers to industrial methods or processes) involved in the manufacture and also keeps product design, software development, and product management in the United States (Kraemer, Linden, and Dedrick 2011, 2). Analyses of the value generated by intellectual property show that revenue disproportionately flows to the rights holders, and, by extension, to the rights holders' home countries. In the case of Apple's iPads, China receives only a sliver of the iPad's value for its manufacturing role, while the United States benefits from Apple's retention of high-value services in the United States.

This is why countries that benefit from strong intellectual property rights regimes, particularly the United States, aggressively seek ever-increasing standards of protection. The U.S. government, globally the strongest proponent of greater protection for intellectual property rights, uses bilateral and multilateral trade agreements to pursue its preferred policies on intellectual property worldwide (Drahos and Braithwaite 2002). Intellectual property is a core feature of international agreements like the Trans-Pacific Partnership Agreement (TPP). Negotiations for the TPP began in 2005 among multiple countries, including the United

States, Australia, Canada, Japan, and Malaysia, and concluded in 2015. The TPP has incited protests and heated debate in many countries because, among its provisions, it would institute strengthened enforcement provisions to protect intellectual property in ways that critics charge would grant too much power to corporations (Flynn et al. 2012).

As the next chapter discusses, the economic and political importance that the U.S. government and the European Union accord to the protection of intellectual property is the result of policy decisions dating back to the 1970s. At that time, prominent rights holders and their trade associations persuaded the U.S. government and other governments to adopt rules to protect intellectual property that would disproportionately favor both U.S. industries and rights holders in a handful of other industrialized countries (Sell 2003). The influence of prominent U.S. and European rights holders and their trade associations continues today. They lobby countries worldwide to toughen laws protecting intellectual property and increase enforcement against the infringement of intellectual property rights. They also pressure companies that they contend are involved in or facilitate infringement to adopt suitably tough (i.e., U.S.-style) enforcement policies and processes. Private enforcement agreements that target the online trade in counterfeit goods are the latest incarnation of efforts to ramp up enforcement activities.

Purpose of Trademarks

We all encounter hundreds of trademarks in the course of daily life, even if we do not consciously recognize them as such. Trademarks are the logos and symbols that adorn our clothing, vehicles, food, and beverages, and the signs on stores and restaurants. Trademarks can consist of words, letters, numerals, drawings, symbols, colors, audible sounds, fragrances, three-dimensional shapes, logos, pictures, or a combination of these or other characteristics (Ricketson 1994). Well-known trademarks are McDonald's golden arches, Nike's swoosh, and Toblerone's distinctive triangle-shaped chocolate bars.

Trademarks serve, or are supposed to serve, a dual purpose. First, they are intended to enable individuals or companies who develop and cultivate trademarks to protect their marks from misappropriation by others. Second, for consumers, trademarks are supposed to serve a public good, designed to assist consumers in identifying the commercial origin of goods (e.g., Apple). They are also intended to prevent the likelihood of confusion among consumers by enabling individuals to differentiate among similar offerings in the marketplace (Ricketson 1994). Trademarks allow someone to distinguish Apple's iPhones from Samsung's Galaxy phones, or lesser-known brands' phones that may otherwise closely resemble these popular trademarked products. Consumers thus rely upon trademarks for information about products and as indicators of a product's quality or consistency. Trademarks promise, but do not legally guarantee, reliability or adherence to certain standards.

Trademarks owners typically register their trademarks with national intellectual property agencies, such as the U.S. Patent and Trademark Office, although registration of trademarks is not required in all jurisdictions. Internationally, trademark registration occurs through the Madrid System at the World Intellectual Property Organization (WIPO) in Geneva, Switzerland. WIPO, as an organization of the United Nations, is responsible for the administration of various international treaties pertaining to intellectual property.

The 1994 Agreement on Trade-Related Aspects of Intellectual Property (TRIPS), discussed in chapter 2, sets worldwide standards for the protection of trademarks. According to TRIPS, the owner of a registered trademark has the exclusive right to use that mark and prevent all others from using "identical or similar signs for goods or services which are identical or similar to those in respect of which the trademark is registered where such use would result in a likelihood of confusion" (art. 16.1). Limited exceptions to this exclusive right are permitted, such as the use of a competitor's trademark for comparison in advertising. Counterfeit goods are unauthorized reproductions of products or packaging that infringe a rights holder's registered trademark. TRIPS, which provides the main global framework for domestic trademark legislation, defines counterfeit goods as "any goods, including packaging, bearing without authorization a trademark which is identical to the trademark validly registered in respect of such goods, or which cannot be distinguished in its essential aspects from such a trademark, and which thereby infringes the rights of the owner of the trademark in question under the law of the country of importation" (art. 51[a]).

Billion-Dollar Trademarks

Developing and protecting trademarks is a serious, multibillion-dollar business. This is because trademarks have no expiry date and can be renewed indefinitely, as long as they are in use. Therefore, unlike copyrights and patents, which have limited terms of protection, trademarks can provide a potentially unending source of revenue. That trademarks can hold significant value explains rights holders' efforts to protect them from unauthorized use.

Trademarks are often considered synonymous with brands. Brands, however, are better understood as "the soul of a product" (Rothacher 2004, 2), embodied within a specific trademark. Marketers strategically shape trademarks into brands to cultivate value in the trademarks. Consumers may imbue brands with certain personality characteristics, whether real or perceived (de Chernatony, MacDonald, and Wallace 2011). When people see the distinctive Apple logo (Apple's trademark), for example, they may think of cutting-edge design with reliable operating systems (its brand). Consumers use brands to convey aspects of their personal identities to others, such as creativity or rebellion, or to signal their status through the consumption of luxury products. Purchasing a premium watch from the high-end Swiss company Blancpain, for instance, may imbue the wearer with a sense of urbane distinction because each watch is individually handcrafted.

Based upon the characteristics and sentiments attached to brands, certain brands can accumulate significant value. The brand-valuation firm Interbrand, for example, estimates Nike's brand at $23 billion, whereas the brand of France-based Louis Vuitton is valued at $22 billion and that of Germany-based Adidas is worth an estimated $7 billion (Interbrand 2015). Large Internet firms also possess lucrative brands. Google's brand is worth an estimated $120 billion, which is in second place among the top one hundred brands, just behind Apple at $170 billion (Interbrand 2015). Brands are intangible assets, so these figures are only estimates. The value ascribed to brands shifts over the years and also rises and falls with firms' fortunes and scandals. There are also variances among brand-valuation companies in their appraisals of brands. Nonetheless, these large figures indicate the importance of corporate brands and show that firms have considerable economic interest in protecting their trademarks.

The challenge for rights holders is that brand attachment is an intensely subjective process. Consumers develop strong preferences for one brand over another, even when there are few differences between products, and shift their loyalty among brands. For those who produce and sell counterfeit goods, their value is the trademark. Consumer surveys show that people may purchase some counterfeit goods as trial versions or as substitutes for genuine branded goods (Rutter and Bryce

2008). Individuals desire products with certain trademarks because of what that mark represents (Gentry 2001). People who desire a particular product may knowingly purchase a counterfeit version and find satisfaction because of the characteristics they associate with the brand. As a result, people may choose to consume a brand (e.g., Gucci) but not a specific product (e.g., authentic Gucci purse). Simply put, consumers may desire counterfeit goods because they are "counterfeits of some brand" that they desire (Gentry 2001, 264). Although this is not a problem for these consumers, companies that invest considerable resources to create and market brands they hope will inspire and maintain consumers' loyalty see it as a serious problem.

The actual harm caused by counterfeiting of such goods is not cut-and-dried. Counterfeited products indicate that the goods—and the associated brands—are popular. "The unfortunate part is: if your brand isn't being counterfeited, you're in more trouble," explains David Lipkus, an associate with the Toronto-based law firm Kestenberg, Siegal, and Lipkus (interview, Lipkus 2012). Given varying degrees of consumer support for counterfeit goods, rights holders acknowledge that they cannot entirely eliminate the problem. "The goal of a good enforcement program is not to let it [counterfeiting] overwhelm the brand," comments Roxanne Elings, former cochair of global trademarks/brand management practice, with the law firm Greenberg Traurig in New York City (interview, Elings 2012).

Why Care about Anticounterfeiting Efforts?

Why should we be interested in studying online regulation that occurs through non-legally binding agreements? It is important to understand the specific nature of online anticounterfeiting enforcement efforts. Studies of copyright infringement are contributing to a rapidly growing literature of interest to scholars, activists, and industry (see Haggart 2014). Trademark infringement, in contrast, is woefully underexamined (a notable exception is Raustiala and Sprigman 2012). This book's focus on counterfeit goods represents an effort to address the paucity of studies that examine how states or corporate actors regulate this issue.

A key reason to study anticounterfeiting efforts is that, as noted above, the harms typically associated with counterfeiting are not as clear-cut or substantial as industry officials typically portray. In fact, as discussed in the next section, it is difficult to calculate with any certainty the economic losses to rights holders from this problem, given the scarcity of reliable data. Purchases of counterfeit products by willing consumers do not represent lost sales to rights holders, since those consumers may have never intended to buy authentic products. However, rights holders may argue that their brands are still damaged because the counterfeits may be of poor quality or harm the consumer in some way.

Anticounterfeiting rhetoric often equates "authenticity" (i.e., authorized branded goods) with quality and safety. Counterfeit goods may be shoddily constructed and pose safety risks, but so can genuine, legitimately trademarked goods. For example, the widely publicized scandal of food products containing traces of horsemeat in Great Britain in 2013 and the scare over melamine-contaminated food in China in 2008 respectively appear to be problems of supply-chain management and deliberate adulteration, not counterfeiting (Castle and Dalby 2013; Gillan 2008).

Not all counterfeits are poor imitations. Some counterfeits are perfect replicas that are virtually indistinguishable from genuine goods. This is why a test purchase—purchasing and testing a suspicious product—is generally the most accurate way to determine whether a product is counterfeit or not. There are "many criteria that help you assess whether it's likely to be a counterfeit," explains Jeremy Newman, a partner with Rouse Legal in London. "You'll never be sure until you see that physical sample" (interview, Newman 2012). Test purchases can be time-consuming and costly, because the products must be shipped from the seller to the examiner. Intermediaries generally only require rights holders to make a good-faith statement in relation to their complaint regarding counterfeit goods, not conduct test purchases. Test purchases are not a requirement within the nonbinding agreements. Without test purchases, however, which provide clear evidence of trademark violation, rights holders' may inaccurately identify genuine or secondhand goods as counterfeit.

Examining corporate regulation through non-legally binding agreements uncovers systemic problems with due process measures. The case studies in chapters 3 through 5 reveal serious problems with rights holders or intermediaries mistakenly targeting lawful behavior. Even if we spare little thought for the due process of merchants selling counterfeit goods, we should be concerned about law-abiding individuals and businesses who may be swept up in enforcement dragnets with little opportunity to appeal their cases. Regulatory efforts that emphasize speed and mass policing, especially through automated tools, are typically vulnerable to problems of false positives, as is the case with the nonbinding agreements.

Equally, this type of enforcement—using macrointermediaries to institute chokepoints in the absence of legislative or judicial requirements—raises serious questions about regulation on the Internet in general. Macrointermediary-facilitated regulation illustrates the capacity of private actors to set and enforce rules globally in ways that tend to benefit narrow corporate interests at the expense of the general public. As the practice of governing through chokepoints expands, there are no reasons why it cannot be adapted to other problems. This is an emerging governance practice that echoes the private, unaccountable nature of the national-security surveillance state. As such, it provides a preview of one possible future for governance, one that is unaccountable, open to abuse, and highly reliant on constant surveillance. It prompts us to ask: is this the type of future we want?

PROBLEM OF COUNTERFEIT GOODS

Most people have likely encountered or even purchased counterfeit goods at some point in their local flea markets, dodgy strip malls, or along Canal Street in New York City. Counterfeiting affects a broad range of goods from luxury clothing and accessories, especially sunglasses and purses, to cosmetics and perfume, food and alcohol, and personal care items like toothpaste and condoms. Companies interviewed for this book investigated cases of counterfeit clothing, hats, and sunglasses sold in open-air flea markets and outside concert venues. They discovered counterfeit beer and wine poured into bottles recycled from high-end manufacturers, and luxury perfume adulterated with animal urine to achieve a particular hue. Industrial products, such as commercial circuit breakers, vehicle brake pads, and pumps for mining operations may also be counterfeited. Counterfeit goods are manufactured in many countries. China, however, is the largest global producer of counterfeit goods. This should be unsurprising given that China also legitimately produces many of the world's best-known brands. Apple's iPhones and iPads, for instance, are manufactured at the Taiwanese-owned Foxconn Technology Group's factories in Shenzhen, China.

It is important to recognize that consumers may knowingly purchase counterfeit goods, as discussed earlier, a practice termed "nondeceptive counterfeiting," in order to benefit from lower prices. People may also unknowingly purchase counterfeit goods, a phenomenon termed "deceptive counterfeiting." Companies that are most publicly prominent in their anticounterfeiting efforts are typically those with sought-after brands in the apparel and accessories sector, such as Louis Vuitton, Chanel, Gucci, Coach, Nike, and Adidas. These companies are motivated, at least in part, by consumer surveys that demonstrate that people who knowingly purchase counterfeit goods do not perceive counterfeit apparel and accessories as harmful. For example, a 2009 study that examined nearly four hundred reports of consumers' perceptions of counterfeit goods, and surveyed consumers in five countries, including the United Kingdom, found that consumers believe counterfeit apparel to be less harmful than counterfeit pharmaceuticals (Business Action to Stop Counterfeiting and Piracy 2009).

Framing Counterfeiting as a Serious Offense

Industry actors have been very successful in framing counterfeit goods as a serious economic issue and a criminal offense. Framing is a concept that explains how actors employ certain ideas to construct issues as "problems." Actors can use ideas and metaphors as discursive frames to present events or behavior in certain ways and suggest alternatives (see Odell and Sell 2006). Effective framing is vitally important. "One must convince people that one's arguments are good, one's institutional innovations necessary, and one's horror stories disturbing," says James Boyle (Boyle 2007, 18, quoted in Sell 2003, 3). As discussed earlier in this chapter, rights holders made intellectual property enforcement a priority for the U.S. government in the 1970s by strategically constructing an association between intellectual property and international trade. Proponents of tougher enforcement against online intellectual property infringement draw upon arguments they have successfully employed since the late 1970s: counterfeit goods cost jobs, threaten innovation, and endanger public health (Halbert 1997).

Counterfeiting undoubtedly causes economic losses to rights holders. As in the case of other illicit markets like drugs, however, there is a lack of reliable, detailed data on the size of the market for counterfeit goods, and few estimates of economic losses to rights holders. Industry and government officials often cite studies from the Organization for Economic Cooperation and Development that calculate economic losses related to counterfeit goods. In its most recent report, in 2016, the OECD estimated that the value of counterfeited and copyright-infringing goods moving through international trade was as much as $461 billion annually (Organization for Economic Cooperation and Development 2016). According to Business Action to Stop Counterfeiting and Piracy, an organization created by the Paris-based International Chamber of Commerce, counterfeit and copyright-infringing goods internationally is estimated between $770 billion and $960 billion (Business Action to Stop Counterfeiting and Piracy 2009).

Industry actors use estimates of losses from counterfeit goods to advocate particular policies and enforcement responses and to legitimize such demands to governments. Critics, however, argue that these estimates are weakened by poor methodologies, a reliance on anecdotal information, and political self-interest from rights holders and industry associations (see, e.g., Staake, Thiesse, and Fleisch 2009). As with other illicit markets, efforts to generate reliable, comprehensive data on counterfeiting and any related negative effects are open to charges of bias, distortion, politicization, and fabrication (Andreas 2010).

Rights holders' emphasis on counterfeiting as a criminal act downplays any responsibility companies may bear for weaknesses or problems in their corporate processes. There is a common misconception among big companies with problems of counterfeited products "that there's some kind of boogeyman counterfeiter or evil empire. Nine times out of ten it's their own suppliers" (interview, lawyer, Hong Kong law firm, 2012). Vincent Volpi, CEO of the U.S. security firm PICA Corporation, explains that factories contracted to manufacture products for a rights holder may exceed their orders. "They're flooding your primary marketplace with the same products that you've designed and authorized," Volpi says, "That's a supply chain issue, because it's technically a counterfeit; but at the end of the day, what you have is unauthorized production" (interview, Volpi 2012).

The complexity of global supply chains and outsourcing production from the United States and Europe to China also creates vulnerabilities (Mackenzie 2010). At an Alibaba Group investor meeting in Hangzhou, China, in June 2016, the founder and executive chair, Jack Ma, pinpointed outsourcing as a contributing factor in counterfeiting. Ma stated that "fake products today are of better quality and better price than the real names" because they are manufactured in "exactly the same factories, [with] exactly the same raw materials but they do not use the names" (Dou 2016). Companies that use production brokers, especially in China, also face the risk of having unauthorized versions of their goods manufactured for sale in China or shipped to overseas markets. Production brokers help rights holders choose manufacturers, particularly in China, to produce their goods, and this involves distributing product designs and specifications to multiple factories to determine which factory has the skills, equipment, and competitive bid. Volpi highlights the problems inherent in this outsourcing process:

> I'm using a production broker, and I'm giving my designs to a production broker with the idea that they are going to go out and shop my designs all over Asia-Pacific to try to get me the best quality for the least amount of price—then that sounds like a good deal, right? At the end of the day, what I've just done is I've just distributed all of my designs all over Asia-Pacific to companies that are capable of producing them—I'm only going to choose one . . . to actually produce. That means that if I've shopped 300 companies, 299 [others also] got my specs. I don't even know who those people are, because the broker's job is to shop those guys. (interview, Volpi 2012)

Counterfeiting is therefore a much more complex problem than the unauthorized production of trademarked goods. Rights holders should bear some responsibility for logistical and financial decisions that introduce vulnerabilities into their manufacturing and distribution processes and weaken their supply chains. The question, however, is how much responsibility rights holders should assume and how much other actors—Internet intermediaries and the state—should bear. In some cases, problems framed as "counterfeit goods" may be more accurately described as problems of parallel trade or contractual disputes between rights holders and manufacturers that could be addressed by changing how manufacturers conduct their business.[5] By framing these problems as a criminal offense (counterfeiting), not a contractual dispute, rights holders have a stronger case to petition for state assistance.

Rights holders tend to condemn all instances of counterfeit goods, but counterfeiting can serve a useful economic purpose since it points to consumer needs or desires in the marketplace. In fact, some companies use counterfeit versions of their products as a form of market research. Peter Vesterbacka, CEO of the Finnish firm Rovio, which owns the popular Angry Birds game, argued that counterfeit Angry Birds merchandise in China helped the company. At a conference in Beijing in 2011, Versterbacka states, "Angry Birds is now the most copied brand in China, and we get a lot of inspiration from local producers. The way we look at it is: of course we want to sell the officially licensed, good quality products, but at the same time we have to be happy about the fact that the brand is so loved that it is the most copied brand in China" (Kidman 2011).

Alongside claims of economic losses, rights holders emphasize serious public health and safety risks posed by counterfeit goods. "I don't envy my colleagues in the copyright field because I think they have a bigger task of proving harm," remarks Ruth Orchard, head of the Anti-Counterfeiting

Group in England, a prominent trade association. "We can demonstrate harm—all sorts of harm—much more easily with concrete goods" (interview, Orchard 2012). Some counterfeit goods, such as medication, food, drink, and electrical goods, can cause harm if the goods malfunction, are substandard, or lack safety features. A U.S.-based manufacturer of commercial electrical components, including circuit breakers for apartment buildings, found counterfeit versions of its products for sale in China that violated safety standards (interview, Garner 2012).

Despite media coverage and anecdotal reports, there is little comprehensive data on the health and safety harms caused by counterfeit products. One reason is rights holders' reluctance to reveal their problems to their competitors and customers, fearing a loss of competitive advantage or decline in their brand's reputation. Another reason is that rights holders may consider data of counterfeit-related harms to be proprietary. For example, the U.S.-based Pharmaceutical Security Institute, a trade association representing the largest pharmaceutical companies, holds the most comprehensive data on counterfeit pharmaceuticals but does not release that information publicly (interview, Kubic 2012).

Rights holders may be motivated to associate all counterfeit goods with safety risks if they are trying to solicit assistance from government officials. Many counterfeit products, such as clothing and accessories, generally do not pose health and safety problems to consumers. The head of the nonprofit Electrical Safety Foundation International, in the state of Virginia, alluded to this slippage between harmful and non-harmful goods when he spoke about the risks from counterfeit electrical products: "You plug it in and it sets on fire. There's no gray area in that. That's the difference between what we're talking about and the Louis Vuitton handbag" (interview, Brenner 2012).

The idea that intellectual property infringement should be treated as a harmful crime can oversimplify certain inherently complex cases. What is often defined as a problem of "counterfeit pharmaceuticals," for example, can be much more complicated. Intellectual-property actors sometimes conflate issues of generic medication, counterfeit pharmaceuticals, parallel trade medication, and substandard medication.[6] For some of these issues, such as the sale of counterfeit and substandard medication, the public interest is obvious. People need to be protected from medication that may be contaminated or adulterated with dangerous substances. Similarly, medication that contains too little or too much of the active medical ingredients could lead to serious side effects, overdoses, or untreated health conditions. The presence of generic medication in a marketplace may have a beneficial effect, by lowering drug costs on legitimate, licensed medication via increased competition. Such slippage among different issues can enable actors to portray a counterfeiting problem as larger or more serious than it is in reality. More broadly, the conflation of generic medication with counterfeit can decrease public—and government—trust in generic medication, which materially benefits the manufacturers of nongeneric pharmaceuticals.

Regulating Counterfeit Goods

Counterfeit goods must be physically manufactured and shipped from production sites to consumers. This is in contrast to copyright-infringing copies of movies or music, which can be digitally copied and illicitly downloaded from sources like the Pirate Bay or Kickass Torrents. Consequently, rights holders concerned about counterfeit versions of their products often have both real-world enforcement programs that address the manufacture of counterfeit goods in particular physical locations, and online programs targeting the advertisement and distribution of counterfeit goods using the Internet.

Real-world anticounterfeiting efforts can be legally complex, time-consuming, costly, and challenging. Government and local officials may be unwilling or incapable of providing assistance. In some areas corruption of local and state officials is a significant problem, and counterfeiting may provide benefits to the local economy through employment (Mertha 2007). Foreign production facilities, many based in China, can be difficult to locate and surprisingly resilient to raids, because there "are lots of small on-the-ground facilities" (interview, lawyer, Hong Kong law firm, 2012). When one factory is closed, workers may simply shift production to another site. In developing countries, the protection of foreign companies' trademark rights is often not a priority for law enforcement agencies, which understandably must focus on more serious offenses, like social unrest or terrorism. Even within industrialized countries, anticounterfeiting efforts can pose challenges. Enforcement efforts aimed at flea markets or discount outlets, for example, can be resource-intensive and ineffective, since sellers shift locations or rapidly replenish their stocks if counterfeits are seized.

Online anticounterfeiting efforts have two goals: to deter consumers from purchasing counterfeits on stand-alone websites and online marketplaces, and to interrupt the distribution and advertisement of counterfeit goods. Most Internet users have probably come across advertisements for counterfeits or sites selling suspiciously cheap brand-name goods. Some products may be euphemistically described on sites or in market-places' sales listings as "replicas" or "lookalike" products. Many of these sites are obviously fraudulent, with spelling and grammatical errors or poor-quality web design. Other sites are carefully designed to replicate exactly the official sites of popular brands. These mirror sites are intended to deceive consumers who wish to purchase authentic products and believe the sites they visit to be genuine.

How significant is the online trade in counterfeit goods? As with efforts to quantify economic losses to rights holders from counterfeit goods, there is little reliable data. Enforcement actions by rights holders give some indication of the scale of the problem. Deckers Outdoor Corporation, owners of the famous Ugg brand of footwear, identified eleven thousand sites between 2007 and 2011 that sold counterfeit versions of its products (Outdoor Industry Association 2011). Similarly, in a series of U.S. court cases between 2008 and 2012, Coach, True Religion, and Tory Burch (based in the United States); Hermès and Chanel (France); and Gucci (Italy), companies selling high-end clothing and accessories, each identified hundreds of sites selling counterfeit versions of their products.

Alongside stand-alone sites, rights holders are also concerned about the sale of counterfeit goods through online marketplaces like eBay and the massive China-based Taobao. These marketplaces are important because they have hundreds of millions of users and are responsible for a significant volume of trade. It is difficult, however, to estimate the proportion of counterfeit goods flowing through legitimate marketplaces. Private security companies that monitor marketplaces on behalf of rights holders can identify thousands, or even tens of thousands of sales listings for counterfeit versions of popular brands, as I discuss in chapter 5.

Those in the business of policing copyright and trademark infringement refer to websites selling counterfeit goods as "infringing sites" or, more colorfully, "rogue sites." There is no commonly accepted definition for infringing sites. Many in the intellectual-property-protection industry define the term in a manner similar to the definition proposed in the Stop Online Piracy Act. SOPA's section 102 defines "foreign infringing sites" as sites or a "portion thereof" that are directed toward and used by individuals in the United States in which the site operator "is committing or facilitating the commission of criminal violations," including trafficking in counterfeit goods or services. SOPA's definition would have applied to sites selling counterfeit goods and those offering copyright-infringing content. The breadth of SOPA's definition alarmed critics, who argued that a "portion thereof" could be interpreted to include sites that had only a small problem with infringement. This could include a site that offered for sale one counterfeit good among all its other, legitimate products. It could also include legitimate sites that had hyperlinks to sites that sell counterfeit or copyright-infringing goods. Fan sites for popular books, movies, or video games may sell branded clothing or memorabilia that violate rights holders' trademarks.

If SOPA had passed into law, its legal definition of infringing sites would have been subject to judicial interpretation and scrutiny. This process would have given critics and defendants a chance to raise objections. Legal rulings on SOPA would have shaped how the definition could have been used and to what types of situations the legislation should apply. In contrast, non-legally binding agreements provide no similar opportunity for scrutiny. For advocates of nonbinding enforcement agreements, the expansive nature of the term *infringing sites* is highly useful. It means that there is no defined threshold of criminality. As a result, regulators have the flexibility to target any sites that they believe are selling, distributing, or advertising counterfeit goods, even if only one item. For critics, however, this looseness is extremely problematic. Sites that, deliberately or unintentionally, sell a mixture of legitimate and infringing goods—or that are even accused of doing so—could be crippled commercially instead of given an opportunity to challenge the allegations or address any problems.

Despite these challenges, in this book I employ the term *infringing site* because it is commonly used. However, I do so with the proviso that such sites are designated as infringing based on allegations, not proof, of infringement by rights holders. In the informal agreements, macrointermediaries typically require only a statement of good faith from the rights holders, not any definitive proof of infringement. Enforcement is undertaken rapidly, often using automated tools, which can make it difficult for the accused to appeal the allegations, as is discussed in chapter 2.

Rise of the Macrointermediaries

Proponents of more policing by intermediaries contend that the online distribution of counterfeit goods is too large, complex, and difficult for rights holders to address alone. It is relatively simple for vendors of counterfeit goods to set up a website, name it something catchy like "www.Nikeoutletsale.com," and spam consumers with advertisements. Vendors may also open multiple seller accounts in online marketplaces

TABLE I   MACROINTERMEDIARIES' ENFORCEMENT CAPABILITIES

Macrointermediary	Enforcement Action
PayPal, Visa, MasterCard, American Express	Withdraw payment processing
Google, Yahoo, Bing (Microsoft)	Withdraw advertising services
Google, Yahoo, Bing	Remove search results
GoDaddy	Withdraw and/or disrupt domain name services
eBay, Taobao	Remove sales listings

and sell their wares to unsuspecting customers or those looking for too-good-to-be-true deals. Laws prohibiting these activities are in place, but enforcement in the online environment is often complex, time-consuming, and difficult. Offenders can operate anonymously and shift among different legal jurisdictions. They can locate in countries infamous for their governments' reluctance or inability to address online offenses. Those wishing to evade the law can strategically choose web hosts or payment providers who may be unaware of or turn a blind eye to illicit activities. Site operators may also strategically move from one jurisdiction or service provider to another in response to enforcement pressure. Those involved in policing intellectual property online, commonly termed the "brand-protection industry," refer to this challenge as "whack a mole," in a reference to the popular arcade and carnival game. Bob Barchiesi, president of the International Anti-Counterfeiting Coalition, an influential trade association based in Washington, D.C., explains that rights holders would "take websites down and they'd pop right back up. Within twenty seconds, they'd knock a site down and it would pop back up with a number one or a dot, just something a little bit different [in the domain name]. It just wasn't doing anything. It didn't have any effect at all" (interview, Barchiesi 2012).

Rights holders argue that intermediaries are better placed and equipped to counter these problems. In this book, I focus on the following macrointermediaries, which are signatories to the informal enforcement agreements: PayPal, Visa, MasterCard, American Express, Google, Yahoo, Bing (Microsoft's search engine), eBay, and the domain registrar GoDaddy (see table 1). I also examine the Taobao marketplace, which primarily caters to consumers in China.

Macrointermediaries' regulatory capacity stems, in part, from "their positions at the nexus points between communications networks" (Murray 2011, 27). PayPal, Visa, MasterCard, and American Express collectively dominate the online payment sector. If you want to buy something online, chances are you'll do so using their services. Google operates the world's largest search engine and largest digital advertising marketplace, distantly trailed by Yahoo and Microsoft. Many of the advertisements users see online are part of Google's advertising services. eBay runs one of the world's biggest online marketplaces, with country-specific platforms around the world, such as eBay.fr (France) and eBay.de (Germany). GoDaddy, as the world's largest domain name registrar, provides and registers domain names.

These Internet giants collectively comprise a "Big Tech" industry sector that ranks alongside the traditional corporate powerhouses of Big Oil, Big Banks, Big Pharma, and Big Tobacco. The companies are all headquartered in the United States, which indicates the considerable commercial influence of U.S. companies on the Internet. Given their operational scope and ability to facilitate access to important services and online spaces, these macrointermediaries have regulatory capacity similar to or even exceeding that of state-based regulators (Murray 2011).

Terms-of-Service Agreements

Informal enforcement agreements with macrointermediaries offer rights holders a useful opportunity to shift some of their enforcement burden to Internet firms and payment providers. More importantly, these agreements allow rights holders to undertake global enforcement campaigns in a manner that previously would have been unfeasible or prohibitively expensive. With their vast, global platforms and technologically sophisticated surveillance and enforcement capabilities, macrointermediaries can conduct mass policing of Internet networks, platforms, and services. By working with PayPal, for instance, rights holders can target sites offering counterfeit goods worldwide that use PayPal to process customers' payments.

Intermediaries set and enforce rules that govern their platforms through their terms-of-use contracts with their users. Terms-of-service or terms-of-use contracts are ubiquitous online. We click to agree to these legal contracts, often without reading or understanding the contracts, whenever we sign up to Twitter or LinkedIn, update iTunes agreements, or open a PayPal or eBay account. These agreements enable companies to determine how their users can access and share certain content, what items users can purchase, methods of payment, and the personal information users must divulge. Through these agreements, intermediaries may collect personal information, including users' names, mail and email addresses, phone numbers, and payment details. Intermediaries may also collect information relating to the individuals' use of the service, such as web browsing histories, email history, and payment transactions.

These contractual agreements also outline users' obligations and their responsibility to adhere to specific terms in exchange for intermediaries' services. The agreements incorporate laws from countries in which the Internet firms operate, such as laws that prohibit fraud, the distribution of child pornography, and the sale of counterfeit goods. They also incorporate policies that relate to the protection of the intermediaries' intellectual property rights and that of third parties. Intermediaries have significant latitude in deeming certain types of content and activities as appropriate or inappropriate for their services through their terms-of-use contracts. They can also penalize users who violate their policies. Facebook, for instance, formerly had a real-name policy that required people to use names that corresponded to government-issued identification. Although Facebook has recently relaxed this policy somewhat to allow non-government-issued identification, such as library cards, the social network has frozen the accounts of people found in violation of this policy. Facebook's real-name policy has angered those, including transgender people, drag performers, and victims of domestic violence, who often do not use names that match official government identification (Holpuch 2015).

Intermediaries can respond to problematic content or behavior on their platforms in several ways. Depending on the type of services they offer, intermediaries can remove or block problematic information, or they can sanction their users who violate their policies. Web hosts and social networks can remove videos, images, advertisements, and text that the intermediaries decide is inappropriate for their platforms. Search intermediaries can remove search engine results that hyperlink to specific web pages, a process referred to as de-indexing. Intermediaries that provide payment, advertising, social media, web hosting, or domain name services can restrict or limit services to individuals who violate their policies.

PRIVATE TRANSNATIONAL REGIMES

To explain the emergence and operation of the nonbinding agreements, it is necessary to account for all the players involved and trace their varying interests in addressing the online trade in counterfeit goods. The coalition of elite corporate actors—multinational rights holders, influential trade associations, and commercially prominent U.S.-based Internet firms—and government officials constitutes a loosely structured transnational private regulatory regime. Regimes can be understood as encompassing "the full set of actors, institutions, norms and rules" involved in a particular regulatory arrangement (Eberlein and Grande 2005, 91).

The concept of a private regime, borrowed from nonstate governance theory within the international relations discipline, provides a useful framework to explain particular state-corporate regulatory dynamics that produced the non-legally binding agreements. Stephen Krasner, along with other international relations scholars, developed the concept of regimes to account for the influence of nonstate actors in global governance. Krasner's classic definition of regimes refers to "sets of implicit or explicit principles, norms, rules, and decision-making procedures around which actors' expectations converge" (Krasner 1982, 185). Scholars of nonstate governance, particularly Claire Cutler, Deborah Avant, Virginia Haufler, Thomas Biersteker, and Rodney Bruce Hall, have further expanded the definition of regimes to explain nonstate actors' capacity to set and enforce rules transnationally (see particularly Avant, Finnemore, and Sell 2010; Cutler, Haufler, and Porter 1999).

Roles of State and Corporate Actors

Regimes recognize state and nonstate actors, especially corporations, who may play varied roles in designing, implementing, and enforcing particular rules and standards. The concept also explicitly recognizes the capacity of nonstate actors to make and enforce rules, particularly through soft law measures, such as nonbinding codes of conduct or industry-derived best practices. Regimes are thus useful to trace the specific historical and sociocultural context from which actors emerged to form particular regulatory arrangements. They can help uncover and explain, for example, the long history of U.S. rights holders and trade associations in shaping intellectual property policy making in the United States and internationally (Drahos and Braithwaite 2002; Sell 2003). By employing the concept of regimes, one can also account for similarities and differences among actors' material and ideational interests in relation to the governance of a particular issue. Actors may have conflicting, sometimes irreconcilable differences that shape the composition and function of governance arrangements. Regulatory efforts that materially benefit one party may impose costs on the other.

Because government officials are central actors in this private regime, it is important to understand the role of the state. To do so, I have adopted in this book the concept of a "regulatory state" (Braithwaite 2005). Central to this idea is the fact that the state deploys power "through a regulatory framework rather than through the monopolisation of violence or the provision of welfare" (Walby 1999, 123, quoted in Braithwaite 2005, 11). States have shifted, since the 1980s, from providing regulation through the production and enforcement of rules to shaping the provision of regulation by nonstate actors (Jordana and Levi-Faur 2004). This means that states may govern through regulation by shaping discourse and distributing resources to nonstate actors in order to direct regulatory efforts (Rhodes 2012). States may strategically confer authority on civil-society or corporate actors, thus empowering those actors to create or enforce regulatory frameworks (Levi-Faur 2013). Governments, for example, may delegate authority to civil-society organizations to enforce animal welfare legislation, or permit corporations to use self-regulatory programs to monitor their adherence to environmental laws. Although states vary in their capacity and interest in governing, the concept of a regulatory state does not indicate a hollowing out of state authority. States retain the capacity to endorse, influence, or reject regulatory frameworks put forth by nonstate actors (Büthe 2010).

States determine which actors are more authoritative, lend legitimacy to some interests over others, and privilege certain policies (Hall 1993, 288). Not all interest groups, of course, have equal resources with which to persuade states to support their regulatory preferences or command the same degree of influence in shaping policy making processes. In the private anticounterfeiting regime, public advocacy groups are sidelined. Rights holders and their industry associations have an institutional advantage over intermediaries through decades of lobbying for strengthened protection of intellectual property (Sell 2010). Despite rights holders' history of successful lobbying, it is important to emphasize that states retain distinct interests and goals.

Private Enforcement Agreements

Regimes may be defined as transnational according to the scope of the rule-setting actors, the level of the rule-setting institutions, the scope of the rules themselves, or a combination of these factors (Mügge 2006, 179). The private anticounterfeiting regime is transnational because of the global scope of the intermediaries involved and their capacity to impose rules on their users through their terms-of-use policies. Regardless of its scope, a regime may also have roots within a specific territorial base or embody distinctly local features (Graz and Nölke 2008, 10). These local roots may infuse a regime with characteristics that shape its character or operation. Prominent rule-making actors, for example, may all be based within the Global North, creating rules that govern activities in the Global South.

The nonbinding agreements have a distinctive Global North-South arrangement. Actors set rules and standards in the United States and Europe and then export them to shape standard-setting practices in other countries worldwide through intermediaries' global operations, especially in China. Three of the agreements were created in the United States, two in the United Kingdom, one in China, and one covers Europe. Intermediaries participating in the agreements include Google, Microsoft (Bing), Visa, PayPal, MasterCard, GoDaddy, Yahoo, eBay, American Express, and Taobao.

Government officials from the United States, the United Kingdom, and the European Commission employed various methods to compel macrointermediaries to adopt the agreements, including threats of legal action and legislation. These government officials did so in response to lobbying from prominent U.S. and European rights holders and their powerful trade associations like the Motion Picture Association of America and the International Anti-Counterfeiting Coalition. These trade bodies have a well-documented history of influencing public-policy making in the United States and internationally, as is discussed in chapter 2. Rights holders involved in the private agreements are large, well-known companies with multiple, valuable trademarks, including Adidas, Nike, Burberry, Louis Vuitton, Nokia, and the consumer care companies Proctor & Gamble and Unilever. The public, in contrast, was largely sidelined.

Enforcement of intellectual property rights online is not solely the job of intermediaries. A whole industry has arisen to support it. The brand-protection industry provides enforcement services to rights holders and intermediaries and can be understood as a service provider to members of the transnational anticounterfeiting regime. This industry, which is part of the global private security industry, emerged in the 1980s with the outsourcing of manufacturing from industrialized countries to those in Asia, particularly China. Brand-protection services rapidly expanded with the growth of the Internet and rights holders' fears of online infringement in the beginning of the twenty-first century. These firms are part of the "high policing" component of the private security industry that specializes in corporate security and investigative work (see Brodeur 2007). They operate globally on behalf of corporate clients and mostly serve clients from the Global North (see O'Reilly 2011). This is in contrast to "low-policing" actors who perform front-line private security duties, which includes guarding specific spaces like malls or airports, or certain populations, such as prisoners. Brand-protection companies offer a variety of surveillance and enforcement services to rights holders, including automated monitoring and enforcement tools to police the online sale of counterfeit goods, which is explored in chapter 5.

There are important commonalities among these agreements. Each contains broadly worded general principles that lay out minimum requirements to guide intermediaries' practices in the enforcement of intellectual property rights. There are common enforcement strategies. Intermediaries are responsible for removing advertisements or search results for counterfeit goods to make it more difficult for consumers to find and access vendors selling counterfeit goods. Intermediaries also agree to withdraw important commercial and business services from sites involved in selling or advertising counterfeit goods. Payment providers, for instance, terminate their services to targeted sites, thus commercially disabling sites.

The regime functions because of common interests among corporate and state actors. Rights holders and intermediaries have financial and reputational interests in protecting their intellectual property from infringement and in maintaining the confidence of their users by cracking down on any association with criminality. Collaboration with rights holders and trade associations on non-legally binding enforcement measures may offer intermediaries greater flexibility and less onerous conditions than legislation or court-imposed requirements. More broadly, actors in the regime have shared interests, although sometimes differing goals, in expanding their control over the Internet, particularly by governing online flows of information and behavior.

CHOKEPOINTS: TECHNICAL POINTS OF CONTROL

Technology is a key component of the transnational anticounterfeiting regime. Rights holders, their trade associations, and private security companies use technology to monitor sites and marketplaces for the sale of counterfeit goods and to send complaints to intermediaries, These intermediaries, in turn, use technologically sophisticated enforcement programs to remove problematic content or withdraw their services from targeted sites. By withdrawing their services, intermediaries create technological chokepoints that deter consumers from accessing targeted sites and hamper the sites' functioning. The use of the terms *throttle* and *chokepoint* by actors who are intent on strengthening enforcement practices explicitly underlines the punitive nature of withdrawing critical services. This strategy assumes that intermediaries, who often rely upon allegations from rights holders, can surgically disable specific sites without negatively affecting other related sites and services. A common problem, however, is the wrongful removal of lawful content by rights holders or intermediaries.

To understand how intermediaries use technology to target suspicious behavior or content, techno-regulation provides a useful framework. *Techno-regulation* refers to the use of technology as a regulatory instrument to shape human behavior (Brownsword 2004). The concept has roots in science and technology studies, a field of research prominently associated with Bruno Latour (2005). Science, technology, and society are understood as mutually dependent upon and shaping one another. Technology is both real and constructed: its design and use are imbued with norms, concepts, and cultural values that in turn influence people's behavior, beliefs, and practices (Franklin 1995).

The use of new technologies is shaped by existing laws and regulations, as well as by state and nonstate actors promoting certain policy goals (Mueller, Kuehn, and Santoso 2012, 350). In addition, there are actors—individuals, states, companies, and other organizations—with material stakes in the development and use of technologies in certain directions (DeNardis 2014). In other words, with techno-regulation, "one can see technology structuring the politics, and politics constraining and channeling the technology" (Bendrath and Mueller 2011, 1156). Macrointermediaries appear to be ideally suited to regulate a wide variety of activities, since they have specialized technical skills and a global enforcement reach. Intermediaries, however, are not "natural" gatekeepers. People created these companies to provide Internet services, not to control the flow of information or transactions across their platforms on behalf of state or corporate actors. Intermediaries became regulators for intellectual property in response to considerable pressure from states and industry groups. Further, as the rest of the book shows, government officials and rights holders have repeatedly demanded that intermediaries make specific technological changes to their enforcement programs to target and address online infringement.

The recognition that the built environment—and technology generally—is designed in ways to shape and constrain how individuals use these spaces is not new. There is a long history, for example, of improving street lighting or altering traffic flows to reduce crime (e.g., Clarke 1997). Digital architecture, too, can shape and manipulate how people access and use technologies. In the context of the Internet, legal scholars Lawrence Lessig and Joel Reidenberg famously refer to rules designed into digital architecture as "code" (Lessig 1999; Reidenberg 1998).[7] *Code* here refers to rules designed in software that control the various systems, tools, and protocols that compose the architecture of the Internet (Lessig 1999). In other words, code may function as law, since these rules can—in some circumstances—have the force of law. Whoever "controls the underlying 'pipeworks' and the protocols controls the Internet" (Guadamuz 2011, 87).

Automated Regulation

One way of thinking about code-based regulation is to consider how algorithms have changed regulation. *Automated regulation,* sometimes called *algorithmic regulation,* refers to the use of software algorithms to shape or affect human behavior (see O'Reilly 2013). Algorithms are sets of rules that influence our lives in many ways. Financial agencies and insurance companies use algorithms to rate and rank our credit worthiness and health risks, while Amazon suggests books we may like, and Google decides the search results we see. The development of computational systems enables regulators—both state and corporate—to regulate via the use of "big data," which can be understood as "the capacity to search, aggregate and cross-reference large data sets" (boyd and Crawford 2012, 663). Algorithms enable data to be "systematically extracted or disclosed, analyzed," and, ultimately, translated into "actionable data" (Lyon 2014, 3) for use by state or corporate regulators.

Thus, state or nonstate actors could introduce rules or standards into the code of software applications that would shape—or even prevent—certain types of online activities or behavior. For example, following a consumer backlash against Microsoft, in June 2013 the company removed restrictions that required gamers, even when playing offline games, to connect to the Internet daily for Microsoft to authenticate their gaming systems (Stuart 2013). As a result of the outcry, Microsoft now allows players to play games offline, as well as to share games with friends.

Automated regulation is increasingly commonplace in the regulation of intellectual property on the Internet. Major Internet intermediaries, some rights holders, and a growing number of private security firms in the brand-protection industry use automated tools to detect and address online infringement. These actors may employ fully automated programs or use a combination of automated measures and human analysts. For example, intermediaries may employ automated monitoring programs to detect suspicious transactions or behavior on their platforms and may then require human analysts to review those instances and impose penalties if necessary. In fully automated systems, rights holders can use automated tools to detect infringement and then send a notification of complaint to the relevant intermediary. In turn, those intermediaries may employ automated programs to remove problematic content or withdraw services from targeted websites. Criminologist Pat O'Malley, in his analysis of automated traffic enforcement, such as cameras linked to traffic stoplights, describes this process as one in which individuals can be "policed, judged and sanctioned" through their "electronic trace" without any human interaction (O'Malley 2010, 795).

Because they effectively regulate what we can and cannot do, rules embedded in technology can raise serious questions relating to their legitimacy and accountability, and to whether they supersede or conflict with actual laws and regulations. Code-based regulation can operate opaquely, in ways unobservable to those who may be regulated. Those who design and implement certain rules may refuse to allow them to be openly inspected and challenged, and people may be unaware of the rules regulating their behavior. Equally troubling, in some contexts rules drafted by corporate actors may displace—or supersede—public laws (Lessig 1999). In terms of opaque state control, governments may require that firms incorporate particular rules within technology, allowing them to govern indirectly, bypassing constitutional or legal controls on state power (see Lessig 1999).

Automated regulation enables states and corporations to take action in response to wrongdoing. It also enables regulators to identify wrongdoing before it occurs, in what is often called "pre-crime." This means that regulators employ algorithms to "predict and intervene *before* behaviors, events, and processes are set in train" (Lyon 2014, 4). Intermediaries have sophisticated enforcement programs in place to detect possible violations of their policies, such as fraudulent transactions intended to cheat an intermediary or its users of funds. Rights holders want intermediaries to target people who are perceived as being at high risk of copyright or trademark infringement because of patterns of previously suspicious behavior. An important element of techno-regulation, therefore, is examining how technology may constrain or prohibit certain types of behavior, thereby forcing people to comply with the rules and removing individual choice (see Brownsword 2011).

Those who design and deploy automated regulatory processes often portray them as operating objectively, accurately, and in a highly targeted manner. But because humans design this software, "their biases and values are embedded into the software's instructions" (Citron 2008, 1249). Simply put, algorithms are pieces of code, and code reflects the biases, prejudices, and assumptions held by the person who wrote the code. Advertising algorithms, for example, have shown advertisements for high-income jobs to men more often than to women (Datta, Tschantz, and Datta 2015). These rules are also often opaque to those they regulate. Companies designing or using regulatory algorithms often hide them in "black boxes" composed of "laws of secrecy and technologies of obfuscation" (Pasquale 2015, 9) by claiming that they are protected trade secrets. Secretly drafted, opaquely implemented rules pose clear challenges in terms of the legitimacy and accountability of regulation. As a result, we must ask: who do algorithms serve, and to what end?

METHODOLOGY

The regulation of intellectual property rights is a rapidly evolving topic, particularly in regard to the Internet. This book focuses on the period from roughly 2009 until late 2013, when small groups of government and industry actors created a series of nonbinding enforcement agreements aimed at sites that distribute copyright-infringing or counterfeit goods. The book focuses on eight agreements that cover multiple Internet sectors: payment, advertising, search, the marketplace, and the domain name system.

Much of the book focuses on the epicenter of the transnational anti-counterfeiting regime: multiple agreements negotiated by U.S. and U.K. government officials. The book also examines U.S. rights holders' successful effort to institute an informal agreement with the Taobao marketplace, a platform of particular concern to U.S. and European rights holders. In addition, the book discusses an informal agreement negotiated by the European Commission relating to marketplaces, including eBay, which is the first of its kind in the world. Each of these nonbinding agreements represents an important element of the transnational private regime.

The book draws upon ninety semistructured interviews with rights holders, trade associations, Internet firms, policy makers, attorneys, investigative firms, and civil-society groups in the United States, the United Kingdom, Canada, and Australia. Most interviews were undertaken in Washington, D.C., New York City, and London. Initial interviews to gain a detailed understanding of anticounterfeiting enforcement and to identify the main players, trends, and issues in the field were undertaken in my former home base of Australia. Interview subjects were selected for their direct experience in creating or implementing the private agreements and involvement in carrying out online anticounterfeiting enforcement programs. Questions were adjusted in line with the subject's expertise and nature of involvement in anticounterfeiting efforts. Rights holders were selected from a wide range of industries—namely, pharmaceuticals, apparel and accessories, sporting goods, commercial electrical components, and consumer electronics. This diversity facilitated an examination of online regulatory measures targeting counterfeit goods across industry sectors. The interviews were a mixture of in-person, telephone, email, and Skype interviews depending on the participant's availability and preferences. Most agreed to participate in for-attribution interviews, although some interviewees asked that their comments not to be attributed to them.

In addition to conducting these interviews, I attended a three-day industry conference hosted by the International Anti-Counterfeiting Coalition in Washington, D.C., in 2012, which focused on anticounterfeiting enforcement strategies, and which proved invaluable as a window into the state's role in private agreements. The book also draws upon primary government and legal documents relating to the negotiation and creation of the nonbinding enforcement agreements. This includes testimony before government committees, strategic plans to regulate intellectual property, and debates over intellectual property bills. The book also employs information from corporate annual reports, new releases, and blogs, as well as material from trade associations and civil-society groups. This information was supplemented with media sources, particularly from blogs focusing on technology and intellectual property.

BOOK OVERVIEW

The rest of the book is divided into six chapters. Chapter 2 provides the historical and political contexts in which the private agreements emerged. It briefly traces the growing influence of multinational rights holders on the U.S. government's intellectual property policy making processes from the late 1970s to 2012. The chapter then examines in detail four U.S. intellectual property bills, including the unpopular Stop Online Piracy Act, which proposed to reshape fundamentally the online regulation of intellectual property rights infringement. When these bills failed, rights holders redoubled their efforts to establish non-legally binding agreements with Internet firms that incorporated many of the bills' toughest provisions.

Chapters 3 through 5 present the book's case studies and examine how the informal agreements aim to regulate through three types of chokepoint: revenue, access, and marketplace chokepoints. These agreements have received little attention in academic studies or popular media. Chapter 3 focuses on payment (PayPal, Visa, and MasterCard) and advertising intermediaries (Google, Yahoo, and Bing), while chapter 4 examines search intermediaries (especially Google) and domain name registrars (specifically GoDaddy). Chapter 5 then examines enforcement efforts by marketplaces (eBay and Taobao). Drawing upon these case studies, chapter 6 considers the interactions, interdependencies, and overlapping interests among corporate and state actors in the regulation of online infringement.

The book concludes in chapter 7 by exploring ways in which states and corporations can use technology to regulate users online in ways that are fair, proportionate, and accountable, and which adhere to broadly accepted good governance practices. In that chapter, I recommend that Internet firms use industry transparency reports to be more open about their regulatory actions. The chapter ends with a call to strengthen digital rights.

2

Internet Firms Become
Global Regulators

The U.S. government's campaign to destroy the WikiLeaks site in 2010 following WikiLeaks' publication of classified U.S. diplomatic cables is one of the earliest and most publicized cases that shows Internet intermediaries' capacity as powerful global regulators. WikiLeaks, created in 2006 in Iceland and founded by Julian Assange, is a nonprofit journalistic organization with the goal of publishing information leaked by whistleblowers. WikiLeaks garnered public attention in April 2010 when it published a 2007 video from a U.S. military Apache helicopter in Iraq firing upon a group of people on the ground. The video, which WikiLeaks titled *Collateral Murder,* aroused considerable controversy because two of the twelve people killed were journalists for Reuters, and the video shows U.S. soldiers continuing to fire upon wounded individuals as they lay on the ground (Manning 2013).

Following *Collateral Murder,* WikiLeaks released thousands of field reports in October 2010 written by U.S. military commanders in Iraq and Afghanistan. These documents, known as "war logs," revealed that U.S. authorities deliberately recorded civilian deaths as enemy casualties, and routinely failed to investigate cases of torture by Iraqi police and soldiers (Manning 2013). In November 2010, WikiLeaks further angered the U.S. government when it received over 250,000 leaked classified diplomatic cables written by personnel in U.S. embassies and consulates in countries all over the world. In what became known as "Cablegate," WikiLeaks published the cables in cooperation with respected mainstream media outlets from Europe and the United States, including the *New York Times, The Guardian* (United Kingdom), *Der Spiegel* (Germany), and *Le Monde* (France).

U.S. army soldier Chelsea Manning, then known as Bradley, admitted leaking the *Collateral Murder* video, the war logs, and the diplomatic cables. Manning was sentenced in August 2013 to thirty-five years in prison for violation of the Espionage Act and other offenses. Manning, who is a trans woman, argues she leaked the information "out of a love for my country and a sense of duty to others" (Manning 2014). In a written statement at her pretrial hearing in March 2013, Manning stated that the leaked cables could "spark a domestic debate on the role of the military and our foreign policy in general" in relation to Iraq and Afghanistan (Manning 2013).

The case of WikiLeaks clearly illustrates how states can exert control in the online environment by working with private-sector companies that supply essential technical and commercial services on the Internet. In response to the leaks and intense media coverage of the leaked cables, senior U.S. political figures publicly and fiercely denounced WikiLeaks, claiming that publication of the cables would harm U.S. national security and damage foreign policy interests. Although mainstream news organizations like the *New York Times* and *The Guardian* were publishing the cables, the U.S. government focused on WikiLeaks and its leader, Julian Assange.[1] Democratic vice president Joe Biden called Assange a "high-tech terrorist" (MacAskill 2010). Such denouncements show that the U.S. government was explicitly viewing the case through a national-security lens. Despite repeated calls, including by prominent Democratic senator Dianne Feinstein, for Assange to be tried under the Espionage Act, no charges were forthcoming. Similarly, the U.S. government did not use court orders to force WikiLeaks to forfeit its information. Legal scholars observe that WikiLeaks would likely have had a strong defense on First Amendment grounds (see Benkler 2011).

Intermediaries' Attacks on WikiLeaks

Instead of trying Assange, the U.S. government turned to Internet intermediaries and pressured them to take action unilaterally against WikiLeaks. Senator Joseph Lieberman, Democratic chair of the U.S. Senate Homeland Security Committee, called upon Internet and payment companies to cease doing business with WikiLeaks. The U.S. State Department sent a letter to WikiLeaks alleging that the organization had illegally obtained classified materials. This letter, observes legal scholar Yochai Benkler, was "a careful piece of lawyering, insinuating, but not asserting, illegality on the part of WikiLeaks" (Benkler 2011, 341). The letter and calls from Senator Lieberman had the effect of convincing the intermediaries to take action against WikiLeaks for violating their terms-of-service agreements (see Benkler 2011).

Shortly after Senator Lieberman's demand, Amazon stopped providing WikiLeaks' cloud-storage facilities. EveryDNS, a domain registrar company, withdrew its domain name services, meaning that users would not be able to find the WikiLeaks site. PayPal, MasterCard, and Visa discontinued payment-processing services. This campaign did not prevent the publication of the diplomatic cables, and it did not destroy WikiLeaks. The organization acquired replacement cloud storage and domain name services from other companies. The loss of its payment systems, however, was a bigger blow, since WikiLeaks relies upon public donations, and struggled to replace its payment providers. Assange characterized the payment blockade as an "economic death sentence" and reported that it wiped out 95 percent of WikiLeaks' revenue (Press Association 2012).

The campaign against WikiLeaks illustrates the utility of intermediaries as regulators, especially because they operate or control key elements of the Internet's infrastructure and are vulnerable to pressure, at least by powerful states like the U.S. government. States—or other powerful actors—can tap into the regulatory capacity of private-sector intermediaries, even in the absence of direct judicial orders, and take advantage of their latitude to terminate services to certain sites. By using their terms-of-use agreements, intermediaries can regulate activities and impose sanctions when other actors are somehow constrained or unwilling to do so. The attack on WikiLeaks also marked an important shift in terms of regulatory tactics on the Internet. WikiLeaks was the first high-profile case of what Benkler terms a "denial-of-service attack" aimed at halting "technical, payment, and business process systems to targeted sites" (Benkler 2011a, 155). The U.S. government first used this technique to block revenue from and freeze funds related to terrorist organizations (Benkler 2011a, 163).

From National Security to Intellectual Property

At the same time that WikiLeaks was under growing pressure from the U.S. government, the U.S. Congress was considering an intellectual property bill, the Combating Online Infringement and Counterfeits Act (COICA). This bill proposed to apply denial-of-service attacks—which the U.S. government legitimized by ordering one against WikiLeaks when it contended the organization posed a national security threat—to websites involved in the infringement of intellectual property rights. By broadening the use of denial-of-service attacks, the U.S. government extended "techniques from the war on terrorism into the civilian domain" (Benkler 2011a, 155). The WikiLeaks lessons have not been lost on corporate actors keen to protect their intellectual property rights online. Simply put, the lesson is: control key intermediaries and you control the provision and operation of important online services and infrastructure.

There are important commonalities between the WikiLeaks case and the transnational anticounterfeiting regime. Examining the attack on WikiLeaks reveals a public-private partnership between the Internet firms and the U.S. government that enabled WikiLeaks' opponents "to achieve extra-legally much more than law would have allowed the state to do by itself" (Benkler 2011, 342). Similar public-private collaboration and a reliance upon intermediary-facilitated regulation are evident in the case of intellectual property and in regard to regulation on the Internet in general.

TRANSFORMATION OF INTELLECTUAL PROPERTY

To understand the U.S. government's contemporary status as the world's leading proponent of intellectual property, it is important to trace its evolution in this area. The anticounterfeiting regime grew out of efforts, from the mid-1970s to the mid-1990s, in which rights holders and their trade associations persuaded the U.S. government to elevate intellectual property rights to a key economic priority. Many of the industry actors who participate in the anticounterfeiting regime have been active for decades in lobbying the U.S. government to strengthen intellectual property rights.

The United States Becomes an Intellectual Property Champion

The United States was not always a champion for intellectual property rights. It has benefited economically from centuries of disregarding intellectual property laws, as have other industrialized economies (Drahos and Braithwaite 2002; Halbert 1997). By the 1970s, however, there were growing concerns in the United States that other countries would make economic gains that would undermine its position as an economic powerhouse. At that time, U.S. policy makers were preoccupied with the possible loss of U.S. competitiveness, growing trade deficits, foreign debt, and the rise of manufacturing in Asia, particularly in Japan (Drahos and Braithwaite 2002; Halbert 1997).

Fears that these factors were endangering U.S. economic hegemony grew as major U.S. corporations like IBM, Pfizer, and Microsoft loudly complained that infringement of their intellectual property rights by Asian countries threatened their businesses (Drahos 1995). These corporations petitioned the U.S. government for assistance with a nationalistic narrative that compellingly linked strengthened intellectual property rights with a strong U.S. economy (Drahos 1995). Major industries characterized the problem as one of "theft" of American hard work and innovation by "pirates," thus effectively reframing the issue as a moral and economic problem (Halbert 1997). Industry claims over unfair trading practices presented emerging Asian economies as Asian "villains" and improbably transformed wealthy, well-established U.S. industries into "victims" (Halbert 1997).

The U.S. government seized upon this convenient and reassuringly simple explanation for its complex fiscal woes. Based upon rights holders' convincing narrative of "theft," the U.S. government conceptually coupled intellectual property with international trade (Halbert 1997). The link between intellectual property and economic growth is therefore socially constructed and reflects the perceptions and interests of the U.S. government and of certain prominent corporate interests, particularly the interests in the pharmaceutical, software, and movie industries. The conceptual linkage between intellectual property and trade explains the importance that the United States and the European Union accord to the protection of intellectual property rights (Drahos and Braithwaite 2002). There are also economic benefits to owning intellectual property, which disproportionately flow to large multinational rights holders in the United States and Europe (see Sell 2010). From this point on, intellectual property was irrevocably linked with trade, and large corporate rights holders became an integral part of U.S. policy making.

Rights Holders Shape Global Standards

Having convinced the U.S. government of the economic importance of intellectual property, major U.S. rights holders and their trade associations shifted their attention to establishing worldwide standards for the protection of intellectual property rights.

In close collaboration with the U.S. government, these corporate actors pursued this goal in two nearly concurrent efforts between the mid-1970s and mid-1990s. One avenue was to introduce protection for intellectual property into trade agreements, beginning with the General Agreement on Tariffs and Trade (GATT). The second was to set standards globally through the World Intellectual Property Organization (WIPO), the international body that governs agreements on trademarks, copyright, and patents. While the U.S. government and its industry actors played an important role, they did not act alone. Key business interests in Europe and Japan also pushed for tougher standards. The protection of intellectual property rights is thus best understood as a loosely coordinated effort by global corporate actors representing a diverse array of multinational corporations and trade associations (Matthews 2002).

In the United States, the industry actors pushing for global standards for intellectual property represented some of the biggest corporate interests in the country. Companies like IBM were concerned about copyright infringement of their software programs, as was their industry association, the Business Software Alliance (BSA). The music and movie industries were likewise troubled by the mass production of unauthorized versions of their products. The high-profile Motion Picture Association of America (MPAA) and the Recording Industry Association of America (RIAA) represented copyright owners. Global pharmaceutical companies, particularly Pfizer, argued that insufficient protection of their valuable patents meant that their innovations faced threats from India and Brazil. Alongside these groups, the International Anti-Counterfeiting Coalition (IACC) advocated on behalf of a broad array of industries concerned about protecting their trademarks, copyright, and patents. Its corporate members include some of the world's biggest multinational corporations, ranging from Calvin Klein, Nike, and Pfizer to Phillip Morris, Sony, and Walt Disney. Many of these companies and trade associations, especially the IACC, are also involved in the nonbinding agreements on counterfeit goods.

Corporate Actors as Trade Negotiators

In recognition of the growing influence of major U.S. rights holders like Pfizer on trade-policy making, both in the United States and internationally, the U.S. government formalized industry's advisory role in 1981 when it created the Advisory Committee for Trade Negotiations (ACTN).[2] The Office of the United States Trade Representative (USTR) organizes and administers the ACTN and relies upon the committee to provide it with policy advice. The USTR is at the heart of trade-policy making and enforcement in the United States. USTR officials negotiate trade agreements, develop and enforce trade policies, and work with U.S. industries and trade associations to represent U.S. commercial interests abroad.

Members of the ACTN formed a powerful committee, the Intellectual Property Committee (IPC). A small group of executives from major U.S. industries comprised the IPC, including representatives from Pfizer, IBM, General Electric, DuPont, Warner Communications, General Motors, and Johnson & Johnson (Matthews 2002). Through these committees, powerful corporate actors had the authority, legitimized by the U.S. government, to propose and negotiate standards and rules at the transnational level to govern the protection of intellectual property.

Influencing Global Trade Agreements

Members of the Intellectual Property Committee, along with like-minded industry actors from Europe and Japan, continued their campaign, alongside the U.S. government, to set global rules to protect intellectual property rights. Two prominent avenues for doing so were GATT and the WIPO, as discussed earlier.

The General Agreement on Tariffs and Trade, created in 1947, was both a trade agreement and a process for securing international trade agreements, until the World Trade Organization (WTO) replaced it in 1995. The GATT took place through a series of negotiations in distinct iterations, or "rounds," each of which took months or years to complete. Negotiations focused on removing tariffs from industries ranging from textiles and chemicals to steel and agricultural products. Industrialized countries, particularly the United States, pushed for the inclusion of intellectual property in the Tokyo Round, which was held from 1973 to 1979, but developing countries resisted, leading to a stalemate.[3]

In addition to pursuing the GATT negotiations, advocates for intellectual property rights also focused their efforts on the World Intellectual Property Organization. The WIPO, established in 1967 in Geneva, Switzerland, is an agency of the United Nations. It coordinates intellectual property policies among its member countries and administers global agreements, including the Paris Convention for the Protection of Industrial Property, introduced in 1883, which is concerned with the protection of trademarks and patents. In the late 1970s, industrialized countries raised alarms about the WIPO's "toothlessness" (Blakeney 1995, 2) and its apparent inability to counter the growing international trade in copyright-infringing goods and counterfeit products. Trade associations and industrialized countries, again led by the United States, sought to revise the Paris Convention to better enforce trademark and patent laws. However, meetings among signatories between 1980 and 1984 broke down because of irreconcilable differences between industrialized and developing countries, much as occurred during the GATT Tokyo Round (Blakeney 1995).

New Global Regime for Intellectual Property

Following repeated defeats, proponents of intellectual property rights finally succeeded in the Uruguay Round of the GATT, which was held from 1986 to 1994. Members of the Intellectual Property Committee developed the United States' position on protecting intellectual property and then established consensus with trade associations in Japan and Europe (Sell 2003). This industry coalition formally supported the IPC's proposals on intellectual property protection, which in 1994 became the Agreement on Trade-Related Aspects of Intellectual Property Rights (TRIPS).

TRIPS was the first multilateral agreement to incorporate enforcement mechanisms for protecting intellectual property, and it fundamentally reshaped intellectual property rights (Sell 2003). The agreement also established the World Trade Organization in 1995 as a forum for governments to negotiate trade agreements and resolve trade conflicts. All countries that wished to become members of the WTO had to sign on to TRIPS, providing a powerful economic motivation for countries to sign. TRIPS requires all WTO member states to criminalize trademark and copyright infringement and to adopt both civil and criminal penalties.

For the Intellectual Property Committee, the creation of TRIPS was a noteworthy achievement. Twelve executives from U.S.-based corporations had created a law that fundamentally changed the enforcement of intellectual property rights worldwide (Sell 2003). In two decades, a small group of mostly U.S. rights holders and trade associations had persuaded the U.S. government to elevate intellectual property to an economic priority and make the issue an integral element of its trade agreements. The role of industry in creating TRIPS demonstrates that the economic interests of the U.S. government and its rights holders and trade associations are intertwined. Equally, this international agreement illustrates the considerable influence that major U.S.—and European—corporations wield in relation to the regulation of intellectual property, both in the United States and internationally.

Influence through Economic Sanctions

U.S. rights holders are not only influential lobbyists and trade advisors to the U.S. government, but they also have access to a powerful tool to enforce their intellectual property rights: the leverage of the massive U.S. economy.

In response to industry pressure, in 1984 and again in 1988, the U.S. government reformed its domestic trade legislation to strengthen its protection of U.S. companies' intellectual property rights. In 1988, the government created the Special 301 Process through the Omnibus Trade and Competitiveness Act. These amendments, drafted in part by industry, allow the Office of the U.S. Trade Representative to impose economic sanctions on countries that do not provide what the U.S. government considers adequate protection for intellectual property or that fail to ensure market access for U.S. firms.

The USTR uses the Special 301 Process to evaluate countries' protection of intellectual property and to impose sanctions against problematic countries. The Special 301 Process has three tiers of sanctions: priority foreign country, priority watch list, and watch list. The U.S. government can pressure countries with unsatisfactory practices and threaten to withdraw trade benefits from or impose duties on a country's goods. The Special 301 Process shows that intellectual property is privileged as a national economic interest of the United States. As a result, the protection of U.S. firms' intellectual property rights worldwide is backed up by the power of the U.S. market and force of the U.S. government.

As part of this process, the USTR publishes an annual survey, called the *Special 301 Report*, that identifies U.S. rights holders' concerns with particular countries. This report names and shames countries, such as China and Russia, that U.S. industry groups consider problematic in terms of safeguarding intellectual property. The report also outlines the legal and regulatory changes that the countries must adopt before the USTR removes them from the Special 301 blacklist.

Industry complaints and industry-provided data drive the Special 301 Process. Rights holders and trade associations provide resources for the "global surveillance network" required by the initiative, as well as data for estimates of industry losses (Drahos and Braithwaite 2002, 107). In turn, the U.S. government provides the bureaucratic infrastructure that negotiates with, threatens, and sanctions targeted countries (Drahos and Braithwaite 2002). This means that U.S. corporations command a powerful tool—the clout of the U.S. government—in their efforts to strengthen rules that govern intellectual property rights worldwide. The Special 301 Process is also a stark indication of the alignment of U.S. rights holders' and the U.S. government's economic interests.

Blacklisting Notorious Markets

In 2006, the USTR updated the *Special 301 Report* to target problematic real-world and online marketplaces, again in response to industry lobbying. This report, called the *Out-of-Cycle Review of Notorious Markets,* identifies problematic marketplaces based on industry complaints. Notorious markets include physical marketplaces, like the Silk Market in Beijing, and online platforms, such as the Pirate Bay.

As in the case of the *Special 301 Report,* rights holders submit industry data and analysis alleging that specific Internet companies, websites, or platforms are failing to protect intellectual property rights in a manner that rights holders consider adequate. When the USTR names companies or websites as "notorious markets," it pressures them to make specific changes to their enforcement policies and practices that have been identified by U.S. rights holders as deficient. The USTR also pressures countries in which the notorious markets are located by threatening to impose sanctions or withdraw access to U.S. market. Through the Special 301 Process, rights holders thus use the authority and market dominance of the U.S. government to back their efforts to export their desired standards globally and shape policy making by corporations and countries alike.

The Special 301 Process is controversial, not least because it fundamentally relies upon industry data and analysis to make determinations of wrongdoing. Critics argue that it lacks credibility and legitimacy and is biased toward industry interests. The Electronic Frontier Foundation and Public Citizen, U.S.-based civil-advocacy groups, contend that the process the USTR uses for determining "adequate" and "effective" protection for intellectual property rights lacks methodological rigor (see

Electronic Frontier Foundation 2015). In fact, the alleged activity need not violate a trade agreement with the United States in order for the USTR to censure the country in which it takes place (Flynn 2010, 5). This flexibility provides U.S. rights holders with considerable latitude in censuring countries and marketplaces that do not meet tough U.S. standards for the protection of intellectual property.

TRACING THE INTERNET'S POLITICAL ROOTS

Having established how a small group of rights holders transformed intellectual property from a purely commercial concern into a national economic priority for the U.S. government, and then helped shape global standards to protect intellectual property, I now discuss regulation in the online environment. To understand how Internet intermediaries, especially those based in the United States, became such powerful regulators, it is necessary to explore the political roots of the Internet. The U.S. government strategically developed policies that would favor its economic and security interests, as well as privilege its commercial enterprises. The commercial dominance of U.S. intermediaries—Google, Microsoft, eBay, Visa, PayPal, and GoDaddy—is not a coincidence but the result of decades of investment and policy making by the U.S. government.

Those who developed the Internet imbued, whether consciously or not, its technologies, policies, and protocols with particular norms and values (Carr 2012). Understanding the emergence of intermediaries as global regulators involves exploring the values and assumptions embedded within certain technologies and examining how they may privilege certain political and legal orders. In relation to the anticounterfeiting regime, this requires critically examining the ideas that privilege intellectual property rights and designate intermediaries as regulators responsible for enforcing those rights online.

State power, particularly that of the U.S. government, is embedded in the Internet. The U.S. government played a key role in the development of the Internet through its Department of Defense, with academic institutions in the United States and Europe also playing central roles.[4] As the primary state actor involved in creating the Internet, the U.S. government has shaped the Internet's legal, economic, and security policies in ways that tend to favor large U.S. companies and serve broadly Western economic interests (Carr 2015; Powers and Jablonski 2015).

Beginning in the early 1990s, during President George H. W. Bush's administration, the U.S. government fostered research on information and communications technologies with the strategic goal of "information as a form of state power" (Carr 2012, 184). Control over information is central to the so-called knowledge economy. President Bill Clinton's administration in the 1990s further emphasized a free-market ideology in relation to the development of the Internet through private-sector-led research and commercial enterprise (Carr 2015; Powers and Jablonski 2015).

Growth of the Information-Industrial Complex

Intermediaries that are now global regulators emerged from decades of U.S. government investment in "information industries" involved in the production, storage, processing, and distribution of information (Powers and Jablonski 2015, 51). The result of these public-private partnerships in this area is an information-industrial complex in which the government facilitates the growth of Silicon Valley through subsidies, direct investment, and policy making (Powers and Jablonski 2015, 51).[5]

As part of this initiative, the U.S. government was strategic in its funding of important early academic and private-sector research that created technologies and applications foundational to the Internet through the Defense Advanced Research Projects Agency, established by the U.S. Department of Defense (Ziewitz and Brown 2013). For example, former vice president Al Gore, while still a senator, introduced the High Performance Computing and Communication Act of 1991, which helped develop Internet technology by funding, among other things, the first commercial web browser, Mosaic (Carr 2012, 184). The Clinton administration in the early 1990s shifted billions away from Cold War–related military initiatives to the U.S. technology industry under the Defense Reinvestment and Conversion Initiative (Powers and Jablonski 2015, 59).

The U.S. government also invests in developing new technologies through the Central Intelligence Agency's nonprofit venture capital firm, In-Q-Tel, which was created in 2000 (Harris 2014). In-Q-Tel primarily invests in firms that are creating technology to process and analyze data, such as in relation to mapping applications and monitoring information flows (Powers and Jablonski 2015). Overall, the government's goal is to cultivate a communications and information technologies sector that serves its security interests and will expand U.S. economic dominance. The close ties between the government, especially the National Security Agency, and U.S. Internet companies were revealed in the Snowden files.

The NSA relies heavily on siphoning information from U.S.-based companies and, in return, protects these companies from threats, including foreign hackers (Harris 2014). As a result, U.S. intermediaries serve as a (sometimes reluctant) arm of the government. In doing so, these companies facilitate national-security-related goals, such as cracking down on WikiLeaks and expanding U.S. surveillance capabilities. These intermediaries also serve U.S. economic interests by expanding the enforcement of intellectual property rights online.

In addition to funding the development of communications and information technologies, the U.S. government has also for decades instituted and promoted policies that commodify information as a good to be acquired, stored, and monetized (Powers and Jablonski 2015). One way the government did this was to campaign for agreements, such as TRIPS, to protect intellectual property rights. The government also normalized the commodification of information by enacting (and exporting) policies that favor advertising-based consumerism through radio, television, and the Internet (Powers and Jablonski 2015). By emphasizing the monetization of information, the United States strategically expanded the global market for software, hardware, and content such as music and movies; and at the same time, it exported its preferred standards, norms, and regulations to govern the flow of this information (Powers and Jablonski 2015, 22).

The commodification of information is a central element of many Internet firms' business models. Advertising-based business models are also standard. These policies gave an advantage to new U.S. companies, such as Google, Amazon, eBay, and Yahoo, all of which were created in the 1990s, as well as to established companies like Microsoft (founded in 1975). The policies also helped pave the way for the subsequent generation of Internet companies like YouTube, Facebook, Twitter, LinkedIn, and Instagram, all founded in the first decade of the twenty-first century.

Many Internet firms, like Google, have advertising-driven applications that rely upon siphoning vast amounts of personal data from their users to sell to advertisers. Their business models are built upon surveillance (Schneier 2013), which makes these Internet companies valuable regulatory allies for state security agencies or corporations combating problems as diverse as leaked classified information (WikiLeaks) and counterfeiting. U.S.-based companies have a commercially dominant presence on the Internet (with some exceptions, such as China, where local firms have a controlling market share in the search and payment industries). As a result, major U.S. companies have the ability to globally shape policies that serve their interests and favor their business models.

EVOLUTION OF INTERMEDIARIES AS REGULATORS

The political roots of the Internet—the particular policies and business models that privilege U.S. economic and security interests—also shape Internet firms' roles as regulators. Regulation on the Internet has changed dramatically since the early days of the Internet. To understand how a handful of U.S.-based Internet firms became powerful global regulators, it is important to consider briefly how the idea of Internet intermediaries has evolved significantly, along with expectations regarding their regulatory roles.

In the early days of the Internet, from the 1970s to the early 1990s, many people argued that the Internet was a novel, ungovernable space that operates beyond the reach of nation-states. Proponents of this perspective, often called cyber-libertarians, promoted the online environment as a space where governments have no control. As discussed earlier, the U.S. government, particularly its Department of Defense but also its academic institutions, played a key role in the development of the Internet. However, the U.S. government was not directly involved in regulating the Internet during this phase but instead took a "passive" approach (Goldsmith and Wu 2006, 32). Even in this early phase the Internet was not completely unregulated. Governance was largely left to the group of academics, engineers, and dedicated users who created its various applications and networks, and who chose a self-regulatory style of setting and enforcing rules (Ziewitz and Brown 2013).

The promise of Internet intermediaries as de facto regulators became clear early in the development of the Internet. In a landmark speech in 1994, for example, Vice President Gore outlined a shift from a "traditional adversarial" regulatory relationship between business and government to one based on "consensus" in relation to the Internet (Gore cited in Powers and Jablonski 2015, 61). Such consensus does not necessarily denote a fully cooperative relationship. Governments may work indirectly with intermediaries by setting regulatory targets or prescribing specific regulatory frameworks or enforcement practices that intermediaries must adopt. As is the case with the informal agreements, governments may prefer to direct intermediaries to act in the absence of specific legislation or court orders.

Regulation through intermediaries offers states (and in the case of intellectual property, rights holders) certain advantages. Corporate actors like intermediaries may be more responsive and adaptive to changes in technology or circumstances than regulation through legislation or international law or agreements (Büthe 2010). Proponents of using intermediaries argue that third parties are often able to regulate targeted activities more efficiently and in a more cost-effective manner than can state authorities (Mann and Belzley 2005). This depends on the third party's resources and willingness to act as a gatekeeper and bear any costs it may incur. By working through third parties, states or corporate actors facing controversial or unpopular regulatory options can delegate actions to nonstate actors and govern indirectly, a practice often termed "policy laundering" (Mueller 2010, 209).

To be effective, intermediaries acting as regulators must be both willing to act in this capacity and capable of governing their platforms in response to certain types of wrongdoing. Intermediaries, however, vary in their willingness to act as regulators on behalf of states or rights holders. Internet firms, which, after all, tend to be profit-seeking enterprises, often express reluctance to serve as de facto regulators and, more importantly, lack the capacity to distinguish legal from illegal activities online or to mediate among competing legal claims. "In general, Google does not want to be a gatekeeper," argues Rachel Whetstone, Google's director of global communications and public affairs (Whetstone 2007). Intermediaries also vary in their regulatory capacity. Their ability to identify and control different types of wrongdoing depends on how they operate, their scope, and the services they offer. They also may have interests that conflict with their regulatory duties and can incur financial and other costs while fulfilling those duties.

Uncertainty over Intermediaries' Roles

The concept of the Internet intermediary has been rapidly evolving since the beginning of the twenty-first century. In the early 1990s, intermediaries that were commonly understood to work as regulators were web hosts, Internet service providers like Verizon, marketplaces, and search engines, especially Google. At that time, governments around the world began designating these intermediaries as responsible for addressing a wide range of illegal and inappropriate behavior, from online harassment and child pornography to copyright infringement (see Zittrain 2006).

Since the first years of the twenty-first century, however, there has been an increase in the number and type of intermediaries. Social media platforms like Twitter, Facebook, and Instagram have emerged, as have file-hosting services like Dropbox. Music- and movie-streaming services, such as Netflix and Spotify, have become ubiquitous. However, legal or policy definitions of the term *intermediary* have not kept pace. Thus, there is a lack of clarity in terms of law and policy making concerning which Internet companies should be regarded as intermediaries (Gasser and Schulz 2015, 17). This is not simply an arcane legal debate. It means there is considerable legal uncertainty as to which Internet actors (under formal definitions of the term *intermediary*) have legal responsibility for policing their platforms for wrongdoing (see McNamee 2011). Further, there is little clarity about the nature of their regulatory responsibilities in relation to wrongdoing carried out by their users (see McNamee 2011). This means that the very idea of Internet firms as regulators is in flux. As a result, there is considerable uncertainty—and protracted legal disputes—about the legal responsibility that different types of companies have for policing copyright and trademark infringement occurring on their platforms (see McNamee 2011).

At the same time that intermediaries face this legal uncertainty, states and, increasingly, rights holders are demanding that intermediaries take on expanded regulatory roles. This is because intermediaries generally have valuable technical skills, access to specialized information or systems, and the capacity to monitor or control flows of information across their platforms. Because of the key roles they play in regulating flows of online information and activity, Internet intermediaries, particularly large U.S.-based companies like Google and PayPal, have emerged as de facto global regulators of online life. The rules they set through their terms-of-use agreements govern the activities of the hundreds of millions of people who use their services. In setting their rules, they exercise considerable authority in deciding what information people can access, use, and share, and what items they can purchase and how. They are also central players with regard to online privacy, they possess the considerable latitude necessary to require their users to divulge certain personal information, and they can track their users' digital footprints across their platforms and related services.

In recognition of intermediaries' centrality to online life, observers have referred to them as "chokepoints" (DeNardis 2014, 11), "natural points of control" (Zittrain 2006, 254), "bottlenecks" (Bracha and Pasquale 2008, 1161), and even "sovereigns of cyberspace" (MacKinnon

2012, xxvi). As these descriptors suggest, it is no exaggeration to say that "Internet intermediaries govern online life" (Pasquale 2010, 105) and can be understood as "builders of our social reality" (Laidlaw 2015, 42) that have varying degrees of influence over the ways people may participate in social, political, and economic life on the Internet.

Targeting Content and Disabling Sites

Despite the diversity of intermediaries, they all generally employ common practices to deal with problematic information on their platforms or behavior by their users. They can block access to or remove information from their platforms, or they can withdraw their services from particular websites.

Intermediaries that facilitate information flows, such as search engines, web hosts, or social media platforms, may block access to specific web pages, specific keywords, entire websites, or certain services, such as social networking sites. They can create "white lists" (permitted content) or "blacklists" (prohibited content) to determine what information users can access. For instance, intermediaries in the United States and United Kingdom use blacklists to block access to sites distributing child pornography. The U.K. government also operates a secretive, voluntary website-blocking program targeting "violent extremism" sites, which host content that violates the country's antiterror laws (see McIntyre 2010). Intermediaries may also be required to block access to sites promoting human rights, freedom of the media, or opposition parties, as is the case in China, Egypt, and Iran (see Deibert et al. 2011). Blocking access to targeted sites does not remove content but merely deters access. Users may bypass blocks by using virtual private networks to access the desired content by another route.

Intermediaries can also remove content from the Internet. A common way of doing so is through so-called notice-and-takedown programs. Under such programs, which emerged in the late 1990s, intermediaries are responsible for promptly removing certain content from their platforms (the takedown) upon receiving a notification from an authorized party (the notice). Notice-and-takedown programs are used to deal with a range of unwanted content, from offensive material and defamation to the infringement of intellectual property rights. Complainants may use automated tools to send notifications to intermediaries, which, in turn, may remove material through automated programs.

More recently, around 2010, intermediaries began employing another approach, the use of what may be called notice-and-termination programs. While notice-and-takedown programs remove certain types of content, notice-and-termination programs remove certain technical or commercial services from targeted sites. In these programs, intermediaries withdraw their services from certain sites (termination) upon receiving a complaint (notice) from rights holders. Depending on the services they offer, intermediaries may withdraw payment, advertising, or domain name services.

The goal of content-removal techniques like notice-and-takedown programs is to make certain problematic content inaccessible. The website itself remains functional. The goal in withdrawing services is to impair the functionality of the website. By terminating services to targeted sites, the intention is to make it more difficult for potential customers to find and access sites and to push website operators away from mainstream intermediaries toward less-reputable service providers. Programs that rely upon intermediaries receiving complaints before acting are known as ex-post enforcement. They are reactive programs in which intermediaries respond to specific complaints. Intermediaries may also act in the absence of specific complaints by removing content or terminating services. This is known as ex-ante enforcement, because it involves intermediaries acting in a proactive manner.

UNCERTAIN REGULATORY ENVIRONMENT

A principal reason that the nonbinding agreements are central to rights holders' enforcement programs is that efforts to legislate in this area were largely unsuccessful. In the United States, rights holders argued for a decade that legislation was urgently needed to update the existing legal framework, the 1998 Digital Millennium Copyright Act (DMCA). Advocates also lobbied for legislation that would include provisions for targeting the online trade in counterfeit goods, since the DMCA is limited to copyright issues. Rights holders were successful in getting legislation before the U.S. Congress in the form of the Stop Online Piracy Act and the Protect Intellectual Property Act. However, these bills died after the massive online protest and Internet blackout described in chapter 1. In the United Kingdom, while the 2010 Digital Economy Act updated the online protection of copyright, implementation of the law was stalled because of intractable conflicts between rights holders and intermediaries.

Before discussing these unsuccessful legislative efforts and the resulting emphasis on non-legally binding agreements, it is important to highlight the legal frameworks that helped set the standard for dealing with the online trade in counterfeit goods. Two pieces of legislation enacted in Europe and the United States provide a baseline for addressing the online infringement of intellectual property rights: the 2000 Electronic Commerce Directive (E-Commerce Directive) in Europe and the DMCA in the United States.

In 2000, the European Parliament introduced the E-Commerce Directive. All member states of the European Union implemented legislation in line with the requirements of this directive. It harmonizes the conditions under which intermediaries can be held liable for third-party infringement throughout the European Union. It also employs a notice-and-takedown scheme for infringing content similar to that of the DMCA. However, in contrast to the DMCA, the E-Commerce Directive applies to a range of activities, including copyright and trademark infringement, as well as defamation. The directive does not provide a legal definition of intermediaries, but it employs the term *information society service providers*. This includes intermediaries that cache or host information or provide conduits for information, a group that includes search engine operators, web hosts, Internet service providers, social network providers, and operators of e-commerce platforms like eBay and Amazon.

Copyright Rules Shaping Anticounterfeiting Efforts

The DMCA, which deals exclusively with copyright, also shaped online enforcement measures against the distribution of counterfeit goods in the United States and internationally. In general, rights holders' push for greater online protection of copyright has also shaped enforcement efforts in relation to trademark infringement. Understanding copyright regulation is important to comprehending online regulation of counterfeit goods.

The copyright lobby is a tightly knit, highly coordinated group dominated by a handful of large firms and prominent trade associations, like the Motion Picture Association of America, that represent the music, movie, book, and software sectors. Lobbying efforts are organized and cohesive, since several key problems, such as unauthorized downloading of copyrighted material, affect all copyright industries. In contrast, those in the trademark lobby describe themselves as "a bit of a hodgepodge" (interview, Croxon 2012). Counterfeiting affects a broad range of industries and makes it difficult for rights holders to adopt a coordinated or standardized approach. Corporate online anticounterfeiting efforts involve rights holders from industry sectors ranging from pharmaceuticals, sporting goods, and alcohol to apparel, consumer electronics, and industrial electrical products.

The regulation of copyright also shapes anticounterfeiting efforts. The DMCA introduced the notice-and-takedown regime, which has been broadly adopted to deal with complaints of trademark infringement. The DMCA grants specific intermediaries conditional immunity from liability for the infringement if, among other criteria, they remove the allegedly infringing content. This is known as the safe harbor provision. Simply put, if intermediaries act promptly in response to a complaint of infringement, they satisfy their legal responsibilities. This idea of limited liability is a core element many of legal frameworks worldwide that deal with online infringement, in relation to both copyright and trademark.

Following the introduction of the DMCA in 1998, intermediaries began to adapt its measures to deal with the online distribution of counterfeit goods. For example, the same year the U.S. government introduced the DMCA, eBay created a notice-and-takedown program called VeRO, the Verified Rights Owner Program. In this program, rights holders submit complaints to eBay regarding sales listings for counterfeit goods, and eBay removes the listings, as is discussed in chapter 5.

Under notice-and-takedown programs, rights holders (or their representatives such as attorneys or private investigators) deal directly with intermediaries. Under the terms of both the DMCA and the E-Commerce Directive, no court or government body verifies rights holders' takedown requests. Nor is there judicial or government oversight of informal regulatory programs like eBay's VeRO program. Critics of notice-and-takedown programs, such as the digital-rights group Electronic Frontier Foundation, point out that these programs are based solely on accusations, not proof, of infringement (Samuels and Stoltz 2012). All that is required from rights holders is a declaration in good faith that they believe their intellectual property rights are being violated. The informal anticounterfeiting agreements are intended to make enforcement more streamlined and rapid, and in fact intermediaries are processing an increasing number of cases of infringement, based only on rights holders' complaints.

Expanding Intermediaries' Enforcement Roles

Between 2009 and 2012, there were increasingly heated debates in the United States and United Kingdom on the enforcement roles and responsibilities of intermediaries. Rights holders and their trade associations in both countries lobbied for tougher online enforcement efforts, arguing that intermediaries should assume greater regulatory responsibilities. Unsurprisingly, intermediaries mostly resisted, arguing that the responsibility to protect intellectual property should remain with rights holders. Civil-society organizations pointed out that the intermediaries' growing regulatory responsibilities were not accompanied by effective oversight measures. These advocacy groups raised the troubling possibility that reliance on private-sector regulation would lead to wrongful targeting of lawful content and behavior, as well as censorship, because unaccountable corporations would have too much say in determining what constituted wrongdoing.

Regulation by intermediaries was an integral part of four U.S. federal bills on intellectual-property enforcement introduced between 2010 and 2012, and of the U.K.'s 2010 Digital Economy Act. In addition to the much-maligned Stop Online Piracy Act and Protect Intellectual Property Act, the U.S. Congress also debated the Combating Online Infringement and Counterfeits Act, which preceded SOPA, and the Online Protection and Enforcement of Digital Trade Act (OPEN Act). SOPA opponents proposed the OPEN Act as an alternative, but it, like the other three bills, failed.

While the four U.S. bills were popularly referred to as copyright bills, they proposed to regulate both the online distribution of counterfeit goods and copyright-infringing content. There are commonalities among the four bills. They adopt an expanded notion of intermediaries, which includes payment providers, advertising platforms, and domain registrars. They propose that intermediaries adopt notice-and-termination programs to withdraw their services from targeted sites. The bills also propose that intermediaries should be able to act voluntarily (that is, without court orders) against sites that unlawfully distribute pharmaceuticals. These similarities indicate a degree of consensus among U.S. policy makers and legislators in terms of enforcement strategies.

In the eyes of their proponents, the bills legitimize the idea that disabling sites through intermediaries' withdrawal of services is a proportionate response to trademark and copyright infringement. More troubling, the bills legitimize the idea that intermediaries are qualified to identify the unlawful distribution of prescription medication and should be able to act freely in the absence of court orders. The Digital Economy Act similarly formalizes the notion of intermediaries' expanded responsibility for dealing with infringement by their users.

Four U.S. Anticounterfeiting Bills

When Senator Patrick Leahy, a Democratic senator from Vermont, introduced COICA in the Senate Judiciary Committee in September 2010, there was no indication that intellectual property would captivate millions of people less than two years later and spark a massive online protest. Under the bill, the attorney general could seek court orders against domestic and foreign domain names that hosted (or linked to) sites that distributed counterfeit goods or copyright-infringing material. Domain names are those names given to Internet protocol addresses, such as "ThePirateBay.se." One domain name may pertain to multiple websites. COICA's Section 2(e) proposed that domain name registrars, payment providers, and advertising platforms be required to withdraw their services from targeted domains involved in trademark or copyright infringement. COICA's Section 2(e) also would have granted these intermediaries the right to act voluntarily against domains they reasonably believed were "dedicated to infringing activities." This means that intermediaries could operate without court orders simply based on their reasonable belief that sites were involved in trademark or copyright infringement.

Given the breadth of COICA's proposals, some degree of opposition from stakeholders, if not yet the general public, was inevitable. Protest against the act came from technologists, civil-society groups like Electronic Frontier Foundation, and others who argued that the bill would facilitate censorship of legitimate speech. Senator Ron Wyden, a Democrat from Oregon and a fierce opponent of the bill, announced he would vote against it in a full Senate vote. COICA, he said, was "almost like using a bunker-busting cluster bomb when what you really need is a precision-guided missile" (Anderson 2010). Although the Senate Judiciary Committee passed COICA, Wyden's opposition halted the bill's progress through the Senate, and the Senate withdrew COICA.

Much like SOPA's rebirth in the form of nonbinding agreements, COICA did not disappear but was reborn months later with another name. In May 2011, Senator Leahy introduced the Preventing Real Online Threats to Economic Creativity and Theft of Intellectual Property Act, or Protect Intellectual Property Act (PIPA), in the Senate Judiciary Committee. If opponents had expected that PIPA would address problems posed by COICA, they were largely disappointed.

Under PIPA, the attorney general could seek court orders to require intermediaries to withdraw their services from particular infringing websites (not domain names, as COICA would have done). Like COICA, PIPA would have granted intermediaries the right to act without court orders against certain types of sites. PIPA's Section 5(b) would have allowed intermediaries to act against sites unlawfully selling or dispensing medication without a valid prescription. PIPA also went further than COICA. Under Section 4, PIPA proposed to grant rights holders the ability to seek a court order to compel payment providers and Internet advertising networks to suspend the services they provided to infringing sites. This measure would have given rights holders the capacity and flexibility to target infringing sites without going through the attorney general. Like COICA, PIPA attracted considerable criticism from civil-society activists, who argued that the bill would wrongly censor protected speech and grant corporate actors too much power to determine whether content and activities infringed upon their intellectual property rights, as described in chapter 1.

While protests over PIPA were growing, Representative Lamar Smith, a Republican from Texas, introduced SOPA in the House Judiciary Committee in October 2011. SOPA, as noted in chapter 1, proposed measures similar to those in PIPA. For example, SOPA's Section 103 would have granted rights holders the ability to seek a court order to force intermediaries to withdraw their services from targeted sites (known as a "private right of action"). Similarly, SOPA's Section 105 would have allowed intermediaries to withdraw their services from sites involved in trademark or copyright infringement, and from sites unlawfully distributing prescription medication (termed a "voluntary right of action").

In an attempt to defuse rising protests over SOPA and PIPA, two critics introduced an alternative, the Online Protection and Enforcement of Digital Trade Act, in December 2011. Senator Wyden brought it to the Senate Finance Committee, and Representative Darrell Issa, a Republican from California, introduced the bill in the House Judiciary Committee. OPEN differed substantially from the previous bills. Instead of depending on the attorney general to seek court orders against infringing sites, the OPEN Act proposed to use the U.S. International Trade Commission (ITC), an independent, quasi-judicial federal agency with an investigative mandate for trade-related issues. Under OPEN's Section 337A, the ITC would grant orders to rights holders that would compel payment-service providers and advertising intermediaries to withdraw their services from infringing sites.

U.K. Conflict over Intermediaries' Roles

In the United Kingdom, similar debates flared up over the limits of intermediaries' regulatory responsibilities and the enforcement techniques that intermediaries should use to control wrongdoing on the Internet. The catalyst for the public debate—and the heated conflict between rights holders and intermediaries—was the 2010 Digital Economy Act. Although this law focused solely on copyright infringement, its failure led to informal agreements that targeted both counterfeit goods and copyright infringement.

For intermediaries, the controversial aspect of the Digital Economy Act is its requirement that Internet service providers, like Virgin Media, that give users access to the Internet must pass on complaints from rights holders to subscribers involved in downloading copyright-infringing content. After sending the third warning letter, Internet service providers must terminate the subscribers' Internet access. This measure is known as a "three-strikes," or "graduated response," program. Intermediaries and rights holders disagreed over who should bear the cost of implementing the three-strikes system.

The U.K. Department for Culture, Media and Sport, which is responsible for administering the Digital Economy Act, admitted in July 2014 that the three-strikes program was essentially dead (*Out-Law* 2014). Instead of seeking to negotiate or legislate a solution to the conflict, unnamed government officials stated that an "industry solution" was now the government's "preferred option" (*Out-Law* 2014). During the protracted industry conflict over the three-strikes system, rights holders, particularly the U.K. music industry, lobbied the government to take action. In response, the Department for Culture, Media and Sport hosted a series of roundtables for intermediaries, rights holders, and their trade associations to explore informal regulatory responses that would deal with both trademark and copyright infringement, as is discussed in the next section.[6]

Debates in the United States and United Kingdom over the nature and limits of intermediaries' regulatory responsibilities for counterfeit goods and copyright infringement form an important part of the backdrop to the creation of the non-legally binding agreements. Rights holders broadly supported the U.S. bills and the Digital Economy Act. For rights holders, the legislation represented a much-needed update to protect their trademarks and copyrights in the rapidly changing online environment.

For opponents, however, the U.S. bills and Digital Economy Act were controversial, because they shifted greater enforcement responsibility to intermediaries without a corresponding increase in oversight or accountability. Critics in both countries argued that the legislation would result in censorship, delegate power to unaccountable industry actors, and impose disproportionate penalties on offenders, including the termination of users' Internet services and impairment of sites' functionality when key services were withdrawn. Opponents of the U.S. bills also emphasized the potential for the miscarriage of justice in relation to intermediaries' voluntary right of action. Trevor Timm, a journalist and activist with the Electronic Frontier Foundation, referred to the voluntary measures as a "vigilante provision" and argued that the "standard for immunity is incredibly low and the potential for abuse is off the charts" (Timm 2012).

As the following sections discuss, this voluntary measure, a highly controversial provision within SOPA and PIPA, is a central element of the nonbinding agreements. Government officials involved in the informal agreements would pressure intermediaries to exceed their legal responsibilities and independently and proactively target sites that the intermediaries believed were distributing counterfeit goods.

EMERGENCE OF "VOLUNTARY" ENFORCEMENT INITIATIVES

The transnational private anticounterfeiting regime is rooted in the United States and Europe, particularly the United Kingdom, where small groups of government and corporate actors set rules and standards that are then exported worldwide through the macrointermediaries' global platforms. China is a key target of the regime, given its status as the primary manufacturing site for counterfeit goods. Three government bodies are principally involved in facilitating nonbinding agreements in relation to online copyright and trademark infringement: the Office of the U.S. Intellectual Property Enforcement Coordinator; the Department for Culture, Media and Sport; and the Directorate General Internal Market and Services within the European Commission.

There is strong government support for non-legally binding efforts to target trademark and copyright infringement in the United States and Europe. In December 2011, for example, member countries of the Organization for Economic Cooperation and Development (OECD) endorsed a set of fourteen principles for policy making in relation to the

Internet. Among the principles that OECD members supported was fostering voluntary codes of conduct (Organization for Economic Cooperation and Development 2011). Non-legally binding enforcement efforts got another endorsement from the G-8 nations—which include the United States, United Kingdom, and European Union—in May 2012 at a meeting at Camp David in the United States. In an official statement, leaders affirmed the importance of "private-sector voluntary codes of best practices" in dealing with intellectual property rights (White House 2012).

The European Commission's commitment to industry self-regulatory programs and to regulation that exceeds what is required by law (known as "compliance-plus" enforcement) is drawn from its consumer agenda, which encourages industry to draft voluntary codes of conduct (European Commission 2012). The 2000 E-Commerce Directive, which was described earlier, explicitly recognizes and endorses voluntary action by intermediaries against online wrongdoing. Article 40 of the E-Commerce Directive calls upon member states of the European Union to develop "rapid and reliable procedures for removing and disabling access to illegal information," and it allows that these could be developed "on the basis of voluntary agreements between all parties concerned." In 2004, the European Commission called upon industry to take an active role in anti-infringement efforts and promoted the development of non-legally binding codes of conduct as "a supplementary means of bolstering the regulatory framework" (European Commission 2004, 4).

The United Kingdom's support for voluntary industry actions against online infringement is grounded in these European Union directives. U.K. government officials also endorse intermediaries' adoption of greater responsibility for policing Internet content and their users' behavior. For example, the government's 2011 Intellectual Property Crime Strategy recommends that advertising, payment and marketplace intermediaries should play more active roles in addressing online infringement (Intellectual Property Office 2011).

Office of the U.S. Intellectual Property Enforcement Coordinator

In the United States, the department behind the informal agreements— the Office of the U.S. Intellectual Property Enforcement Coordinator— is small and almost entirely unknown to the general public. Despite its size, IPEC has had an outsized influence on the creation of multiple nonbinding enforcement agreements. The U.S. Senate created the office with the Prioritizing Resources and Organization for Intellectual Property Act (PRO-IP Act) of 2008 and located it within the Office of Management and Budget in the Executive Branch. IPEC's mission is singular: it coordinates and enhances the U.S. government's federal enforcement efforts solely in relation to intellectual property rights.

Victoria Espinel was appointed as the first head of IPEC by President Barack Obama in 2009 and served until she left in August 2013. After departing IPEC, Espinel became the president and chief executive of the Business Software Alliance, the main trade association representing the interests of software companies internationally.[7] During her tenure at IPEC, Espinel was popularly referred to as the intellectual property "czar." This is a fitting title for Espinel, who announced that her goal was to "change the enforcement paradigm" (Intellectual Property Enforcement Coordinator 2012, 5) in relation to online infringement by working "to encourage practical and effective voluntary actions to address repeated acts of infringement" (Espinel 2012). The term *intellectual property czar* further indicates the priority that the U.S. government accords the protection of intellectual property.

In 2010, IPEC published its first strategic plan, which announced plans to work with the private sector voluntarily and "collaboratively" through "carefully crafted and balanced agreements" to address online infringement (Intellectual Property Enforcement Coordinator 2010, 17). Beginning in 2010, Espinel coordinated a series of meetings among Internet firms and payment providers to create sets of industry-generated best practices to address the online trade in counterfeit goods and copyright-infringing content. She strongly endorsed intermediaries' withdrawal of services from targeted sites, arguing, "Starving illegal online businesses of revenue for unlawful goods or services will disrupt, and even cripple, the business model of many illegal websites" (Espinel 2011).

IPEC's closed-door negotiations with Internet firms occurred at the same time that Congress was considering COICA, SOPA, and PIPA, and protests were slowly growing against the bills. Following these closed-door meetings, Espinel announced a series of informal agreements. The agreements cover a wide range of Internet services, including search, payment, advertising, and domain name services, and involve major Internet firms and payment providers—namely, Google, Microsoft, Visa, PayPal, MasterCard, GoDaddy, Yahoo, AOL, Bing, Taobao, and American Express. See table 2.

Although it was not involved in creating an informal agreement, another U.S. department plays a key role in convincing intermediaries

TABLE 2   U.S. AGREEMENTS

Macrointermediary	Scope	Nonbinding Agreement
MasterCard, Visa PayPal, and American Express	Global	Agreement with payment providers (IPEC)
MasterCard, Visa PayPal, and American Express	Global	Payment-termination program (IACC)
Google, Yahoo, AOL, and Bing	Global	Ad networks' statement of best practices (IPEC)
American Express, Visa, MasterCard, PayPal, Google, GoDaddy, Yahoo, and Microsoft	Global	Center for Safe Internet Pharmacies (targets unlawful distribution of medication) (IPEC)
Taobao	China	Memorandum of understanding to remove counterfeit goods from Taobao marketplace (USTR)

to work with rights holders. The Office of the U.S. Trade Representative (USTR) pressured Taobao to work with U.S. rights holders and trade associations, especially the International Anti-Counterfeiting Coalition.

Department for Culture, Media and Sport

While negotiations were under way in the United States over non-legally binding agreements, U.K. rights holders began pushing government officials to hold similar discussions. In the United Kingdom, two government departments share responsibility for intellectual property: the Department for Culture, Media and Sport (DCMS) and the Department for Business, Innovation and Skills. Given its subject matter of culture and sport, the DCMS is known colloquially as the "Ministry of Fun."

Two senior government officials play key roles in the coordination of nonbinding agreements. Jeremy Hunt served as secretary of state for culture, media, and sport between May 2010 and September 2012 and is a Conservative member of Parliament. Ed Vaizey served as parliamentary under secretary of state for culture, communications and creative industries within DCMS between May 2010 and July 2014. Following his tenure as under secretary, Vaizey, a Conservative member of Parliament, became minister of state at DCMS and the Department for Business, Innovation and Skills in July 2014. As parliamentary under secretary, Vaizey had responsibility for Internet and creative industries, culture, and broadband, spectrum, and telecommunications, among other duties.

TABLE 3   U.K. AGREEMENTS

Macrointermediary	Scope	Nonbinding Agreement
Google, Yahoo, Bing	United Kingdom	Digital Trading Standards Group (advertising)
Google, Yahoo, and Bing	United Kingdom	Search intermediaries code of conduct

As discussed earlier, industry demands for informal enforcement measures to address online trademark and copyright infringement arose during
the delay in implementing the three-strikes program of the 2010 Digital
Economy Act. In late February 2011, Vaizey began organizing and hosting
a series of roundtables with rights holders, trade associations, and intermediaries. Despite the series' name, the Online Infringement of Copyright
Roundtables also considered measures to address the online distribution
of counterfeit goods. The roundtables included discussions about creating
informal agreements for payment, advertising, and search intermediaries.
The stated mission of the roundtables was to "check on progress that is
being made both in the regulatory environment and in terms of industry-
led initiatives to reduce the level and viability of online infringement of
content" (cited in Bradwell 2012). Between 2011 and 2013, Vaizey helped
coordinate discussions among intermediaries and rights holders, create a
nonbinding code of conduct for search engines, and push forward the
implementation of a new self-regulatory program for the U.K. digital
advertising industry (see table 3). Major Internet and telecom firms participated in the roundtables, including Google, Yahoo U.K., Bing, Microsoft, Facebook, Virgin Media, and British Telecom.

European Commission

In 2009, even before IPEC had started negotiations in relation to its informal agreements, unnamed representatives from the Directorate General
Internal Market and Services began closed-door negotiations with industry stakeholders. In relation to intellectual-property policy making, the
directorate focuses on making enforcement measures more effective and
establishing cooperation "between authorities at all levels in the fight
against IP infringements." In terms of the negotiations to address counterfeit goods, officials from the European Commission coordinated "a structured dialogue between stakeholders to facilitate mutual understanding"
(European Commission 2009, 10). For the negotiations, the commission

TABLE 4   EUROPEAN AGREEMENT

Macrointermediary	Scope	Nonbinding Agreement
eBay (European operations)	European Economic Area	Memorandum of understanding to remove counterfeit goods from eBay marketplace

provided administrative and logistical support, and it also reported playing a role by "safeguarding, where necessary, a fair balance between all the different interests at stake, including the legitimate rights and expectations of EU citizens" (European Commission 2009, 10).

The goal of these discussions was to strike a nonbinding agreement in relation to the sale of counterfeit goods through online marketplaces (see table 4). In early May 2011, the European Commission quietly posted online an agreement titled simply "Memorandum of Understanding." The agreement sets out general principles for marketplaces and rights holders to work together in cracking down on the sale of counterfeit goods in the European Economic Area (European Commission 2011). This informal agreement gives industry stakeholders "the flexibility to adapt quickly to new technological developments" (European Commission 2009, 10). Thirty-nine marketplaces signed the agreement, including the European operations of eBay and Amazon, such as those located in the United Kingdom, Sweden, Italy, and Germany.

Regime Participants

There is no comprehensive listing of all the industry participants of the nonbinding agreements. Macrointermediaries' involvement, however, is more easily discernible from press releases announcing the agreements. Macrointermediaries who are signatories to the agreements are headquartered in the United States and have operations in multiple other countries. Many of the intermediaries that participate in the regime dominate their respective industry sectors: Google for the search and digital advertising industries; Visa, PayPal, MasterCard, and American Express for the payment industry; GoDaddy for the domain industry; and eBay for marketplaces. The only non-U.S. company among the intermediaries is Taobao, part of the massive e-commerce Alibaba Group that dominates the consumer-to-consumer marketplace in China. See table 5.

TABLE 5   EIGHT NONBINDING ENFORCEMENT AGREEMENTS

Initiative	Coordinator	Macrointermediaries
Ad networks' statement of best practices	IPEC	Google, Yahoo, AOL, Bing (Microsoft)
Payment account termination program	IPEC	MasterCard, Visa PayPal, American Express
Payment account termination program	IACC	MasterCard, Visa PayPal, American Express
Center for Safe Internet Pharmacies (payment, advertising, and domain)	IPEC	American Express, Visa, MasterCard, PayPal, Google, GoDaddy, Yahoo, Microsoft
Memorandum of understanding (marketplace)	USTR	Taobao
Digital Trading Standards Group (advertising)	DCMS	Google, Yahoo, Bing
Search intermediaries code of conduct	DCMS	Google, Yahoo, Bing
Memorandum of understanding (marketplace)	European Commission	eBay

Several influential trade associations also played a prominent role in lobbying for and shaping the informal agreements. In the United States, the International Anti-Counterfeiting Coalition worked with the USTR to establish a nonbinding agreement with Taobao, and created a payment-termination program with major providers, which IPEC helped to coordinate.

The European Commission's agreement brought together sixteen trade associations, representing the software, textile and clothing, pharmaceutical, film, and sporting goods industries. These include the U.K. Anti-Counterfeiting Group, the Business Action to Stop Counterfeiting and Piracy, the Motion Picture Association, and the Interactive Software Federation of Europe. Since the 1980s, these associations have helped to shape intellectual property-related laws and policies at the national and international levels.

In the United Kingdom, copyright trade associations played a prominent role in lobbying the government to coordinate nonbinding agreements to address not only copyright infringement but also the trade in counterfeit goods. Participants included major trade associations: the Federation Against Copyright Theft, the British Phonographic Industry, the Motion Picture Association of America, and the Internet Advertising Bureau, which represents the digital advertising industry in the

United Kingdom and is concerned with both trademark and copyright infringement.

In terms of rights holders, there is no comprehensive listing of those participating in the anticounterfeiting regime because, in contrast to their trade associations, they generally maintain a lower profile. Only the European Commission names rights holders and trade associations that are signatories to its agreement. Fourteen companies, many with multiple well-known brands, joined the marketplace memorandum. These include Adidas, Burberry, Louis Vuitton, Dior Couture, Mattel (makers of Barbie and Fisher-Price), Microsoft, Nike, Nokia, Proctor & Gamble, Richemont (owners of Cartier), and Unilever. An indication of other participating rights holders can be gleaned by examining the membership directories of the participating trade associations, especially the IACC. It represents companies from the apparel, sporting goods, and pharmaceutical industries, including Pfizer, L'Oréal, Nike, and Johnson & Johnson.

The final element of the private enforcement agreements is the brand-protection industry, which is composed of a wide array of companies offering monitoring and investigative services to police copyright and trademark infringement. These companies identify and seize counterfeit goods from locations where they are manufactured. They also monitor marketplaces and stand-alone websites for sale of counterfeits or distribution of copyright-infringing content, use automated tools to send takedown notices in relation to search results and sales listings, and target repeat offenders and those selling bulk quantities of counterfeit goods.

As this discussion shows, the informal agreements discussed in depth in the following chapters did not emerge out of thin air. Political, legal, and technological developments shaped the way for intermediaries to become global regulators, with important consequences. As the following case studies show, these informal agreements raise fundamental problems with oversight and accountability that are natural consequences of the breadth and volume of intermediaries' enforcement activities. In particular, macrointermediaries' considerable latitude in setting and enforcing rules for huge populations that depend on their services gives them the potential to negatively affect entire businesses, technologies, and services on the Internet. Effectively, they can govern—somewhat arbitrarily and with little oversight—how people can access, use, store, and share information and creative content; what goods they may trade and purchase and how; and the technologies and platforms they can use. These informal agreements are a key way that they exercise this power.

3

Revenue Chokepoints

Payment providers, particularly those with global operations, have emerged as powerful regulators, given their ability to control the online flow of funds. By withdrawing their payment services, these intermediaries can seriously disrupt the capacity of businesses or individuals to generate revenue by raising donations or selling goods and services. The largest payment providers—Visa, PayPal, and MasterCard—are particularly active gatekeepers for states and other corporate actors. As discussed in the previous chapter, these providers withdrew their services from WikiLeaks in 2010 after intense pressure from the U.S. government. This campaign against WikiLeaks, which significantly disrupted the organization's ability to generate the donations it relies upon, shows the regulatory power of major payment providers.

These payment macrointermediaries also act independently—and sometimes arbitrarily—against companies or organizations that they contend violate their policies. Between 2011 and 2013, for example, PayPal terminated its services to a fund-raising campaign for Chelsea Manning's legal defense, a crowd-funded initiative for an email service in Iceland, and online publishing companies whose books featured erotic content including incest, underage sex, and bestiality (Zetter 2011; Hutchinson 2013; Charman-Anderson 2012). PayPal reversed its decision in each of these cases following criticism of censorship and unfair enforcement practices, as well as arguments by supporters stating that the websites involved were in compliance with PayPal's policies.

People may disagree with fund-raising efforts to help Chelsea Manning, or may find books featuring incest or bestiality as erotic distasteful. In these cases, however, the activity was legal and PayPal took action without a court order. These cases underscore intermediaries' latitude in designating specific content or behavior as inappropriate for their services. Simply put, even when the content or behavior in question is legal, intermediaries can draw upon their broadly worded terms-of-service agreements to withdraw their services from any user at any time.

Payment intermediaries are "an important part of the armory in the fight against counterfeits," explains Siân Croxon, a London-based attorney with the law firm DLA Piper (interview, Croxon 2012). Payment processing and advertising are the lifeblood of sites that generate revenue by collecting donations, selling goods and services, or hosting digital advertising. Sites reliant upon donations or sales must have a functional payment-processing capacity and typically offer several trusted, well-known payment options. Site operators may also generate revenue by hosting advertisements on their web pages. To disrupt infringing sites, payment intermediaries can choke the sites' flow of illicit revenue (funds from the sale of counterfeit and copyright-infringing goods), while advertising intermediaries can choke the flow of licit revenue (advertising). By impairing access to these essential services, intermediaries can starve websites of revenue.

Payment and advertising intermediaries can sanction those who violate their policies by limiting or terminating their services. Payment providers terminate a site's merchant account, which removes the site's capacity to process payments relating to that provider. Advertising intermediaries can similarly withdraw their services by canceling the provision of new advertisements to appear on those sites. Website operators who lose payment services and advertisements can seek alternatives; however, a few large companies dominate each industry. Visa, MasterCard, PayPal, and American Express are the largest online payment providers, and Google operates the biggest digital advertising business.

While both payment and advertising intermediaries can throttle sites' revenue, payment macrointermediaries are the more powerful regulators. This is because sites can function without advertising revenue, but they need payment services to process donations or customers' payments. Further, because the online payment industry is dominated by a handful of providers, affected sites have few commercial alternatives. Payment macrointermediaries can essentially cut off actors deemed "bad" from the global online payment system, crippling, possibly fatally, their means of conducting business. This is the essence of governing through revenue chokepoints.

As the PayPal examples show, intermediaries have significant latitude in determining that certain activities, from pornography and political fund-raising to the sale of counterfeit goods, violate their policies. A discussion of case studies will demonstrate how intermediaries, particularly those with a dominant market share in an industry, raise the serious problem of anticompetitive, or other types of, unfair regulatory behavior. By virtue of their market share and regulatory capacity, payment and advertising macrointermediaries may inadvertently—or, more troublingly, deliberately—target lawfully operating sites. Macrointermediaries, especially payment providers, thus can act as private arbiters of legality. In doing so, they can affect what Internet users can purchase and how they can use payment systems, even with respect to situations where the goods or services in question are legal.

DIGITAL PAYMENT INDUSTRY

For those looking to shop online, make donations to their favorite charity, or generate funds from their website by selling products there is an increasing number of ways to send and receive funds online. There are digital currencies like Bitcoin. A rapidly growing number of online payment processors, like WePay or 2CheckOut, facilitate the transfer of funds to individuals or businesses by transferring money from credit card accounts or bank accounts. Credit card companies, like Visa or MasterCard, enable people to purchase goods based on the cardholders' agreement to pay off a portion of the monthly balance. PayPal, on the other hand, is an online payment company that enables users to transfer money using their bank accounts, credit cards, or PayPal account.

Despite the wide array of payment options, Visa, MasterCard, and PayPal dominate the online payment industry. Visa, created in 1958, is the largest payment provider, both online and offline, having facilitated payment and cash transactions of $7.4 trillion worldwide in 2015 with 2.4 billion cards worldwide (Visa 2016, 2). According to the industry research company Nilson Report, Visa commanded 58 percent of the global market in 2014 (Nilson Report 2015). Following Visa is Master-Card, formed in 1966, which controls 26 percent of the payment market (Nilson Report 2015), with 727 million credit cards worldwide

(MasterCard 2014). American Express trails Visa and MasterCard in terms of market share but is still a major credit card company worldwide. Created in 1850, American Express had approximately 117.8 million cards in use globally in 2015 that facilitated payments of $1.04 trillion worldwide (American Express 2015, 2).

PayPal is the largest online payment company. Created in 1998, PayPal has 179 million active customer accounts and, in 2015, processed 4.9 billion payments for a volume of transactions totaling $282 billion (PayPal 2016). eBay, which purchased PayPal in 2002, split the company into an independent publicly traded company in July 2015 so PayPal could better compete with its growing number of competitors in the online payment industry.

Sites that want to attract customers or donations, whether they operate legally or illicitly, tend to accept funds from at least one of the major payment providers. A New York law firm, Gioconda Law Group, examined three thousand websites that U.S. federal courts ordered closed for selling counterfeit goods. The study found that Visa, MasterCard, and PayPal are, in that order, the most common payment methods on sites selling counterfeit goods (Gioconda Law Group and RogueFinder 2012). Therefore, by working with these providers, rights holders can orchestrate a significant crackdown on the sale of counterfeit goods online.

How Payment Providers Operate

Given the complexity of the online payment industry, it is important to briefly consider how Visa, MasterCard, and American Express operate and process payments. For the consumer, these credit card companies all function in a similar manner. However, there is an important difference that affects how payment providers terminate merchant accounts. Visa and MasterCard operate what is termed an "open-loop" payment system, while American Express mostly operates a "closed-loop" payment system.

Visa and MasterCard are card associations: they each operate globally through a network of tens of thousands of formally affiliated and licensed financial institutions. An open-loop payment system means that Visa and MasterCard neither issue cards to users, nor grant merchant accounts to individuals wishing to process commercial payments. Instead, these card associations license financial institutions around the world to issue their branded payment cards (e.g., a credit card from Citibank with a Visa or MasterCard logo).

Entities that grant people credit cards are called "issuing" institutions. Financial institutions that grant merchant accounts that can accept payment by Visa or MasterCard are known as "acquiring" institutions. Any bank or credit union can issue credit cards or grant merchant accounts for Visa or MasterCard as long as the card association approves them. "We allow the cardholder sitting in Turkey to do business with a merchant in Germany within a nanosecond," explains Martin Elliott, director of corporate risk management at Visa International. "What we don't do is: We don't issue the cards. We don't sign the merchants. We don't lend money to folks" (Elliott 2012).

The closed-loop system, in contrast, is much simpler. These systems are popular among department stores, where payment cards are limited to use within a particular store. American Express operates a closed-loop system in which it directly issues payment cards to users and has a contractual relationship with merchants. It processes payments made between cardholders and merchants without a network of financial institutions. To make matters more complex, however, American Express primarily operates its closed-loop system in the United States. Outside the United States, it establishes agreements with third-party financial institutions in the American Express network in a manner similar to that of Visa and MasterCard.

Purchasing Goods Online

Anyone who has purchased goods from a legitimate online retailer has an idea of how online payments work at the consumer's end, but there are complex and highly technical transactions behind the checkout page. Imagine purchasing something from your favorite online retailer. You click to the checkout page and enter your payment and shipping information. The site then lists various payment options: Visa, Master-Card, PayPal, and American Express, each with its easily recognizable trademark. Each of these is called a financial or payment channel. On legitimate sites, each of these payment channels is functional. On infringing sites not all channels may function but may be used to give the appearance of legitimacy.

The transaction process varies according to the type of payment you choose (see table 6). If you are in the United States and decide to pay with an American Express card (assuming a closed-loop process), the transaction proceeds as follows. You enter your payment details, and the merchant's system sends the transaction directly to American

TABLE 6 PROCESSING PAYMENTS ONLINE

MasterCard or Visa (Open-Loop)	American Express (Closed-Loop)
Cardholder submits card to merchant's system.	
1. Merchant's bank asks card association (Visa or MasterCard) to determine issuing bank.	1. Merchant's system sends the transaction to American Express.
2. Card association's authorization system validates card's security features and forwards the request to issuing bank for purchase approval.	2. American Express verifies the card and authorizes the transaction.
3. Issuing bank approves purchase. Card association sends approval to acquiring bank.	3. American Express sends approval to merchant.
4. Acquiring bank sends approval to merchant.	
Cardholder completes purchase and receives receipt.	

Express. American Express verifies the card, authorizes the transaction, and sends approval to the merchant.

If you pay with Visa or MasterCard (an open-loop payment system), the transaction goes between the cardholder's issuing bank and the merchant's acquiring bank for approvals by both before it is processed. These transactions take only milliseconds as each of the card associations uses proprietary algorithms to verify the purchase, which includes checking the customer's spending profile, location, and credit limit and the merchant's location, and either approving the purchase or flagging it as suspicious (Fisher 2015). Once these approvals are granted, the merchant's site processes the buyer's credit card payment.

PayPal, in contrast, operates quite differently. Users can pay for goods by transferring money from their PayPal account to the business, or they can pay using the credit card that they linked to their PayPal account.

The differences in how payment providers operate are important because they affect how these providers can target wrongdoing by their users. American Express (through a closed-loop process) and PayPal have a relatively direct relationship with their users, while Visa and MasterCard must work through their networks of banks that issue credit cards and merchant accounts.

Payment Intermediaries' Enforcement Policies

Payment providers each have complex, lengthy terms-of-use contracts that they use to set and enforce their policies. Most people may not read—or fully understand—the contract they sign to get a credit card or to open a PayPal account.

MasterCard and Visa (operating through open-loop networks) have contractual agreements with each of their issuing and acquiring banks. Each bank that works in MasterCard or Visa's network must adhere to that card association's rules when offering payment services. In turn, these banks have contractual relationships with merchants operating real-world or online stores and with cardholders who use their credit cards to purchase goods from those stores. If you have a Visa card from Bank of America, for example, you must abide by all the terms set by the bank and by Visa. As discussed earlier, Visa and MasterCard do not have direct contractual relationships with merchants or cardholders. This means that Visa and MasterCard cannot restrict or terminate access to those accounts since affiliated banks granted them. Instead, the card associations instruct acquiring institutions, say, the Bank of China, to investigate suspicious behavior and take appropriate action, which includes the termination of merchant accounts.

Payment providers' terms-of-service agreements lay out how users and merchants can use the services, what activities are unacceptable, the responsibilities of issuing and acquiring financial institutions, and the penalties for violating policies. The agreements vary somewhat from country to country, reflecting national laws that prohibit the sale of certain goods and services, such as weapons, illicit drugs, and counterfeit products. Visa and MasterCard, for example, state that any transactions "must be legal in both the Cardholder's jurisdiction and the Merchant Outlet's jurisdiction" (Visa 2013). Rights holders and their trade associations refer to these contractual agreements as a "legal linchpin" (Montanaro 2012). This is because these agreements grant payment intermediaries the considerable authority necessary to order the termination of merchant accounts of sites anywhere in the world that violate their policies. PayPal, like other intermediaries, reserves the right to terminate, at its "sole discretion," its agreement with users "for any reason and at any time upon notice to you" (PayPal 2015, 10.3h).

Violation of these providers' terms-of-use policies can result in a range of sanctions. Payment providers may suspend or terminate users' accounts, thereby leaving them without the capacity to process payments.

PayPal, for example, retains the right to freeze users' funds. Visa, Master-Card, or American Express may levy fines on acquiring banks in their network of financial institutions that fail to detect or deal adequately with merchants who violate their policies (see e.g., American Express 2013). As Bob Barchiesi, president of the International Anti-Counterfeiting Coalition, notes, these fines are "the hammer that the credit cards have over" their network of licensed financial institutions (Barchiesi 2012). They help ensure that acquiring banks do not grant merchant accounts to individuals involved in selling illegal goods or otherwise engage in behavior that payment providers disapprove of, for legal or other reasons.

Terminating Merchant Accounts

The big four payment providers all have processes for dealing with violations of their policies that predate their signing the non-legally binding enforcement agreements. Visa, MasterCard, and American Express have similar procedures for terminating merchant accounts. Rights holders may send complaints of infringement directly to providers, or they may work through authorized third parties, such as trade associations that undertake enforcement efforts, and attorneys or private investigative or brand-monitoring firms. The process is relatively straightforward:

1. The complainant provides contact information and evidence of ownership of the trademark(s) in question to the relevant payment provider.
2. Complainants describe the alleged infringement and capture a screenshot of the site showing the product(s) for sale.
3. They note the web address of the site.
4. They provide evidence of payment methods by capturing a screenshot of the site's checkout page showing, for example, the Visa logo.
5. They attest that the merchant is not authorized to sell the products in question.
6. They provide evidence that they have notified the website operator of the infringement through, for example, cease-and-desist letters.
7. They attest that the information is accurate and complete, with statements made in good faith.

TABLE 7 PAYMENT ACCOUNT TERMINATION

Rights holder complains of an infringing site to payment providers	
PayPal investigates the site	Visa and MasterCard require the relevant acquiring bank to investigate the merchant account
PayPal terminates the merchant account, if warranted	Acquiring bank conducts investigation and terminates the merchant account, if warranted
Site can no longer process payments through PayPal	Acquiring bank reports back to Visa or MasterCard
	Site can no longer process payments through Visa or MasterCard

Once the payment providers receive a complaint, they trace the transaction to identify the acquiring bank that granted the merchant account to the website operator in question (see table 7). Visa and MasterCard require that the acquiring bank respond within two business days if law enforcement has initiated the complaint and within five business days for rights holder-generated complaints (MasterCard n.d.). Acquiring banks must conduct an investigation and terminate the merchant account, if warranted. If the bank decides termination is not necessary, Visa and MasterCard demand, in the words of MasterCard, that acquirers "provide compelling, written evidence disproving the violation" (MasterCard n.d.). Banks are thus motivated to fine, and terminate the accounts of, people who are involved in wrongdoing or, indeed, any activities that the card associations deem inappropriate, because the card associations can levy fines upon banks that they find have been negligent in their duties.

PayPal's process for sanctioning users is much simpler since it does not operate through a network of acquiring financial institutions. PayPal has a dedicated internal security unit of analysts who use proprietary software to detect misuses of PayPal's services. PayPal also hires third-party online monitoring firms to "crawl the Internet looking for key words, indicators and PayPal brands and references" that may be in use improperly or without PayPal's permission, explains Julie Bainbridge, PayPal's senior brand protection manager (interview, Bainbridge 2012). If PayPal representatives detect a violation of the company's policies, they conduct an investigation. "If we detect behavior in violation of our terms [of service], the PayPal account is restricted," says Bainbridge. PayPal then sends an email to the user saying the account is restricted because of a violation and that the merchant can no longer accept payment by PayPal.

PAYMENT INTERMEDIARIES AS REGULATORS

Payment intermediaries' regulatory processes serve an important function, as anyone who has been a victim of credit card fraud can attest. These intermediaries have financial interests in ensuring that their systems are secure and trusted, and consumers also benefit from stable, reliable payment systems. Payment providers have valuable brands that they want to protect from any negative association with criminal activity. "Your brand is getting damaged," Bob Barchiesi, president of the IACC, warned payment providers when he campaigned to persuade them to work closely with his association to target infringing sites, "because your brand lends credibility to these [infringing] sites" (interview, Barchiesi 2012).

Payment intermediaries are valuable regulators because they supply critical infrastructure and, given the concentration in the payment industry, affected sites have few viable commercial replacements when the largest payment providers terminate their services. Payment intermediaries thus force site operators to seek less-reputable or lesser-known payment providers. A representative from the IACC says the goal of working with payment intermediaries is to "shrink the universe" of intermediaries that provide services to infringing sites (Johnson 2013, 36). Recent academic research backs up this idea: a study of unlawfully operating online pharmacies concludes that "reliable merchant banking is a scarce and critical resource that, when targeted carefully, is highly fragile to disruption" (McCoy et al. 2012, 1).

For advocates of tougher regulation of intellectual property, creating revenue chokepoints is an effective enforcement tactic. These chokepoints, however, have the potential to affect both lawfully operating sites that may share payment channels with targeted sites, and legally operating businesses whose services may facilitate infringement, such as virtual private networks. Disruption of these legally operating sites is preventable collateral damage resulting from overly broad, mass enforcement campaigns. Because payment intermediaries' efforts occur outside the authority of the courts and public scrutiny, their actions display a troubling lack of accountability and oversight. Instances of wrongful or abusive enforcement come to light only when site operators publicize their cases or warn their users about suddenly inoperable payment systems.

Two early cases, in which payment providers blocked sites selling child pornography and tobacco, illustrate not only intermediaries' regulatory prowess and potential for abuse but also governmental pressure on intermediaries to compel their participation.

From Child Pornography to Online Tobacco Sales

Tackling the online sale of counterfeit goods was not the first time that payment macrointermediaries agreed to work in the absence of court orders or legislation. Payment intermediaries first agreed to work voluntarily in relation to websites that sold child pornography: images and videos of child sexual abuse. Beginning in the late 1990s in the United Kingdom, and in the early twenty-first century in the United States, government officials were rightfully concerned about the growing online black market in child pornography. Law enforcement agencies in both the United States and the United Kingdom found it difficult to shut down these sites, which typically operated outside their legal jurisdictions. Since these sites charged fees to their customers, payment intermediaries were ideally situated to block users' payments related to child pornography and terminate the sites' merchant accounts, thus disabling the sites.

At this time, both the United States and the United Kingdom had legislation prohibiting the sale or distribution of images of child sexual abuse. But government officials wanted payment intermediaries to take a more proactive approach and independently track down child pornography sites instead of merely reacting when law enforcement made an official complaint.

To combat the online sale of child pornography, the U.S. and U.K. governments created nongovernmental organizations with the participation of Internet companies and financial institutions. In 1996, the U.K. government created the Internet Watch Foundation (IWF), which is a nonprofit organization funded, in part, by the European Union and by Internet companies like Google.[1] The U.S. government followed suit in 2006 with the formation of the Financial Coalition Against Child Pornography (FCACP) as part of the National Center for Missing and Exploited Children, a nonprofit organization funded by the U.S. Department of Justice. These organizations bring together payment providers (Visa, MasterCard, and PayPal), banks, search intermediaries, web hosts, and other providers of Internet services. Industry participants agree to voluntarily terminate their services to any website identified by the organizations as involved in distributing child pornography. No court orders are necessary, since the sale or distribution of child pornography violates intermediaries' terms-of-service agreements with their users (as well as constituting a criminal offense).

Despite the rhetoric of voluntary industry involvement, governmental pressure was key in compelling intermediaries to join the IWF and FCACP. The U.K. government explicitly stated that Internet companies would face legislative regulation if they did not create a self-regulatory body to address child pornography websites (Sutter 2000, 360, cited in Laidlaw 2012, 6). In the United States, the pressure was somewhat subtler. U.S. Senator Richard Shelby, a Republican from Alabama, is widely credited by his Senate colleagues for bringing together Internet firms and payment providers in 2005 to create FCACP through his role as chair of the Senate Banking Committee.

Shelby convened a meeting of the leaders of financial institutions, including Visa, MasterCard, and PayPal; and in a letter to these leaders and his Senate colleagues, he wrote, "If people were purchasing heroin or cocaine and using their credit cards, we would be outraged and we would do something about it. This is worse" (cited by Sarbanes 2006, 6). Shelby's statement demanding industry action highlights how references to terrible crimes—the sexual abuse of children—can catalyze enforcement responses. Appealing to businesses and asking them to work together to protect children from horrific abuse is a worthwhile effort, and likely an easy argument. Once an enforcement program is established, however, it is an almost irresistible temptation to expand it from its original purpose (the serious offense of child sexual abuse) to other, more mundane social problems. U.S. government officials did just this when they demanded that payment intermediaries block payments in relation to unlawful online sales of tobacco on the grounds that it constituted a problem for public health and tax collection.

The moral imperative for payment providers to act proactively and independently to tackle sites is less clear-cut in the case of sites that unlawfully distribute tobacco in the United States than in the case of child pornography. It is legal to sell and purchase tobacco online in the United States, provided that retailers meet certain legal requirements, such as by verifying buyers' ages and declaring relevant taxes. In 2005, Visa, MasterCard, PayPal, and American Express agreed to prohibit payment processing for sites in violation of state and federal policies on tobacco sales. Public health researchers lauded the agreement, and an official from the Bureau of Alcohol, Tobacco and Firearms declared that industry participation was "completely voluntary" (*Green Sheet* 2005).[2]

This agreement was not voluntary. To encourage cooperation from payment providers, forty-two state attorneys general warned the providers that they believed the sites were violating U.S. federal and state laws on tobacco and instructed the payment companies to take measures to address these violations (MacCarthy 2010, 1084). In doing so, the state attorneys general underlined the possibility that payment providers could be held accountable for facilitating criminal activity by processing unlawful transactions.

Precursors to the Anticounterfeiting Agreements

The IWF, FCACP, and the tobacco agreements, all non-legally binding arrangements among payment intermediaries and government officials, are important forerunners to informal anticounterfeiting agreements. Participants characterize these programs as voluntary, but coercive pressure by state actors to compel intermediaries' involvement is evident. The U.S. and U.K. governments directly pressured payment intermediaries with the threat of legislation (in the case of IWF) and with legal action (in the tobacco agreement).

Heinous offenses like the trade in child sexual abuse images may, for some, justify any enforcement measures, even those of dubious legality. But it is essential to remember that rule-of-law principles, including due process, are foundational elements of Western, liberal democratic legal systems. These legal systems do not provide exceptions for certain offenses that may inflame public sentiment or excite moral panics. At the time they created the informal agreements, the U.S. and U.K. governments had legislation in place that prohibited the online distribution of child pornography, and the United States had various federal and state laws that regulate sales of tobacco.

For government officials the problem was that the enforcement of laws against these offenses on the Internet is complex and often fraught with difficulty. By turning to payment intermediaries, government officials off-loaded enforcement responsibility and assigned it to private companies instead. This assumes—wrongly—that intermediaries can effectively distinguish legality and illegality online and act accordingly, and narrowly, to target wrongdoing. Regulation through intermediaries is often problematic because they operate absent public or judicial oversight and with little disclosure of their regulatory efforts. When intermediaries have the capacity to stifle legitimate speech or disable websites by withdrawing critical online services, nonbinding regulatory programs warrant close scrutiny.

CITY OF LONDON POLICE'S INFORMAL PARTNERSHIP

Given the secrecy that has surrounded most of the non-legally binding agreements relating to trademark and copyright infringement, it is difficult to determine exactly when they began. One of the earliest informal partnerships relating to intellectual property emerged around 2009 in the United Kingdom between rights holders, payment providers, and the City of London Police. At that time, U.K. copyright owners and their trade associations were concerned about websites operating outside the United Kingdom, especially in Russia and Ukraine, that enabled people to download copyright-infringing files of music for a small fee. As discussed in chapter 2, the well-organized and -funded copyright lobby is typically a leader in terms of enforcement strategies, and is followed by trade associations targeting counterfeit goods. The success of the U.K. music industry in forging a non-legally binding agreement with the assistance of the U.K. government influenced the development of similar programs in the United States that target the online trade in both copyright-infringing and counterfeit goods. Victoria Espinel learned of the informal agreement from the City of London Police soon after becoming head of IPEC, and according to a London police department official, "she was very excited" (interview, Wishart 2012).

Informal Agreements Begin by Targeting Russian Sites

In 2009, U.K. trade associations were trying to shut down Russia-based websites by appealing to Visa and MasterCard to withdraw their services from the sites. When the payment providers refused, rights holders sought assistance from the City of London Police, which has responsibility for addressing intellectual property-related crime in the United Kingdom. Although the City of London Police has a small official jurisdiction—the three-kilometer-square area covering London's financial district—the agency is responsible for investigating financial crime across the country. At that time, City of London Police officers were working with the U.K. music industry on the copyright-infringing sites. The challenge, however, was that U.K. police agencies have no jurisdiction over sites located outside the United Kingdom, and taking action against such sites would have constituted a violation of their policies. This is why rights holders appealed to Visa and MasterCard to remove their services from the copyright-infringing sites voluntarily.

Visa and MasterCard, however, were reluctant to act voluntarily. A key reason, explains Denise Yee, senior trademark counsel at Visa, is that payment providers "are not well positioned to identify counterfeit or copyright-infringing content" (Yee 2011, 13). Yee states, "Where legality is not clear, we have no authority to decide what is lawful," and payment providers are therefore in the "precarious position of either agreeing with the IP owner or the merchant" (Yee 2011, 13). It can be difficult to distinguish trademark or copyright infringement with certainty, especially online, as discussed in chapter 2. If payment providers in that "precarious" position make the wrong call, Yee points out, they may be open to lawsuits (Yee 2011).

In 2006, for example, Visa and its acquiring institution withdrew payment services from the Russia-based site AllofMP3.com, which was distributing unauthorized downloads of music (Yee 2011). AllofMP3.com's site operator sued Visa; and in a decision that Visa found "surprising" (Yee 2011, 13), the Russian courts found that the site did not infringe on copyrights under Russian law and ordered Visa to restore the site's payment services. The AllofMP3.com case illustrates the challenges that payment providers can face in determining wrongdoing when the legality of the activities is not clear, especially if their interpretation of their policies is overruled by courts in particular jurisdictions. However, even in this case Visa retained a certain degree of control over its services. Visa restored its services only between AllofMP3.com and its Russian customers, essentially cutting off the site from the rest of the world (Yee 2011).

"We Reckon We Can Prosecute"

Returning to the 2009 case of the U.K. music industry, the City of London Police adopted a novel approach and forged a partnership with Visa and MasterCard. A key figure in creating the informal agreement with the payment providers was Detective Superintendent Bob Wishart at the City of London Police, head of national operational delivery at the regional fraud project. Wishart went on to head the Police Intellectual Property Crime Unit, operated jointly by the City of London Police and the U.K. Intellectual Property Office, which is discussed later in this chapter in relation to the regulation of digital advertising in the United Kingdom.

Wishart, who was working with U.K. rights holders in 2009, sought legal advice from lawyers at the City of London Police. Based on this advice, Wishart warned the payment providers that unless voluntary cooperation was forthcoming, the City of London Police was prepared to lay criminal charges against them. These charges would relate to money laundering, because the City of London Police would argue that Visa and MasterCard benefited financially from processing payments from the infringing site. Wishart recalls cautioning Visa and Master-Card, saying: "Look, you are effectively supporting these sites. We're telling you that they are illegal. . . . We're telling you that from here on in, everything that you earn out of these sites is potentially proceeds of crime. We're putting you on notice. We checked the legislation, and we reckon we can prosecute" (interview, Wishart 2012).

Given that ultimatum, the providers agreed to work cooperatively with rights holders. "MasterCard stepped up to the plate straightaway," recounts Wishart. "Visa, who had more of the market share, were slightly more reluctant and didn't want us involved." The payment providers argued with Wishart that it was not their responsibility "to police the Internet" (interview, Wishart 2012). Wishart countered this claim by referring to the payment providers' enforcement efforts against child pornography. Visa and MasterCard acknowledged, Wishart explains, that "they pay hundreds of thousands, if not millions, of dollars annually to police the Internet to make sure their corporate branding, logos, everything else is in no way connected with any child pornography" (interview, Wishart 2012). Certainly, both copyright infringement and child pornography are offenses. However, drawing a comparison between the unauthorized sharing of music files and child sexual abuse illustrates the classic problem of "mission creep," in which programs expand beyond their original goals (such as combating child pornography) to other social problems, often in ways that were unintended or unimagined by the program's creators.

Wishart is candid in his acknowledgment that the City of London Police provided the necessary "leverage" to the negotiations and acted as "an honest broker" to facilitate cooperation between the music industry and payment providers (interview, Wishart 2012). As the threat of criminal charges against Visa and MasterCard shows, the City of London Police did far more than just supply leverage. According to Wishart's account, coercive pressure motivated Visa and MasterCard to agree to work voluntarily against sites outside the legal jurisdiction of the City of London Police. The resulting nonbinding arrangement was successful. "Overnight we stopped business," Wishart states. Rights holders do all the legwork, and City of London's requests to the providers are informal, without the force of court orders. Wishart explains, "The music industry would do all the work around the websites, present us with an evidence package that we said was to a criminal prosecution standard. Then we would say to Visa and MasterCard, 'Pull the plug on the merchants,' stopping merchant deposits" (interview, Wishart 2012).

The nonbinding agreement that began with a legal threat grew over several years into a coordinated enforcement program with the participation of an array of payment providers, including PayPal. By March 2011, the International Federation of the Phonographic Industry, a music industry trade association, publicly disclosed the program's existence, although it provided few details of the program's operation (Lasar 2011). In a press release by the International Federation of the Phonographic Industry announcing PayPal's participation, Detective Chief Superintendent Steve Head of the City of London Police praised the program, saying that his agency is "fully committed to pro-active initiatives such as these where we work with the private sector" (International Federation of the Phonographic Industry 2011). This agreement marked the first time that elite corporate actors could direct macrointermediaries to act as their gatekeepers, using a regulatory capacity that was previously available only to powerful states.

As mentioned earlier, officials from the City of London Police discussed the informal agreement with Victoria Espinel, which, says Wishart, "really set the ball rolling" in relation to the creation of nonbinding agreements between IPEC and intermediaries (interview, Wishart 2012). "It's sort of ironic that the Americans sort of stole all the good work we've been doing," Wishart comments, "and turned it into something a lot better" (interview, Wishart 2012). The United Kingdom's informal program with payment providers likely influenced Espinel and the creation of similar agreements in the United States. By 2009, however, there was already a campaign in the United States among rights holders and their trade associations for nonbinding enforcement agreements with key Internet intermediaries. The parallel development of non-legally binding enforcement programs in the United States and the United Kingdom, along with a similar agreement coordinated by the European Commission, demonstrates the U.S. and European roots of the anticounterfeiting regime.

NEGOTIATING SECRET DEALS IN THE UNITED STATES

The idea of voluntary industry initiatives began to gain traction in the United States as early as 2009. In that year, the International Trademark Association (INTA), a New York City–based trade body, recommended that intermediaries assume greater enforcement responsibility for the online sale of counterfeit goods. INTA proposed that online marketplace intermediaries, search intermediaries, and payment providers adopt voluntary measures to address the online sale of such goods (International Trademark Association 2009). Prominent intermediaries agreed to the measures, including Visa, MasterCard, American Express, and PayPal, as well as eBay, Yahoo, and Google. Many of INTA's recommendations focused on educating consumers, encouraging intermediaries to work with rights holders, and establishing clear processes to deal with infringement.

In the case of payment providers, however, INTA recommended they consider terminating infringing sites' merchant accounts (International Trademark Association 2009). INTA is a prominent association in terms of formulating and lobbying for intellectual-property-related policies on behalf of its nearly sixty-seven hundred affiliated organizations worldwide. As a result, INTA's advocacy of voluntary merchant-account termination programs to address the trade in counterfeit goods indicates support for this practice among rights holders and their trade associations.

Less than a year after INTA's report and Victoria Espinel's appointment as head of the Office of the U.S. Intellectual Property Enforcement Coordinator, Espinel began holding closed-door discussions with intermediaries, rights holders, and trade associations. As discussed in chapter 2, the backdrop to IPEC's negotiations was Congress's consideration of controversial intellectual property bills: COICA, SOPA, and PIPA. Public opposition to these bills was growing as civil-society groups like Public Citizen and technology websites, especially *Techdirt,* waged increasingly influential campaigns against the bills. Mike Masnick, *Techdirt*'s founder, played a key role in raising the public's awareness of PIPA and SOPA and in marshaling the anti-SOPA protests.

Criticism of these bills, however, was not confined to civil-society groups and technologists. Even payment macrointermediaries expressed reservations over some of the provisions. In testimony to the House of Representatives in late 2011, Linda Kirkpatrick, a senior executive at

MasterCard, argued that some of SOPA's provisions were too burdensome and pointed out several areas where MasterCard wanted amendments. For example, SOPA would have imposed strict time frames on payment providers, allowing them five days to respond to rights holders' complaints of infringing sites (sec. 102, [c][2][A][i]). In the same provision, SOPA also would have given rights holders an opportunity to seek monetary sanctions against payment providers considered noncompliant with the process. Kirkpatrick urged the House Committee on the Judiciary "not to set an artificial deadline for the performance of a specific action as it may present impossible compliance challenges in some circumstances" (Kirkpatrick 2011, 11). It is reasonable to assume that Visa and PayPal also found SOPA's requirements too onerous, although only MasterCard admitted so publicly.

Pressure from the U.S. Government

Intermediaries in negotiation with IPEC faced a delicate balancing act. On one hand, they were motivated to avoid (or amend) legislation that would have imposed strict requirements and time frames on their dealings with rights holders in relation to infringing sites. Non-legally binding arrangements, in contrast, can allow corporate actors greater flexibility and less onerous conditions than legislation. Intermediaries' involvement in informal agreements can also demonstrate their commitment to being good corporate citizens. On the other hand, intermediaries did not voluntarily enter negotiations with IPEC, and, once there, they faced pressure from Espinel to go beyond their previous enforcement efforts—and their legal responsibilities.

According to the payment providers, Espinel pushed them to take a tougher approach than they had previously to the distribution of counterfeit goods. "We know you're at the table being proactive, but you need to do more," Julie Bainbridge, PayPal's senior brand protection manager, recalls Espinel saying in relation to PayPal's enforcement practices (interview, Bainbridge 2012). Linda Kirkpatrick at MasterCard also candidly acknowledged Espinel's central role in shaping the informal agreements: "We have, thanks to Ms. Espinel, an established best-practices policy that all of us have signed up for, a set of minimum standards that many of us far exceed. But it certainly sets the groundwork and framework for what's appropriate" (Kirkpatrick 2012).

Payment Providers' "Best Practices" Agreements

In June 2011, Espinel announced that major payment providers "reached an agreement to develop voluntary best practices to withdraw payment services for sites selling counterfeit and pirated [copyright-infringing] goods" (Intellectual Property Enforcement Coordinator 2012, 46). Signatories to this agreement were MasterCard, PayPal, Visa, and American Express, along with the U.S.-based Discover credit card company. Two documents set out the nonbinding principles: one outlines best practices for payment intermediaries, and the other sets out a complementary set of practices for rights holders in their work with payment providers.[3] The payment providers' agreement, dated May 16, 2011, is titled "Best Practices to Address Copyright Infringement and the Sale of Counterfeit Products on the Internet." The rights holders' agreement, called "Best Practices for Rights Holders with Payment Processors," is dated July 2011.

The payment providers' agreement, a four-page document, lists its participating intermediaries: Visa, MasterCard, PayPal, American Express, and Discover. The document has thirteen sections that detail policies and procedures for payment providers working with rights holders. In sections 1 and 2, payment intermediaries agree to "maintain a clearly identifiable complaint mechanism" for rights holders on their websites and give contact information so rights holders can make complaints. Section 3 lays out detailed steps that rights holders should take in making requests to payment providers for the termination of infringing sites' merchant accounts:

- Provide a description of the alleged infringement, proof of that infringement, and the address of the site in question.
- Provide a screenshot of the payment systems used on the site in question.
- Make a statement that the targeted site is not authorized to sell the goods or supply a copy of a cease-and-desist letter sent to that site.
- Give evidence of ownership of the trademark or copyright in question.

In sections 4 through 9, the payment providers' agreement describes the intermediaries' process for investigating and sanctioning online merchants accused of selling counterfeit or copyright-infringing goods. Section 7 states that if the payment provider determines "in its reasonable opinion that the merchant is engaged in sales of Illegitimate Products," then, according to section 8, the provider "shall suspend or terminate services to that merchant." Section 10 requires payment providers to have a process for the "prompt review of remedial measures" if a merchant (or acquiring institution) disputes the allegations of infringement. The agreement, however, does not specify what or how much process is due when a merchant requests a review, and no provision exists for a third-party review pending resolution of the review (Bridy 2015, 1552). Section 11 states that the payment provider may request written confirmation from the rights holder supporting the allegation of infringement when the merchant demonstrates "credible evidence" that she or he is not involved in illegal conduct, and the rights holder must not hold the payment provider liable for any costs or liabilities resulting from disputes over merchant-account termination. Section 12 sets out definitions for the agreement, while section 13 allows that policies may vary among payment providers.

Best Practices for Rights Holders

The rights holders' agreement, a two-page document, does not list participating rights holders. Unlike the payment intermediaries' agreement, this document sets out generic best practices for rights holders that want to work with payment providers to terminate the merchant accounts of sites involved in violating U.S. intellectual property laws. The rights holders' agreement covers seven main areas. The first section requires rights holders to agree that all complaints (by rights holders or their designated agents, such as trade associations or private security firms) will be made in good faith.

Sections 2 through 6 set out guidelines for rights holders as they coordinate high-volume submissions of complaints through their trade associations, which the agreement calls "channeling associations." These provisions are designed with the understanding that rights holders' trade associations will play a central role in funneling their members' complaints of infringing sites to payment providers. In fact, the International Anti-Counterfeiting Coalition, one of the main trade associations representing major companies in the apparel, pharmaceutical, automotive, and entertainment industries worldwide, worked closely with payment providers and Victoria Espinel to create a payment-termination program targeting infringing sites for its rights-holder members. The IACC's payment-termination program, called RogueBlock, described in the next section, illustrates the strong ties between the U.S. government and its major industries in terms of protecting intellectual property.

In order to coordinate complaints about infringing sites, section 2 of the rights holders' best practices agreement requires rights holders to "channel all complaints" through their trade associations, which "shall endeavor to consolidate such claims made by its members prior to submission to the payment processors." Section 3 asks rights holders to "respond expeditiously to reasonable requests for additional information" from payment providers. Section 4 requires channeling associations to "develop and utilize a common form or system for notifying a payment processor" about the use of its payment service in activities that violate U.S. intellectual property laws. Section 5 requires channeling associations to use standardized coding (e.g., for counterfeit goods or unauthorized copyright streaming) to assist payment providers' enforcement responses. Section 6 asks channeling associations to notify all payment providers when complaints are sent simultaneously to multiple providers to ensure that each knows of ongoing investigations. The last part, section 7, requests channeling associations to provide "baseline training to payment processors on detecting counterfeit products or infringing works."

Government and industry officials involved in drafting the payment providers' informal agreement describe the procedures as "voluntary" (Intellectual Property Enforcement Coordinator 2012). Similarly, in the payment providers' agreement, section 13 clearly stipulates that the procedures it lays out are "voluntary and non-legally binding," and that its best practices "shall not replace, modify or interpret existing law or legal framework." While these agreements do not introduce new, or amend existing, laws, they are explicitly designed to push payment intermediaries to go beyond their legal responsibilities and institute new procedures to process mass numbers of complaints from rights holders. Simply put, the agreements require payment providers to create an enforcement apparatus that exists outside law enforcement agencies and judicial orders and relies upon good-faith declarations from rights holders.

The IACC's RogueBlock program, much like the informal agreements, is a product of governmental pressure on payment intermediaries. The IACC and the payment providers candidly acknowledge the role of IPEC and, especially, Victoria Espinel in coordinating the informal agreements. The RogueBlock program clearly illustrates how non-legally binding agreements can fundamentally alter the way intermediaries address online wrongdoing.

International Anti-Counterfeiting Coalition's RogueBlock Program

The RogueBlock program is an excellent example of how intermediaries' non-legally binding best practices can be translated into concrete enforcement efforts. Bob Barchiesi, IACC president, first heard about payment providers' participation in nonbinding enforcement programs at a White House event. "I think it's a great concept," Barchiesi says he told the providers, "so we want to do it, too" (interview, Barchiesi 2012). Following this encounter, Barchiesi and the IACC staff worked closely with IPEC, especially Espinel, and the payment providers. At the heart of these discussions was how the IACC could play a more active role in combating infringing sites on behalf of its rights-holder members. These discussions, according to Barchiesi, shaped the "Best Practices for Rights Holders with Payment Processors" agreement (interview, Barchiesi 2012).

In the IACC's public announcement of its program, the trade association thanked Espinel "for her leadership in bringing together representatives of the financial industry and rights holders" (International Anti-Counterfeiting Coalition 2011). This again shows the key role of the U.S. government, particularly Victoria Espinel, in forging so-called voluntary industry agreements. Without Espinel's direct involvement, it is doubtful that the nonbinding agreements or RogueBlock would exist. These informal agreements cannot be understood as "voluntary," given the direct involvement of the U.S. government in their creation.

RogueBlock began in January 2012. The program operates through a series of memoranda of understanding between the IACC and payment providers. Signatories to the program are Visa International, Visa Europe, MasterCard, PayPal, and American Express, along with Western Union, MoneyGram, Diners Club, and Discover. There is no public listing of the rights holders that participate in the program. However, in October 2012, the IACC prepared a report on the RogueBlock program and detailed its successes and challenges for Victoria Espinel, which illustrates IPEC's continued interest in a program that the department helped create. This report does not name participating rights holders but says that, in October 2012, there were thirty-one participants, representing industry sectors including "apparel, footwear, and luxury goods, electronics, automotive, tobacco, pharmaceutical, business and entertainment software, and consumer products" (International Anti-Counterfeiting Coalition 2012, 3).

RogueBlock is a software system that tracks and coordinates complaints from all IACC members and funnels them through a portal to payment providers. The program is intended to "create a streamlined, simplified procedure" for rights holders to submit complaints "to credit card networks across multiple platforms," explains Barchiesi (Barchiesi 2011). The goal is to "shrink the universe of third-party acquiring banks willing to do business with rogue merchants" (International Anti-Counterfeiting Coalition 2012, 3). The program does so by partnering with payment intermediaries and pushing them to strengthen their enforcement practices in relation to online infringement. By working through the providers' terms-of-service agreements, the IACC's members can target the sale of counterfeit goods globally. "Whereas in the past, with litigation, where it's been difficult to find the infringer or locate what jurisdiction applies," comments Kristina Montanaro, former director of special programs at IACC, "in this program it doesn't matter; because if the transaction is illegal, it's enough to facilitate the termination of the merchant account" (Montanaro 2012). If the payment intermediary determines that its terms-of-service policy has been violated, then it terminates the site's merchant account.

Rights holders who pay an annual fee to participate in the RogueBlock program (including non-IACC members) can make complaints in three areas: counterfeit goods, copyright-infringing content, and the trade in circumvention devices. Circumvention devices are hardware or software that breaks rights-holder-imposed digital locks. These digital locks can dictate how individuals can access, share, or use particular information covered by copyright. They can, for example, prevent information from being copied or can restrict the way users access information by, for instance, confining a video game to a particular device.[4] The creation or trafficking in circumvention devices is unlawful in many jurisdictions, including the United States, where it is prohibited under the 1998 Digital Millennium Copyright Act.

The process for terminating merchant accounts works as follows. Rights holders—or the lawyers or private security firms who act on their behalf—submit complaints electronically to RogueBlock. Complainants must include screenshots of the targeted site's home page, the product(s) in question, and the payment methods listed on the checkout page. They must also indicate ownership of the trademarks or copyright in question and provide a statement attesting that they make the complaint in good faith. IACC staff review all complaints and identify the relevant acquiring bank that granted the merchant account in question by tracking the site's financial transactions. The IACC then sends the complaint directly to the relevant payment providers for investigation and, if required, account termination.

The IACC does not publicly disclose details of RogueBlock's enforcement efforts, but it publishes some general information on its website that indicates the scale of enforcement. The IACC reports that between RogueBlock's launch in January 2012 and August 2015, it investigated over ten thousand sites and terminated over five thousand individual merchant accounts, which the IACC says affected over two hundred thousand sites (International Anti-Counterfeiting Coalition n.d.). The difference between the number of sites under investigation and merchant accounts terminated may reflect the fact that some sites remain under investigation. In other cases, merchant accounts may have been inactive or terminated before the investigation began.

Although details are scarce, it is clear that payment macrointermediaries are terminating thousands of merchant accounts operated by sites that rights holders deem "infringing." Linda Kirkpatrick, a senior MasterCard executive, confirmed the scope of MasterCard's enforcement involvement. Kirkpatrick, in a presentation at the IACC's anticounterfeiting conference in May 2012, said that MasterCard and Visa have had "hundreds and hundreds—even thousands, over the last few years — of merchants terminated as a result of our collective efforts" (Kirkpatrick 2012).

"THANKS TO MS. ESPINEL"

By their own admission, payment macrointermediaries responded to direct pressure from the U.S. government, especially from Victoria Espinel. Linda Kirkpatrick, says that, "thanks to Ms. Espinel," the payment providers have "a set of minimum standards that many of us far exceed" (Kirkpatrick 2012). This statement emphasizes the central role of the U.S. government, particularly IPEC, in creating the informal regulatory response to infringing sites. Trade associations, too, publicly acknowledge the importance of the informal regulatory agreements that were established in mid-2011, especially given the failure of the Stop Online Piracy Act, which Congress withdrew in January 2012. "While folks were depending on SOPA and PIPA," noted IACC president Bob Barchiesi, "we already had our voluntary agreements with the card networks" (Barchiesi 2012).

Kirkpatrick's acknowledgment also underlines the degree to which payment macrointermediaries significantly strengthened their enforcement practices—to the point that they "far exceed" (Kirkpatrick 2012) their legal responsibilities. For example, payment providers agreed to amend their enforcement actions in order to facilitate the mass, rapid termination of merchant accounts on behalf of rights holders. "The one-at-a-time approach doesn't work," explains Bainbridge; "but if we can do a carpet-bombing of multiple sites, it will be more effective" (interview, Bainbridge 2012). Overall, providers' enforcement efforts following the nonbinding agreements are more organized and better resourced, as compared with their previous measures.

Payment providers described their enforcement efforts as being relatively uncoordinated and unstructured before they adopted the nonbinding agreements. Kirkpatrick recalls that before the nonbinding agreement, providers each had a "different, fragmented approach to attacking the problem" and "no formal process for addressing inquiries" (Kirkpatrick 2012). Julie Bainbridge, a senior manager at PayPal, similarly concluded that "usual efforts are not enough to win the battle against" infringement (interview, Bainbridge 2012).

Intermediaries were motivated to sign on to non-legally binding agreements in order to avoid possible stricter legislative requirements. As discussed earlier, the Stop Online Piracy Act would have set timelines for payment intermediaries to withdraw their services from sites and financial penalties for noncompliant payment providers. Kirkpatrick said such measures could "present impossible compliance challenges" (Kirkpatrick 2011, 11), a view likely shared by other intermediaries. By adopting nonbinding agreements, even those that push intermediaries to exceed their legal enforcement responsibilities, intermediaries can demonstrate to government that they are responsible corporate actors dealing with illegality on their platforms. Providers want to be able to go to "the White House and say, 'We don't really have as big an issue as folks thought,'" explains Barchiesi, IACC president (interview, Barchiesi 2012). This statement, too, illustrates the U.S. government's direct involvement in directing negotiations and creating nonbinding agreements. If the informal agreements had been truly voluntary, industry-led efforts, intermediaries would perhaps be less motivated to demonstrate their compliance to government.

Sustained governmental pressure on payment providers resulted in macrointermediaries working together collaboratively for the first time. For proponents of tougher enforcement against infringing sites, nonbinding agreements that encourage coordinated or standardized regulatory practices within Internet sectors provide a useful global consistency in efforts against trademark and copyright infringement. During the 2012 IACC conference on counterfeiting and copyright infringement, and while sitting alongside her colleagues from PayPal and Visa, Kirkpatrick underlined the novelty of the big-three payment providers acting cooperatively: "Some of us are competitors in our space. But on this particular topic, I think we've unified and rallied against the common goal of follow the money. It's not often that you get MasterCard, PayPal, and Visa on the same panel. Our lawyers don't let us. But again, on this topic, there's no question that we need to be unified" (Kirkpatrick 2012).

Kirkpatrick's observation that the providers' lawyers "don't let us" work together refers to concerns about anticompetitive or unfair behavior that can result when companies with dominant market shares in an industry collaborate to set rules and standards. Knowing that Visa, MasterCard, and PayPal, which together overwhelmingly dominate the online payment industry, are working together on behalf of prominent multinational rights holders raises the troubling possibility that they may set rules that benefit their interests and those of other corporate actors at the expense of the general public. Kirkpatrick's statement is a testimony to state power that can bring together powerful corporate actors, and to the importance that the U.S. government accords the protection of intellectual property rights. Her words demonstrate that the U.S. government has signaled that state-corporate efforts to expand the protection of intellectual property rights on the Internet are more important that the possible appearance of anticompetitive actions.

Private Payment Blockades

Payment providers' supply of critical infrastructure makes them valuable intermediaries and regulators. They can enact revenue chokepoints to target donation-dependent organizations (like WikiLeaks) or commercially oriented sites that sell, for instance, child pornography or counterfeit goods, based on a violation of the intermediaries' broadly worded terms-of-service agreements. Governing through revenue chokepoints can be highly problematic when payment intermediaries expand their enforcement efforts from protecting their platforms and users from fraud to acting as global regulators on behalf of states or powerful corporate actors. We may support payment providers' expansive enforcement efforts against child pornography even in the absence of law enforcement warrants or court order. The case of WikiLeaks, however, raises troubling questions about intermediaries' unfettered regulatory power to remove content and disable sites. At the time of the anti-WikiLeaks campaign, no representative of Wiki-Leaks was facing criminal charges and the site was not subject to a court order.

Payment intermediaries are legally entitled to set the conditions under which companies and individuals use their services. Intermediaries' conditions can have public benefit when they reduce fraud or deter the sale of dangerous or substandard goods and services. In other cases, however, payment intermediaries are acting unfairly and arbitrarily determining that entire technologies and business models, not merely individual websites, violate their policies. As a result, some macrointermediaries are acting as private—and unaccountable—arbiters of legality in regard to a wide range of Internet services and technologies.

PayPal takes a particularly aggressive approach to technologies and applications that it determines may violate, or potentially have a high risk of violating, its policies. As discussed at the beginning of this chapter, PayPal has withdrawn its services from a publisher of books with distasteful (but not illegal) erotic content, a legal fund-raiser for Chelsea Manning, and a crowd-funded email service (Charman-Anderson 2012; Zetter 2011; Hutchinson 2013). The provider restored its services in these cases following public protests. PayPal has also withdrawn its services from technology companies that offer BitTorrent file-sharing protocol, online file storage services, and virtual private networks (VPNs), which are private, often encrypted networks that enable people to access the Internet securely while protecting their privacy. PayPal contends that these services pose a high risk for facilitating unauthorized downloads of music, movies, and software (see Enigmax 2013; Ernesto 2012, 2016).

Certainly, many people who download unauthorized content may do so through BitTorrent file-sharing services and use virtual private networks to conceal their location and IP address. However, these are all legal technologies that enable users to store and share information easily, cheaply, and, in the case of VPNs, securely. More importantly, VPNs are essential tools for activists, dissidents, or anyone who needs to access, share, or publish information without fear of state censorship or reprisal. For journalists, democracy activists, and civil-rights groups operating in authoritarian countries like China, Egypt, or Iran, VPNs are critical lifesaving tools. Intermediaries' withdrawal of services from a company offering legal technologies and applications because they can facilitate wrongdoing is an unfairly broad and unduly harsh regulatory approach.

DIGITAL ADVERTISING INDUSTRY

The other half of the revenue-chokepoint equation involves intermediaries controlling the online flow of advertisements. Rights holders are concerned with two interrelated problems in relation to digital advertising: bad ads and bad sites. *Bad ads* refers to the unlawful advertisements of illegal goods and services, such as counterfeit versions of Nike sneakers and Apple iPhones. These ads are intended to entice—or deceive—people into purchasing counterfeit versions of their favorite brands. *Bad sites,* in contrast, refers to the mistaken placements of legitimate advertisements on sites with illegal or inappropriate content, such as sites selling counterfeit goods. Some illegally operating sites seek to generate licit revenue by hosting legitimate ads.

Bad ads and ad misplacement on bad sites make up a small percentage of the overall digital advertising industry. While the scope of the problem may be relatively small, advertising intermediaries take the issue of ad misplacement on infringing sites seriously. Sites "that sell counterfeit products and pirated content are really in the same category as pornography," argues Dick O'Brien, executive vice president and director of government relations, for the American Association of Advertising Associations (O'Brien 2012). Few mainstream brands want any association with pornography.

For rights holders, ad misplacement on bad sites can be a problem because of concerns that it may damage the company's reputation or brand. The public backlash from "one bad story could ruin a brand for a very long time," explains Amit Kotecha, a senior mobile and networks manager for the U.K. branch of the Internet Advertising Bureau, the digital advertising trade association (interview, Kotecha 2012). Rights holders are aware that ad misplacement is a relatively small problem. "From a brand's perspective," Kotecha explains, even if the ad on an infringing site is worth "just a penny," rights holders do not want their ads on infringing sites (interview, Kotecha 2012).

Rights holders play a central role in shaping advertising regulations because they spend considerable sums within the advertising industry to craft certain images of their brands. As a result, explains Kotecha, rights holders "fund the whole industry, and everyone has to meet those demands" (interview, Kotecha 2012). Companies with valuable, well-known trademarks want ads featuring their products and services placed on sites with lawful activity and legitimate content. Advertising intermediaries, meanwhile, have a strong economic interest in adopting measures that encourage rights holders to continue expanding their digital advertising presence.

Digital Advertising Ecosystem

Everyone has seen—and probably tried to avoid—online advertisements. Advertisements can be static (with simple images or text), animated, or interactive, in which the user is invited to play a game or watch a video. Some ads "pop up" above the web page that you are viewing, while banner ads that sit within a web page may be static or may incorporate video, audio, and other interactive elements. Search engines like Google incorporate ads alongside search results, while social media platforms like Facebook and Twitter insert ads into users' feeds. We've all seen advertisements tailored for us on our social media feeds or alongside our search engine results. This is because advertising pays for "free" online services, from search engines and social media platforms like Facebook and Twitter, to email services.

Digital advertising is a rapidly growing billion-dollar business. For 2016, the projected total for global spending on digital advertising is approximately $168 billion, compared with a projected total for media advertising in 2016 of $542 billion (Bagchi, Murdoch and Scanlan 2015; eMarketer 2016). The United States remains the largest advertising market, estimated at $50 billion (PEW Research Center 2015). Google operates the largest digital advertising business globally, in addition to running the most popular search engine worldwide. Google continues to command over a third (38 percent) of the U.S. digital advertising industry, which is down slightly from its share of 40 percent in 2013 (PEW Research Center 2015).

We may think of Google as primarily a search engine, but from a business perspective it is primarily a massive advertising platform. Google generates the vast majority—90 percent—of its revenue from its advertising business. In its 2015 annual report, Google recorded revenue of $75 billion, with revenue from the United States accounting for $38.4 billion, the United Kingdom $7.1 billion, and the rest of the world accounting for the remaining $33.1 billion (Alphabet 2016, 23). Google can be understood as "a transaction platform whose primary purpose is to match buyers and sellers" (Powers and Jablonski 2015,

93), since the more Google knows about its users, the more valuable its data to advertisers. Far behind Google in the advertising market are four companies, Facebook, Microsoft, Yahoo, and AOL, which together generate the majority of the remaining digital advertising revenue in the United States.

Creating a Digital Advertisement

The digital advertising industry is even more complex than the online payment industry because there are more players involved in creating, selling, and distributing advertisements than processing payments. Amit Kotecha, a senior manager for the Internet Advertising Bureau in London, has spent many hours explaining the complexity of digital advertising to rights holders concerned that their advertisements will end up on bad sites. Many of the rights holders with whom Kotecha meets do not fully understand the complex process of buying and placing advertisements in the digital environment. They think it is "a one-to-one relationship between the advertiser and the publisher," Kotecha says, "when in fact most of the time there are over five relationships or five transactions before it ends up on the site" (interview, Kotecha 2012).

To understand the complexity of the digital advertising ecosystem, imagine you work for an advertising agency that has created an ad for the latest line of Nike shoes. As many as nine different types of intermediaries may be involved in creating, selling, and delivering ads that will be placed on web pages. Advertisers—in this case, Nike—work with advertising agencies that create advertisements and produce advertising campaigns.

Ad networks serve as brokers between rights holders producing ads and websites selling space on their platforms. These ad networks determine how much advertising they can sell to sites, contract with rights holders to buy that space, and then deliver the ads to websites. Ad networks may represent sites in a particular sector like health or electronics, or buy access to sites meeting certain criteria, such as those with users in a particular demographic or with certain recreational interests. Google dominates the ad networks with its Google AdSense; other ad networks include AOL Advertising, and Media.net from Yahoo-Bing's advertising network.

An ad exchange is a technology platform that facilitates automated, auction-based pricing and real-time buying. Sellers put ads on the exchange, and buyers bid for ads much like people bid on "eBay or the stock market" (interview, Kotecha 2012). Google's DoubleClick Ad Exchange is the largest ad exchange; others are OpenX and AppNexus, which are funded by Microsoft. Finally, the publisher is the individual website that displays ads to users. One website operator may strike deals to show ads on thousands or tens of thousands of web pages.

Companies that create, sell, and place advertisements increasingly rely upon automated and real-time bidding to purchase and deliver ads to sites in microseconds, similar to the operation of stock exchanges. "The advertising world is like spaghetti," observes David Wood, director of antipiracy at the British Phonographic Industry, which represents the U.K. music industry. "God knows how they pay each other" (interview, Wood 2012). This means that it can be difficult for advertising intermediaries to know when ads end up in the wrong place, such as a site selling counterfeit goods. As discussed in the following sections, it is also challenging to prevent ad misplacement.

ADVERTISING INTERMEDIARIES' ENFORCEMENT POLICIES

Online advertising is subject to a complex mix of national laws, informal industry guidelines and advertising companies' policies, such as those set by Google. National laws regulate or prohibit advertisements in many subject areas, including pornography, weapons, hate speech, tobacco, and illicit drugs. Laws vary among countries in regard to allowing ads on topics like alcohol, abortion, and gambling. Advertising trade associations set out guidelines that echo state laws to avoid placing advertisements on sites with content relating to pornography, tobacco, illicit drugs, violence, or the infringement of intellectual property rights. The Interactive Advertising Bureau, a New York City–based global advertising trade association, sets out guidelines and policies for its members in its "Standard Terms and Conditions for Internet Advertising" (see Interactive Advertising Bureau 2013).

The digital advertising industries in the United States and the United Kingdom set domestic guidelines and policies that prohibit placing advertisements on sites that distribute counterfeit goods or provide unauthorized downloads of copyright-infringing content. Advertising platforms can also institute their own rules regarding advertising content. In its advertising policies, Google forbids ads with content that is "likely to shock or disgust," including "blood, guts, [or] gore," as well as ads seeking to exploit a "natural disaster, conflict, death, or other tragic event" (Google n.d.). Companies that operate advertising networks and exchanges, like Google's DoubleClick Ad Exchange, have policies that explicitly prohibit advertisements that relate to the infringement of copyright or trademarks. Google also prohibits ads that use certain keywords to describe counterfeits, such as *knockoff, replica, imitation, clone, faux, fake,* and *mirror image* (Google n.d.).

To reassure rights holders that their advertisements will not go astray, most major advertising intermediaries seek some sort of industry certification. The Interactive Advertising Bureau, for example, certifies advertising intermediaries, including Google, Yahoo, and AOL.

Bad Ads and Ads on Bad Sites

As discussed earlier, advertising intermediaries face two problems in relation to the online trade in counterfeit goods: bad ads and legitimate advertising on bad sites. As with any product, those who manufacture and sell counterfeit goods use advertisements of their products to attract customers to their sites. Merchants may advertise their goods as counterfeit through the use of coded terms like *replica* or *knockoff,* or they may deceive people who believe they are purchasing genuine products into buying counterfeit goods. Operators of lawfully operating websites typically do not want ads for illicit products on their sites, especially since the advertisement of counterfeit goods is illegal in most countries.

To remove bad ads, advertising intermediaries like Google, Yahoo, and Bing operate notice-and-takedown programs, similar to the program that eBay uses for removing sales listings for counterfeit goods (see chapter 5). Advertising notice-and-takedown programs generally require complainants to identify the web address of the web pages in question, provide a screenshot of the advertisement, and attest that the complaint is accurate and made in good faith. Google, for example, uses a combination of automated systems and human analysis to detect and act upon ads that violate its policies. In 2014, for example, Google removed more than 524 million bad ads, up from 350 million in 2013, touting malware and fraudulent scams as well as counterfeit goods (Gupta 2015).

Advertising intermediaries may also take action against those who distribute bad ads. In its advertising policies, Google warns that it may freeze the placement of ads that violate its policies until the problem is addressed, a practice termed "ad disapproval." Google also banned more than 214,000 advertisers from its advertising services in 2014, including 7,000 advertisers for promoting counterfeit goods, down from 14,000 advertisers of counterfeit products in 2013 (Gupta 2015). Advertising intermediaries may also suspend accounts, which means that they will no longer accept advertisements from specific websites. These policies are intended to push bad-advertising actors out of the legitimate advertising industry.

The second problem for rights holders is the misplacement of legitimate ads on bad sites. Legitimate ads sometimes mistakenly end up on sites selling counterfeit goods. Sites that provide copyright-infringing content are more popular than those selling counterfeit goods, because more people download copyright-infringing content than shop for counterfeit goods. The Pirate Bay, for example, has about 400 million visits monthly, which far outstrips sites selling counterfeit goods (Halimi 2015). Although ad misplacement on sites selling counterfeit goods is a smaller problem than copyright-infringing sites, rights holders focus their efforts on both trademark and copyright infringement. From all indications, however, the amount of legitimate advertising mistakenly placed on infringing sites is relatively small. A 2013 survey of marketing managers in the United Kingdom, for example, found that only 1 percent of all advertisements end up on sites with inappropriate content (Digital Strategy Consulting 2013).

To deter the misplacement of legitimate ads, advertising intermediaries use ad-verification technology. These tools use software that automatically scans web addresses, website source code, and words in web pages for prohibited keywords supplied by the advertiser. If any of those keywords are present, such as those that pertain to pornography or counterfeit goods, the tools block the real-time delivery of advertisements (Interactive Advertising Bureau 2013). Buyers and sellers of advertising can also institute placement restrictions before selling ads and incorporate these terms into their sales contracts. Larry Allen, senior vice president in charge of business development and global platform sales at the U.S. advertising firm 24/7 Media, said in a presentation at the 2012 industry conference on counterfeit goods hosted by the International Anti-Counterfeiting Coalition that his company monitors all websites it works with on "a daily basis" (Allen 2012). When the company detects violations of its policies, Allen explains, the company terminates the publisher's account and "withholds retroactively monies that would be owed to them [the publisher] which helps them do things more appropriately" (Allen 2012).

Advertising intermediaries may also develop lists of verified sites, which in advertising jargon are known as "whitelists" or "appropriate schedules." Rights holders and intermediaries may also compile lists of prohibited sites known as "blacklists" or "inappropriate schedules." Joe Barone, managing director in charge of digital advertising operations with the advertising firm GroupM, explained to rights holders at the 2012 IACC conference how his company uses legal contracts with publishers selling website space to GroupM, which is one of the world's largest firms in terms of buying advertising space on websites. In GroupM's contract, Barone explained, the company includes a hyperlink to a blacklist of prohibited websites and requires publishers to agree "that they will not run our advertising or our clients' advertising on sites that are identified as rogues" (Barone 2012).

Using blacklists to prohibit certain behavior or information has a troubled history on the Internet. In 2011, for example, GroupM created a blacklist of over two thousand URLs (uniform resource locators, or web addresses) to ensure that its advertisements were not misplaced on sites involved in unlawful activity. In a commendable spirit of transparency, GroupM released its blacklist to a BitTorrent-focused technology news site, *TorrentFreak,* to examine, which revealed that the blacklist mistakenly included many legitimate sites (see Ernesto 2011). Sites listed in error included a digital library (Archive.org), a technology company (BitTorrent, Inc.) and video- and music-sharing sites (SoundCloud and Vimeo) (Ernesto 2011). Because such blacklists are compiled without the site operators being aware they are blacklisted, legitimate operators can lose revenue and customers, as well as suffer reputational damage as they try to appeal their designation. Further, as shown by research on sites that offer unauthorized downloads or streaming in breach of copyright laws, such sites do not rely heavily on advertising revenue from mainstream firms and lucrative blue-chip brands. Instead, they may generate funds from donations or less-reputable advertisements, such as for gambling and the sex industry (see Karaganis 2012; Watters 2014). As GroupM's problematic blacklist shows, it is often difficult to determine lawful behavior in relation to copyright—and trademarks—online. Moreover, the risks associated with blacklisting legitimate sites appear to outweigh any benefits from advertising blacklists in relation to trademark and copyright infringement, since research indicates that infringing sites do not rely upon mainstream advertisements.

U.K. REGULATION OF DIGITAL ADVERTISING

Rights holders' fear of damage to their brands was the impetus for regulation of the U.K. digital ad industry in 2005. In that year, the U.K.

television program *Panorama,* the BBC current affairs show, ran a documentary that exposed how the advertising industry misplaced advertisements on websites with illegal and controversial content. "We are talking about some pretty grim websites," recalls David Ellison, a marketing services manager for the advertising trade association Incorporated Society of British Advertisers, speaking in an interview in relation to the *Panorama* documentary (Ellison 2012). Some websites contained videos of illegal boxing or street-fighting matches. The sites were "at best distasteful and on the wrong end of the morality scale, and at worst highly illegal" (Ellison 2012). For rights holders, the *Panorama* documentary aroused concern about where advertising intermediaries placed their ads, and was also "really good for the industry, because all of the legitimate ad networks got together," says Kotecha of the Internet Advertising Bureau. Advertising intermediaries said, "'What are we going to do about this? Our business is at threat because we don't want all this money to go away'" (interview, Kotecha 2012).

The *Panorama* documentary prompted the U.K. digital advertising industry to come together in 2006 under the auspices of the Internet Advertising Bureau, the key industry trade body, to create a voluntary code called the Internet Advertising Sales House (IASH), which operated from 2006 to 2011, when negotiations began to replace it with a more comprehensive regulatory program. IASH was an industry-operated certification program with the goal of preventing the misplacement of ads on sites with content that rights holders contend is contrary to their brand's image. IASH certified only one type of intermediary in the digital advertising ecosystem: ad networks, which serve as brokers between advertisers delivering ads and websites selling advertising space. This means that other advertising intermediaries, such as ad exchanges, were not covered by IASH.

Under the IASH program, ad networks vetted every website they represented and allowed rights holders to choose whether or not they would place their ads on sites featuring sexual content, alcohol, or violence. IASH proved popular with rights holders. Rights holders with the biggest accounts, such as British Airways, decided that they "only want[ed] to buy from the ad networks that have been certified by the industry," explains Kotecha (interview, Kotecha 2012).

As the digital advertising industry evolved between 2006 and 2011, new intermediaries emerged in the advertising ecosystem, particularly ad exchanges. Intermediaries' distribution and placement of ads also became more complex, because ad exchanges buy and sell ads in real time, much like stock market exchanges. Rights holders wanted an expanded regulatory program to cover the entire digital advertising industry, especially ad exchanges.

Ad Industry Negotiations

In 2011, the London-based Internet Advertising Bureau began negotiations with all intermediaries in the advertising industry in an effort that would lead to the creation of the successor to IASH, the Digital Trading Standards Group (DTSG). The IAB consulted a wide array of intermediaries, as well as trade associations representing the advertising industry and those for rights holders. The biggest trade associations representing rights holders that were pushing for change were those from the copyright lobby, particularly the Federation Against Copyright Theft (FACT) and the British Phonographic Industry (also known as the British Recorded Music Industry, or BPI). Trade bodies that focus on anticounterfeiting efforts, as discussed in chapter 2, are generally smaller, lower-profile groups in comparison with the highly coordinated, well-funded, and prominent copyright groups. This holds true both in Europe and in the United States. The U.K. Anti-Counterfeiting Group, which is the lead body for anticounterfeiting policy making in the country, did not have a visible presence in lobbying the government or IAB in relation to the DTSG.

Although copyright trade associations played a prominent role in pushing for the DTSG, they did so for rights holders concerned about both trademark and copyright infringement. Rights holders, focused on protecting their trademarks, lobbied advertising intermediaries to strengthen efforts to remove ads for counterfeit goods. Trademark owners also pushed advertising intermediaries to do more to counter ad misplacement. FACT and BPI monitored infringing sites for years looking for legitimate advertisements, according to Kotecha: "If they saw a big brand like Tesco or BP [British Petroleum] or someone like that, they would screenshot it and send a formal letter to their marketing director," who would then complain to the Internet Advertising Bureau (interview, Kotecha 2012). In addition to protecting their brands, rights holders wanted advertising intermediaries to create revenue chokepoints to prevent revenue generated by legitimate ads from flowing to sites offering unauthorized downloads of music or movies.

"Political Imperatives from Government"

For the Internet Advertising Bureau, two years of negotiations over a comprehensive new self-regulatory program with a wide array of advertising intermediaries was necessary. Kotecha observes that such a program "has to be passed around before they can say yes to it" (interview, Kotecha 2012). For rights holders worried about damaged brands and about funding the sale of counterfeit goods and copyright-infringing content, two years was too long. Unsatisfied with the pace of negotiations, representatives from BPI and FACT lobbied the U.K. government to pressure the advertising industry.

As discussed in chapter 2, government officials from the Department for Culture, Media and Sport, which is responsible for intellectual property, convened a series of closed-door roundtables between 2011 and 2013 among rights holders' trade associations, advertising intermediaries, and the Internet Advertising Bureau. Ed Vaizey, the parliamentary under secretary of state for culture, communications and creative industries at the Department for Culture, Media and Sport, hosted the meetings. "Political imperatives from government" pushed the advertising industry forward, recalls Kotecha. "Brands have made things move pretty quickly" (interview, Kotecha 2012).

Vaizey's pressure on the advertising industry is documented in the minutes of the meetings between government officials and the advertising industry obtained by the civil-society organization Open Rights Group via Freedom of Information requests (see Bradwell 2011, 2012). The minutes of the roundtable meetings show that Vaizey pushed the advertising industry to "fast-track" the creation of the Digital Trading Standards Group (Bradwell 2012). Advertising intermediaries were also motivated by the U.K. government's threat of legislation if the advertising industry did not make sufficient progress. Kotecha explains: "They really believe in self-regulation. The last thing they want to do is legislate. We definitely don't want that. It just leads to this black hole. We don't know when they are going to legislate again. They could just push something through. If they do it once, they can do it again" (interview, Kotecha 2012).

While governmental pressure was not responsible for the creation of the DTSG—that impetus came from rights holders—direct governmental pressure hastened the program's implementation. The DTSG is therefore a product of both rights holders' pressure on the advertising industry and governmental intervention. Given the advertising industry's close working relationship with and economic dependence on rights holders, negotiations would have eventually concluded successfully. Governmental pressure, says Kotecha, pushed the advertising industry "to get their ass in gear really quickly" (interview, Kotecha 2012).

Introducing the Digital Trading Standards Group

After nearly two years of negotiations, the U.K. advertising industry introduced the Digital Trading Standards Group in December 2013. Unlike its predecessor, IASH, the DTSG covers all advertising intermediaries, including ad exchanges, which buy and sell advertisements in real time. Signatories to the DTSG include the ad exchanges operated by Google, Microsoft, Yahoo UK, and AOL, along with multiple other advertising intermediaries. The DTSG's guidelines, which are publicly available online, are called the "U.K. Good Practice Principles" (Joint Industry Committee for Web Standards 2015). The Joint Industry Committee for Web Standards, the main standard-setting body for the digital advertising industry, approved and formally endorsed the principles as an industry standard in the United Kingdom. The DTSG's objective is to reduce the risk of advertising being misplaced on websites offering illegal or inappropriate content. "No other country in the world has got this far," says Kotecha in reference to the DTSG's coverage of the entire ad ecosystem. "It's a massive step forward" (interview, Kotecha 2012).

The DTSG has two main components. Participants agree to allow independent, industry-approved firms to verify their ad misplacement-minimization policies within six months and, thereafter, annually. Second, signatories agree to follow the DTSG's processes that govern where advertisements can be placed online. To comply with this principle, participants must institute content-verification measures that block the placement of advertising on sites with illegal content, such as those offering counterfeit goods or other content deemed inappropriate by some clients, like pornography, gambling, or alcohol. Advertising intermediaries must have their content-verification systems audited and certified in an industry-approved, independent process.

A key component of the DTSG is the creation of a comprehensive, industry-compiled blacklist of websites. The blacklist is primarily composed of sites offering unauthorized downloads of copyright-infringing music and movies, because these sites attract far more people than those selling counterfeit goods. For this element of the DTSG program, then, enforcement efforts are directed toward starving copyright-infringing sites of revenue from legitimate ads. Overall, however, rights holders with valuable trademarks, who are, as noted earlier, keen to protect their trademarks from mistaken placement on infringing sites, also stand to benefit from regulation through the DTSG program. Trademark owners are also motivated to stamp out any ads for counterfeit versions of their products.

Industry groups, especially FACT and the BPI, compile lists of sites with inappropriate content for the DTSG blacklist. The City of London Police's Police Intellectual Property Crime Unit (PIPCU) hosts the advertising industry's blacklist, which it calls the Infringing Website List. Created in September 2013, PIPCU is funded by the U.K. Intellectual Property Office, which is responsible for policy making and administration in regard to intellectual property rights in the United Kingdom. Before adding sites to the list, officers from PIPCU verify that those sites are distributing content in violation of copyright. PIPCU then contacts the website operators to warn them that the sites violate intellectual property law. Officials from PIPCU also offer the website operators "the opportunity to engage with the police, to correct their behavior and to begin to operate legitimately" (City of London Police 2015). If a site operator declines to comply, PIPCU can add the site to the Infringing Website List.

That PIPCU officers verify that sites contain copyright-infringing content and contact site operators before adding sites to the blacklist instills the process with a degree of due process. Similarly, PIPCU's involvement adds some regulatory legitimacy to the process. However, neither the Infringing Website List nor the criteria used to designate sites for the blacklist are publicly available, and PIPCU has not explained how site operators can challenge their inclusion on the list.

U.S. REGULATION OF DIGITAL ADVERTISING

In the United States, too, government officials and rights holders placed considerable pressure on the digital advertising industry. The resulting regulatory framework in the United States, however, is strikingly different from that of the United Kingdom. While U.K. rights holders successfully campaigned for an industry-wide regulatory program, U.S. efforts focused on major ad networks operated by Google, which dominates the industry, along with Yahoo, Bing, and a handful of other companies.

As in the U.K., where advertising intermediaries faced the government's threat of legislation, advertising intermediaries in the United States faced potential legislation in the form of COICA, PIPA and the

Stop Online Piracy Act. These bills, which were all defeated, would have required advertising intermediaries to withdraw their services from sites involved in counterfeit goods and copyright-infringing content. U.S. legislators and policy makers made clear their preferences for more action from the advertising industry. In 2011, Victoria Espinel argued before the House of Representative Subcommittee on Intellectual Property, Competition, and the Internet that ads on infringing sites help "these sites obtain legitimacy and confuse the public" (Espinel 2011a, 48).

Similarly, the U.S. Congressional International Anti-Piracy Caucus, which was created in 2003, and which changed its name in 2014 to International Creativity and Theft-Prevention Caucus, provides briefings on intellectual property policy making in the United States and internationally to congressional delegations. In letters to the largest U.S. advertising associations in October 2011, members of the caucus demanded that they choke off revenue to sites involved in distributing infringing goods (Sandoval 2011).

Google, the world's biggest digital advertising company, faced additional coercive pressure, in the form of criminal charges from the U.S. Department of Justice, to modify its advertising practices. While Google was in talks with Espinel and the Office of the U.S. Intellectual Property Enforcement Coordinator about strengthening its advertising policies, the search/advertising giant was also under investigation for allegedly accepting ads from so-called illegal online pharmacies.

The term *illegal online pharmacies* refers to sites that distribute over-the-counter or prescription pharmaceuticals that may be unsafe, poor quality, counterfeit, unapproved, or issued in the absence of appropriate prescription processes (Government Accountability Office 2013). This is a broad concept that combines safety concerns (e.g., poor quality and counterfeit medication) with procedural concerns (how prescriptions are issued and to whom). It encompasses sites peddling misbranded, unapproved, or adulterated medication, as well as pharmacies that offer professional services and legitimate, safe medication, but which operate in violation of U.S. federal and state laws regarding the distribution of prescription medication. In terms of intellectual property, pharmaceutical firms targeting these illegal pharmacies typically emphasize the problem of counterfeit pharmaceuticals in terms of the medicine itself or the associated packaging.

In 2011, Google settled the case by forfeiting $500 million, one of the largest forfeitures in the United States. Under the terms of the agreement with the U.S. government, Google admitted that it improperly allowed Canada-based online pharmacies to run ads for their products in the United States through Google's AdWords program (Department of Justice 2011). These Canadian pharmacies were not licensed to distribute prescription medication to U.S.-based customers under U.S. federal and state laws. According to U.S. Department of Justice officials, the case involved "the patently unsafe, unlawful, importation of prescription drugs by Canadian on-line pharmacies with Google's knowledge and assistance, into the United States, directly to U.S. consumers" (Department of Justice 2011). Department of Justice officials frankly acknowledged that the forfeiture was intended to "get Google's attention" (Department of Justice 2011).

Online pharmacies that sell prescription medication to U.S. consumers may pose a health and safety risk. Google's admitted unlawful involvement in ads for pharmaceuticals, however, highlights the complexity of the global distribution of pharmaceuticals, especially through online channels, where the lines between parallel trade and counterfeit goods may become blurred and are subject to intense debate between pharmaceutical companies and online pharmacies (see Drahos and Braithwaite 2002). The case against Google also showcases the importance that the U.S. government accords to the protection of intellectual property. More broadly, the case indicates the degree of protection that the U.S. government offers the U.S. pharmaceutical industry. This industry has successfully advocated for ever-stronger intellectual property laws since the late 1970s, and it has a long history of shaping U.S. policies and trade agreements in this area, as discussed in chapter 2.

U.S. Advertising Industry

Given the proposed legislation, government coercion, and rights-holder lobbying, pressure on the advertising industry to take action was considerable. In May 2012, the largest advertising associations in the United States released a shared statement of non-legally binding best practices. The Association of National Advertisers (ANA), the American Association of Advertising Agencies, and the Interactive Advertising Bureau (IAB) together represent the U.S. advertising industry. The IAB is a U.S.-based global advertising trade association whose U.K. chapter is the Internet Advertising Bureau, which was discussed earlier.

Representatives from these organizations announced their best practices on May 3, 2012, to applause from rights holders, government officials, and brand-protection companies attending the International

Anti-Counterfeiting Coalition conference in Washington, D.C., to address counterfeiting and copyright infringement. "Many of our members have in the last year or two been coming to us and stating that they are deeply concerned about the problems of both piracy and counterfeiting," said Daniel L. Jaffe, executive vice president of the ANA, in announcing the best practices. "They thought that we should do something about it" (Jaffe 2012). There is no apparent link between this industry initiative and the U.S. government. Rather, as Jaffe notes, the impetus for an industry-wide set of best practices for digital advertising came from rights holders.

In the best practices statement, the advertising associations emphasize that "U.S. advertisers must also have confidence that their corporate brands and images are not being harmed by association with such unlawful activity" (Association of National Advertisers 2012). To ensure rights holders' confidence, the advertising associations outlined three areas in which its members would institute policies. They urged their members to take measures to remove misplaced ads from sites that infringe intellectual property rights and to exclude those sites from their services. They also called upon advertising intermediaries to prevent the misplacement of ads and to refund or otherwise credit advertisers in relation to ad misplacement.

Ad Networks' Best Practices Agreement

While the largest U.S. advertising associations announced best practices intended to safeguard rights holders' intellectual property, Espinel coordinated a series of meetings between 2010 and 2013 with Google, Yahoo, and Bing to institute similar informal agreements on digital advertising practices. In July 2013, IPEC and the major ad networks reached a deal following what an Microsoft executive says was a "multi-year effort with the White House to develop these best practices" (Humphries 2013).

The agreement, titled "Best Practices Guidelines for Ad Networks to Address Piracy and Counterfeiting," is publicly available online, in contrast to most of the nonbinding enforcement agreements studied in this book (Ad Networks 2013). Signatories to the agreement are Google, Bing, AOL, Yahoo, and the prominent advertising firms 24/7 Media and Condé Nast. The agreement states that the "sale of counterfeit goods and copyright piracy are issues Ad Networks take seriously, and Ad Networks have policies and practices in place to address this problem" (Ad Networks 2013). In their agreement, the ad networks say their enforcement measures should be "consistent with all applicable laws" and undertaken in ways that respect "privacy, free speech, and fair process" (Ad Networks 2013). The ad networks also emphasize that the agreement sets out "voluntary best practices" that "should not, and cannot, be used in any way as the basis for any legal liability" of the networks for infringement by third parties on their advertising platforms (Ad Networks 2013).

The ad networks' agreement sets out guidelines in three areas. First, the "General Commitment" section states that the participating ad networks agree to institute policies prohibiting advertising on infringing sites and post these policies on their websites. The networks also commit to an "ongoing dialogue" with all interested parties, including consumer organizations and free-speech advocates (Ad Networks 2013).

Second, the section titled "Identification and Verification Process" states that the ad networks agree to be certified, either through the Interactive Advertising Bureau, which is the trade association for online advertising in the United States, or through an independent process (Ad Networks 2013). Before the creation of this informal agreement, however, the Interactive Advertising Bureau had already certified major advertising networks, including those operated by Google and Yahoo.

Third, the "Complaint Process" section states that the ad networks agree to institute notice-and-termination programs. In these programs, the intermediaries prevent the misplacement of ads on sites selling counterfeit goods or distributing copyright-infringing content, by withdrawing their advertising services from those infringing sites. In the agreement, this section sets out a detailed process for rights holders to submit "valid, reasonable, and sufficiently detailed" complaints to ad networks. Complainants must do the following:

- Describe the alleged sale of counterfeit goods and provide information about the specific web pages where the items are being sold.
- Provide evidence of advertising from a specific ad network with screenshots of the web pages in question.
- Attest that the illegitimate activity is not authorized by the rights holders or the law.
- Affirm in good faith that the information provided to the ad networks is accurate, and that the complainant owns the trademark(s) in question (or is authorized to act on behalf of the owner).
- Provide the complainant's contact information and signature.

After undertaking an investigation of the complaint, the ad networks may request the infringing sites to cease their illicit activity, may halt the placement of ads on those sites (or on web pages within those sites), or may remove the sites from the ad network. Halting ad placement or removing the sites from the ad network means the targeted sites will no longer receive advertising services from that intermediary, thereby choking the flow of ad revenue to the sites.

In addition to the information given in these three sections, the ad networks' agreement also outlines what they perceive to be their enforcement responsibilities. These largely entail responding to rights holders' complaints that relate to infringing sites, but the agreement does not impose a duty on any ad network "to monitor its network to identify such websites" (Ad Networks 2013). The networks contend that rights holders are "in the best position to identify and evaluate infringement." Without specific complaints, the ad networks argue, they "lack the knowledge and capability to identify and address infringement" independently and cannot "engage in extensive or definitive fact finding to determine a particular party's intellectual property rights."

These statements reveal considerable tension between intermediaries and rights holders in regard to the division of enforcement responsibilities. Intermediaries' resistance to monitoring their platforms independently for infringement is a common theme throughout the nonbinding agreements. Internet firms' reluctance in this area is also evident in relation to search engines (see chapter 4) and marketplaces (see chapter 5). The ad networks' statement clarifying their regulatory duties also underscores the difficulty that intermediaries have in identifying infringement online.

"We're Never Going to Get Rid of It"

Rights holders' efforts to crack down on bad ads and ads on bad sites have two principle motivations: to choke revenue flows to merchants selling counterfeit goods, especially in relation to funds from legitimate advertising, and to protect their brands. As Kotecha notes, rights holders want to avoid sending even "a penny" of their ad money to infringing sites (interview, Kotecha 2012). Any strengthening of intermediaries' enforcement efforts, however, is not likely to affect infringing sites significantly. Advertising insiders candidly admit that a small proportion of ads will continue to be inadvertently placed on inappropriate sites. "We're never going to get rid of it," explains Kotecha, "but we can reduce the risk" (interview, Kotecha 2012).

The advertising industry relies upon companies' need to create ads to sell their products and services. Companies, especially those with valuable, sought-after brands "fund the whole industry," and the "pressure from brands" is a powerful force that shapes the regulation of the digital advertising industry (interview, Kotecha 2012). Pressure from rights holders stimulated the development of the Digital Trading Standards Group program in the United Kingdom, and the U.S. advertising associations' best practices agreements. When rights holders' pressure on intermediaries fell short, however, they successfully lobbied the U.S. and U.K. governments to intervene and compel advertising intermediaries to amend their regulatory practices in relation to infringing sites.

U.K. advertising actors credited "political imperatives" (interview, Kotecha 2012) from the Department for Culture, Media and Sport for pushing the ad industry to accelerate its implementation of the DTSG. Similarly, U.S. advertising actors candidly admit that the ad networks' agreement was the result of years of negotiation with Victoria Espinel and IPEC (Humphries 2013), while Google faced legal pressure from the U.S. Department of Justice. Nonbinding agreements, however, offer intermediaries and rights holders the promise of harmonizing regulatory differences among countries. Big global players like Google want "a global initiative," argues Kotecha. "They don't want to have different laws in different countries" (interview, Kotecha 2012). More importantly, by adopting nonbinding measures, intermediaries hope to stave off legislation or legal action by governments for facilitating illicit activities.

PRIVATE ARBITERS OF LEGALITY

State pressure and coercion were central to the creation of private enforcement agreements among payment and advertising macrointermediaries. The U.S. and U.K. governments both employed threats of legislation and legal action to convince the macrointermediaries to adopt and implement nonbinding enforcement practices. Advertising and payment actors, in addition to facing coercive measures, have varying financial and reputational interests in adopting private agreements. Interests of industry and states, however, largely overshadow consumers' interests, and the private enforcement agreements raise serious concerns about unfair and anticompetitive regulatory practices.

Macrointermediaries are powerful regulators, given their capacity to set and enforce rules governing hundreds of millions of people who use their services. When they institute rules—sometimes arbitrarily and unbeknownst to their users—they govern how people can access, use, store, and share information and creative content, and what goods they may trade and purchase, and how. Payment providers, particularly the major intermediaries, have a greater regulatory capacity than advertising intermediaries because they can commercially cripple targeted sites by withdrawing payment-processing facilities. Site operators that lose the big-four payment services will likely struggle to secure equivalent payment methods, a finding that accords with studies of illegal online pharmacies (see McCoy et al. 2012). In contrast, sites that lose revenue from specific advertisers can more easily replace their services because site operators can seek less-reputable advertising companies or less-conventional advertisements, such as for escort agencies. Given the market dominance of a handful of payment providers and the significant commercial sanctions they can impose—by starving sites—these intermediaries are the most powerful, effective regulators in the transnational anticounterfeiting regime.

Revenue chokepoints are based on the follow-the-money enforcement strategy that law enforcement agencies first used to target terrorist financing (for a critical assessment, see Levi 2010) and then adapted to throttle the for-profit trade in child pornography. Given how seriously society takes these crimes, we may accept the risk that legitimate organizations may be targeted in error. Trademark and copyright infringement, however, typically represent a distinctly less significant threat. As a result, we have to question what types of social problems we consider serious enough to warrant extrajudicial enactment of payment blockades. Revenue chokepoints may be deemed appropriate for sites distributing counterfeit goods that pose health and safety risks, but not for those that sell less harmful counterfeit clothing and accessories. Further, there needs to be a public discussion regarding the means by which payment intermediaries impose such sanctions, such as by seeking a court order or operating with oversight from an independent third party, as well as any reasonable limitations to their actions. Finally, it's important to remember that intermediaries' enforcement efforts do not result in the seizure of counterfeit goods or the arrest of bad actors. Intermediaries can only endeavor to disable infringing sites or deter people from accessing such sites. While this is important, targeting site functionality in itself does not provide an effective enforcement response to counterfeit goods.

In addition to the problem of wrongfully targeting lawful behavior, the potential for unfair enforcement actions by payment macrointermediaries is of particular concern. This is because, among all macrointer-mediaries, major payment providers have the capacity to act as private arbiters of legality. All macrointermediaries have considerable latitude in determining the legality or appropriateness of content and behavior. When payment macrointermediaries terminate their services to websites or companies, targeted sites are commercially disabled and must struggle to replace their payment-processing services. These intermediaries have the authority through their terms-of-service agreements to withdraw their services for any reason. Macrointermediaries' efforts extend, as was discussed earlier in relation to PayPal, to companies that are offering legal services or technologies. Entities are targeted based on the intermediaries' preemptive determination that those companies *may* breach the intermediaries' policies, particularly if those companies offer services perceived as likely to facilitate infringement of intellectual property rights.

This sledgehammer approach to enforcement can stifle competition and unfairly limit users' access to legal services and technologies, such as virtual private networks and encryption tools. More broadly, intermediaries' denial of services can stifle the development of technologies and services that may pose a threat to the established corporate interests and business models, such as the next YouTube or PayPal.

4

Access Chokepoints

Search intermediaries and domain registrars facilitate access to the web,[1] and both provide critical Internet services. Search engines enable individuals to access knowledge and ideas from around the world and to tap into previously difficult-to-retrieve sources of information. Google, created in 1998, dominates the search market worldwide, to the extent that the company has become synonymous with online search services. In fact, Google has entered our common vernacular as a verb ("to Google"), and the term often refers to any kind of online search. Given its market share and the billions of searches it facilitates daily, Google arouses the ire of governments around the world that hold it responsible for illegal or offensive content that appears in its search results, from child pornography, illegal adult pornography, and terrorist- and extremist-related content to the sale of counterfeit goods.

Similarly, rights holders frequently condemn Google for failing to weed out search results that link to web pages distributing counterfeit goods or copyright-infringing content (termed *infringing search results*). Rights holders want Google to strengthen its enforcement practices significantly in order to remove these infringing results and, more broadly, to exclude infringing sites from even being indexed by Google's search engine. The goal is for Google to enact access chokepoints that deter users from finding or accessing infringing sites.

Rights holders also want to enroll another macrointermediary to enact access chokepoints: the U.S.-based domain registrar GoDaddy.

Domain registrars play a key role in maintaining the effective functioning of the domain name system by translating (or in the technical term, *resolving*) easy-to-remember domain names into numerical addresses and allowing users to access websites anywhere in the world. Domain registrars are relatively new regulatory actors in the anticounterfeiting realm. Even individuals within brand-protection circles are more familiar with traditional regulatory actors: search intermediaries, Internet service providers, and operators of online marketplaces.

Enacting Access Chokepoints

Studying search intermediaries and domain registrars together makes sense because they are particularly attractive as regulators to states and corporations wanting to control users' access to certain kinds of content online. Search and domain macrointermediaries, which are key components of the transnational anticounterfeiting regulatory regime alongside the payment and advertising macrointermediaries examined in chapter 3, differ in the manner in which they deter access to certain types of sites. Search intermediaries remove search results that link to web pages that violate their policies. Removing these search results does not affect content on the web pages.

Domain intermediaries, on the other hand, can make it difficult for users to access infringing sites, or they render such sites inoperative. To do so, registrars can seize domain names (such as "www.replicaRolex .com") so that users will see only error messages instead of those desired sites. Registrars may also override normal domain-name resolution to redirect users from sites with messages warning them that they have tried to access a site illegally selling counterfeit goods. These strategies, though, have limited efficacy. Seizing domain names generally does not affect the sites' content. Site operators who lose their domain name to the registrar can easily obtain another name from a different domain registrar and resume operations. However, if the registrar also provides web hosting services to the targeted site (GoDaddy provides both registrar and web hosting services), then the registrar can seize the domain name and the site's content, thereby preventing anyone from accessing that site.

Governments' designation of search and domain intermediaries as regulators with responsibility for controlling the online trade in counterfeit goods raises serious questions about the accuracy, accountability, and, more broadly, legitimacy of intermediaries' regulatory efforts.

Like other intermediaries, search and domain companies sometimes mistakenly target legal content, thereby impeding users' access to that content and negatively affecting lawfully operating websites. Automated enforcement programs exacerbate this problem, because they significantly increase the scale and speed of rights holders' enforcement efforts. Google, long the target of rights holders' criticism for search results that link to infringing sites, uses automated tools to process complaints from rights holders, which totaled 558 million in 2015 (Ernesto 2015). In October 2015, Google processed its billionth takedown notice, a staggering increase from the few dozen complaints it first received in 2008 (Ernesto 2015a).

Such mass-policing-style programs are notoriously inaccurate. Studies of Google's enforcement efforts based on rights holders' complaints reveal that inaccurate complaints lead to the wrongful removal of search results linking to web pages with lawful content (see, e.g., Seng 2014; Urban et al. 2016). As Google continues to receive ever-increasing numbers of complaints about infringing sites, legal content and lawfully operating sites will continue to be swept up in enforcement dragnets. When Google removes search results, websites may, because of Google's market dominance, struggle to attract viewers and remain commercially viable. Any exclusion from Google's search results represents a broader exclusion from society and from full participation in commercial, social, and cultural life.

Domain intermediaries' seizure of domain names in response to allegations of the sale of counterfeit goods raises other serious concerns. Each domain name may contain multiple subdomains for websites that are not engaged in wrongdoing, and the seizure of one domain can affect all subdomains. In 2014, for example, in an effort to fight botnets, Microsoft obtained a temporary restraining order from a Nevada federal court to seize twenty-three domain names from a South Virginia–based domain registrar company called No-IP, and then to transfer those domain names to Microsoft's control (see Cardozo 2014). Botnets are networks of Internet-connected computers that are controlled through software and generally harnessed to conduct illicit activities, which in the Microsoft case was the distribution of malicious code—viruses and worms known as malware. However, in seizing those domain names Microsoft inadvertently terminated service to nearly 5 million subdomains operated by No-IP, which was unaware of the court order or Microsoft's seizures until its customers complained of system outages.

The digital-rights group Electronic Frontier Foundation criticizes Microsoft's operation, saying the seizure order—approved by a federal judge—was "99.6% overbroad" (Cardozo 2014). To explain the significance of Microsoft's overreach, the EFF's Nate Cardozo aptly employs the analogy of a busy shopping mall. The mall is filled with legitimate businesses and one store selling illegal goods, and to counter that single store Microsoft obtained a federal court order in secret to transfer control of the entire mall to Microsoft's "mall cops," who vow only to keep the criminals out of the mall (Cardozo 2014). Instead, "Microsoft's mall cops were apparently overwhelmed by the number of visitors and simply locked the mall's doors, keeping out everyone, including the 99.6% of visitors who had legitimate shopping to do" (Cardozo 2014).

Microsoft's efforts starkly illustrate the degree to which domain seizures can be a blunt enforcement tool that can cause serious collateral damage to subdomains connected to the targeted domain. In this case, however, a federal judge approved Microsoft's actions. Under the nonbinding anticounterfeiting agreements, however, GoDaddy's domain seizures occur in the absence of any judicial approval or oversight. Further, GoDaddy takes action against targeted domains based on legally untested claims made by rights holders stating that the sites are pharmacies operating in violation of U.S. federal and state laws. Ensuring a safe, effectively regulated supply of medicine to consumers is a laudable goal, particularly when some sites may be distributing counterfeit medication. But as the Microsoft case demonstrates, domain seizures can inadvertently throttle lawfully operating subdomains, thus unfairly disabling legitimate sites and wrongfully tarnishing the reputations of the owners of those sites.

As part of the nonbinding agreements struck under pressure from the U.K. and U.S. governments, Google and GoDaddy exceed their regulatory responsibility to target infringing sites. In the United Kingdom, Google adopted a nonbinding agreement with other major search intermediaries—the first of its kind worldwide—at the behest of the U.K. government, which acted on behalf of prominent intellectual property associations. GoDaddy signed on to an informal agreement, negotiated by Victoria Espinel, that targets unlawfully operating online pharmacies allegedly selling counterfeit pharmaceuticals. As in the case of payment providers, such agreements give significant regulatory power to search engines and domain registrars.

SEARCH ENGINES

One company operates the interface through which we experience much of the Internet—Google. It operates the most popular search engine worldwide, trailed distantly by Microsoft's Bing and Yahoo. In the United States, Google's market share is around 65 percent (Sterling 2015). Bing, created in 2009, has 20 percent, and Yahoo, created in 1994, has about 13 percent of the market (Sterling 2015). Google's dominance is even more marked in European Union countries, where it commands about 90 percent of the market. Google's only major rivals are local search engines in China, where the Chinese-language Baidu commands about 85 percent of the domestic search market (China 2015), and in Russia, where Yandex controls about 60 percent of the search market (Gesenhues 2014). For most people worldwide, then, using a search engine means using Google. Given its dominance, it makes sense to focus on Google's changing duties as a regulator and its involvement in the nonbinding agreements.

Search engines provide the vital link between users and the billions of web pages comprising the World Wide Web, the system of hypertext-linked web pages that is one of the services that operates on the Internet. Beneath search engines' simple interfaces—you type your search query in a box—are complex software programs. These proprietary programs, which vary among search companies, use algorithms to scan the web, extract billions of items of information, and deliver them to users organized in a fashion that is relevant to users' search queries. Searches can be conducted for text, images, video, audio, or other types of information. In order to identify and catalogue billions of web pages, search engines use software called "web-crawling bots," or "spiders," to crawl the web and build indices of what is found. Search engines must continually crawl the Internet, because new sites are added and existing sites change. Not all information on the web is searchable. Search engines typically do not index information protected by passwords or subscriptions or contained within proprietary databases.

Once a search engine retrieves information based on a user's keywords, it must present the information in a manner that is useful and relevant, even though the search results may number in the millions. Search intermediaries use complex proprietary algorithms to rank search results, and they closely guard the details of those algorithms. Google's PageRank algorithm, for example, ranks web pages according to multiple variables, including the frequency and location of keywords on that page, and the number of other pages linking to the page in question (Singhal 2012). Search engines present ranked results in listings called "search engine results pages." Each search result contains a hyperlink to the web page where the search terms appear and a brief snippet of text. From that text snippet and the hyperlink, users can choose among search results. Highly ranked search results receive the most traffic. Google's top search results are the most commercially valuable, since Google is the dominant search engine. Because the software underlying search rankings is proprietary, search results vary among search engines, and search engines produce different results in different countries (Spink et al. 2006).

Companies that operate search engines generally argue that they simply deliver information in response to search queries. Google says that it "is a provider of information, not a mediator" and does not "make any claims about the content" of the web pages relating to search requests.[2] However, given the capacity of search engines to sift and index vast amounts of information, search engines, especially Google, can act as an "interface through which we interact with the Internet and thereby with the world at large" (Kohl 2013, 193). It is important to remember that the selection and ordering of information, whether in traditional libraries or indexed search results, is never completely neutral, since it entails making judgments about what information is to be included and how it is to be organized (Kohl 2013). The manner in which search engines order and rank search results is opaque because it is carried out using undisclosed proprietary algorithms. This algorithm is "the ultimate manipulation tool," analogous to the "secret recipe for Coca-Cola" (van Eijk 2012, 146).

Search engines not only index information but also construct and shape meaning by prescribing the information for search queries and filtering information presented to users (Elkin-Koren 2001, 185). They can deliberately or inadvertently exclude certain types of web pages from their search results, privilege search results from paying parties, and incorporate preferences for certain types of content (Kohl 2013). Scholars studying search intermediaries argue that to "exist is to be indexed by a search engine" (Introna and Nissenbaum 2000, 171). This observation aptly captures search engines' critical role in shaping knowledge and meaning, because exclusion from search results can marginalize or disappear certain types of information. Research on search intermediaries' indexing practices indicates that search markets are slanted toward large, commercial, popular sites and risk silencing certain voices and types of content (Introna and Nissenbaum 2000). Google, for example, has a troubling history of privileging its own services in its search results over those offered by competitors, resulting in a situation in which the "intermediary acts as a messenger for itself" (Kohl 2013, 197).

Google Is "a Digital Behemoth"

Google's stated mission, noted on its website, is to "organize the world's information and make it universally accessible and useful." To fulfill this mission, Google amasses, sifts, and rapidly digitizes enormous amounts of data from a dizzying array of sources and employs sophisticated search algorithms to deliver search results to users. Given the scale of Google's search platform and its market dominance, one could argue that to exist is to be indexed not simply by *a* search engine but specifically by Google. As explained earlier in the chapter, when a search giant like Google removes search results or does not index web pages for inclusion in its search results, the related sites may struggle to remain commercially viable or attract viewers. "You should be concerned about those websites that are coming up in the first few pages of the Google search," Damian Croker, CEO of the investigative firm BrandStrike Limited in London, tells his rights-holder clients concerned about counterfeit goods: "That's where your consumer is looking" (interview, Croker 2012).

Google is more than just a search engine: it is also, as was discussed in the previous chapter, the largest global advertising platform, which generates the majority of its revenue. The company also owns YouTube and the popular blogging site Blogger, and it created the Android operating system for phones and tablets. Google provides email, cloud storage, mapping applications, and creative content through its Google Play store, and it is digitizing millions of books and cultural content from museums and collections worldwide.[3]

Google's services, especially digital advertising, rely upon the company collecting vast amounts of information on those who use its many services. This information enables Google not only to match customer data with advertisements but also to develop predictive capabilities so that it can forecast what users will do, want, and think. Google's mass collection (and data mining) of personal information has aroused sharp criticism from privacy advocates for its breach of privacy laws. Equally, Google's commercial dominance in the search and advertising sectors has raised accusations of anticompetitive behavior, particularly in the European Union. Pete Wishart, a member of Parliament for the Scottish National Party, voiced these concerns about Google during a January 2014 debate on an intellectual property bill before the House of Commons in the United Kingdom: "It is a digital behemoth—there is nothing bigger in the digital world—and the gatekeeper for all our content industries. Nothing happens without Google, and nothing can go through its prism without satisfying it in some way" (Wishart 2014, 24).

Given Google's status as a digital behemoth, rights holders have fought a long-running campaign to pressure the search engine company to strengthen its enforcement efforts against infringing sites. With greater cooperation from Google, the thinking goes, counterfeit goods should be more difficult to locate online.

SEARCH INTERMEDIARIES' ENFORCEMENT POLICIES

Because search intermediaries may also provide other services, like advertising or content hosting, it is important to clarify the enforcement policies that relate to search results. In its policies, Google usefully separates its businesses: "We distinguish between search (where we are simply linking to other web pages), the content we host [e.g., YouTube], and ads" (Whetstone 2010).

Search intermediaries typically prohibit the display of certain types of results. A complex array of national laws, judicial rulings, and search intermediaries' internal policies govern the type of information search engines are permitted to display in their search results page and how they remove problematic search results. Rachel Whetstone, vice president of global communications and public affairs at Google, says the company's search policies are the "least restrictive of all our services, because search results are a reflection of the content of the web," and Google wants to avoid engaging in "political censorship." Whetstone further details Google's policies: "We do not remove content from search [results] globally except in narrow circumstances, like child pornography, certain links to copyrighted material, spam, malware, and results that contain sensitive personal information like credit card numbers" (Whetstone 2010).

Like other globally operating search intermediaries, Google complies with national laws in relation to its search content. In its operations in Germany, for example, Google complies with laws that make pro-Nazi material illegal, removing results from its German search engine, www .google.de (Whetstone 2010). Search engines also control search results that are lawful but which may be considered by some as offensive, such as those relating to gambling, adult sexual content, and violence. Search companies also have considerable latitude to determine the types of content that they contend are inappropriate. Google, for instance, removes or blocks images in search results that involve pornography, bodily functions or fluids, vulgar words, or animal cruelty (Google n.d.a).

Most people are likely familiar with Google's copyright infringement policies and its removal of search results linking to sites offering unauthorized downloads of movies, music, and software. Like other intermediaries, Google also deals with trademark infringement. In its policies, Google states that its "trademark policy does not apply to search results, so if you have concerns about websites appearing in search results contact the site owner directly" (Google n.d.b). Google explains that, after the site operator has been contacted and "the webmaster has altered the page in question, Google's search results will automatically reflect this change after we crawl the site" (Google n.d.c). Google's counterfeit-goods policy "concerns the actual goods promoted on the website in question" (Google n.d.b).

Search intermediaries' regulation of trademark infringement varies from country to country because of differing national laws. In the United States, there is no statutory requirement for search intermediaries to remove search results relating to trademark infringement: the Digital Millennium Copyright Act pertains only to copyright infringement. Despite lacking a legal requirement to do so, Google removes search results linking to sites selling counterfeit goods, as is discussed in the next section.

Search engines operating in the European Union, on the other hand, are subject to the European Commission's 2000 Electronic Commerce Directive, as implemented in member states' laws. The directive addresses both trademark and copyright infringement, as explained in chapter 2. The directive's article 14 recommends that search intermediaries institute a notice-and-takedown program to act "expeditiously" to "remove or disable access to" search results linking to web pages involved in the sale of counterfeit goods. Rights holders in the European Union thus have an advantage over their U.S. counterparts, because they have a legal framework through which they can require Google to remove search results linking to sites selling counterfeit goods.

How Search Intermediaries Regulate

Before describing the emergence of the first-ever informal agreement regulating search results in the United Kingdom, it is important to clarify how search intermediaries regulate their search results. A search engine company can de-index (that is, remove) specific hyperlinks from search results that link to problematic web pages, but it cannot remove content from a web page if it does not provide web hosting services to that web page. To remove a web page's content, one must contact the site operator or web hosting service. To remove specific search results, search intermediaries typically require users to identify the nature of the problem, provide evidence, and specify the hyperlink of the search result in question. Complainants must also distinguish between the hyperlinks of search engine results and search engine–related advertisements that typically appear alongside those results. Google has a different set of policies dealing with advertisements that promote counterfeit goods (see chapter 3).

The vast majority of Google's enforcement efforts are directed toward copyright infringement, since significantly more people seek unauthorized downloads of music, movies, video games, and software programs than purchase counterfeit goods. As explained in chapter 2, the highly coordinated and politically prominent copyright lobby is at the forefront of enforcement activities. Complaints to Google over copyright infringement rose from 50 million in 2012 to 345 million in 2014, and reached 558 million in 2015 (Ernesto 2015), and Google removes about 100,000 search results per hour (Ernesto 2016a).

Removing Search Results Linked to Counterfeit Goods

Rights holders concerned about counterfeits damaging their brands are following the lead of copyright owners and submitting complaints to Google about search results that link to sites selling counterfeit goods. Although Google is not legally required to remove search results in the United States in relation to trademark infringement, Google is doing so for various well-known clothing and accessories brands. These brands include the U.S. companies Tory Burch, Nike, Kate Spade, Coach, and Deckers Outdoor Corporation, which owns the popular Ugg brand of footwear, as well as the luxury-brand French companies Chanel and Louis Vuitton. Google documents this counterfeit-related removal of search results in its Transparency Report, which is a stand-alone site

Google established to collect and track complaints its receives from rights holders and requests from governments for data on Google's users.[4] In the report, Google tracks the individuals or organizations who submitted the requests, and the date of the requests, and it indicates the number of requests it complies with and of those it rejects.[5]

Google allows people to search the Transparency Report by three criteria: the name of the organization that submitted a complaint, the name of the rights holder, or the type of request. Search complaints relating counterfeit goods constitute a tiny fraction of the hundreds of millions complaints Google receives for copyright infringement. What is important, however, is that Google removes trademark infringement-related search results without a legal requirement to do so. Between July 2011 and February 2016, for example, Deckers Outdoor Corporation requested the removal of 22,993 search results, while the fashion label Tory Burch requested the removal of 15,621 results between October 2015 and February 2016 (Google Transparency Report 2016). In these cases, Google removed the vast majority of search results.

Although Google classifies its trademark-related complaints as copyright-related removals, they clearly pertain to the sale of counterfeit goods. In relation to Tory Burch, the removed search results linked to sites like http://toryburchoutletstores.com selling counterfeit Tory Burch products. A Chicago-based law firm, Greer, Burns and Cain, which specializes in intellectual property, submitted complaints to Google on behalf of Tory Burch. The law firm also seized the related sites' domain names and placed warning banners on the sites saying the site operators were charged with trademark infringement and counterfeiting, a strategy that is discussed in greater detail in the second part of this chapter.

In the cases of the U.S. brands (Tory Burch, Kate Spade, Nike, and others) and French brands (Chanel and Louis Vuitton) cited in Google's Transparency Report, Google is removing counterfeit-goods-related search results from its U.S. operations, www.google.com. This means that Google is going beyond its legal requirements to work with rights holders concerned about the sale of counterfeit versions of their brands directed at U.S. consumers. These enforcement efforts appear relatively uncoordinated, since rights holders (or their attorneys) work individually to send complaints to Google. In contrast, the nonbinding agreement among search intermediaries in the United Kingdom is designed to strengthen search intermediaries' enforcement practices and clarify their regulatory responsibilities.

SEARCH INTERMEDIARIES AS REGULATORS

Search intermediaries, like payment intermediaries, have long been active in non-legally binding initiatives to stamp out sites selling child pornography. Google, Yahoo, and Bing, alongside Visa, MasterCard, and PayPal, are members of the Financial Coalition Against Child Pornography, which is managed by the U.S.-based National Center for Missing and Exploited Children. These search intermediaries also belong to the Internet Watch Foundation, which tackles the distribution of child sexual abuse images in the United Kingdom. As members of these organizations, search intermediaries agree to block access to or remove search results relating to sites that these organizations identify as involved in child pornography. Speaking about Google's efforts against online child pornography in 2013, Google CEO Eric Schmidt said the company had "fine tuned Google Search to prevent links to child sexual abuse material from appearing in our results" (Schmidt 2013).[6] This means that Google uses algorithms to block results when users search for material using certain child-sexual-abuse queries, and it also removes certain sites from its search index based on blacklists that FCACP and the Internet Watch Foundation compile. Instead of seeing websites with images of child sexual abuse, users will see warnings from Google and child-protection associations telling them that the material related to those search terms is illegal (Schmidt 2013).

Google's Resistance to Addressing Infringing Sites

In the United States, rights holders and their trade associations campaigned to compel search intermediaries, especially Google, to assume greater enforcement responsibilities in relation to the online trade in counterfeit goods and copyright-infringing content. An indication that Google was willing to amend its search practices in relation to trademark infringement came in 2009, when the New York City–based International Trademark Association (INTA) released its report titled "Addressing the Sale of Counterfeits on the Internet." Google and Yahoo contributed to the report, which called for developing "voluntary best practices for trademark owners and Internet-related companies aimed at facilitating the protection of trademarks on the Internet" (International Trademark Association 2009, 3).

In its report, INTA's recommendations for best practices for search intermediaries include having "a clear and effective process publicly available to deal with counterfeiting abuse" (International Trademark

Association 2009, 4). The report also advises that trademark owners and search intermediaries should "work collaboratively in an open, consultative exchange to target counterfeiting abuse," and it notes that such activities may include "blocking or flagging for heightened review certain suspect terms that may be indicative of counterfeiting activity" (International Trademark Association 2009, 4). In terms of blocking, INTA is suggesting that search intermediaries may consider blocking search results related to search queries associated with counterfeit goods, such as those that include the terms *replica, knockoff,* or *lookalike.* INTA also emphasizes that search intermediaries should consider "the technological issues inherent in any attempt to accurately target and eliminate problematic categories of abuse, such as counterfeiting." For example, one issue is the fact that "filtering and blocking can sweep too broadly and encompass legitimate results" (International Trademark Association 2009, 4).

This note of caution indicates that intellectual property trade associations are keenly aware of the problem of intermediaries mistakenly removing access to lawful content by removing search results. Indicators that rights holders and intermediaries use to identify counterfeit goods, such as the terms replica and lookalike, and the sale of goods at unusually low prices, could result in legitimate merchants inadvertently being caught in enforcement dragnets. This is particularly the case for individuals or companies selling secondhand products or parallel-trade goods intended for sale in a different geographical region. These indicators and keywords are typically not available for public scrutiny, since rights holders are concerned that operators of infringing sites would alter their activities in response.

Although Google agreed to the nonbinding recommendations in INTA's report, which asked intermediaries to consider blocking, the macrointermediary strongly opposed a legislative requirement to block sites distributing counterfeit goods. Under Section 102 of the Stop Online Piracy Act, search intermediaries would have been responsible for blocking search results relating to web pages outside the United States that target U.S. consumers for the sale of counterfeit and copyright-infringing goods. Kent Walker, senior vice president and general counsel at Google, testified before a House Judiciary Subcommittee in 2011 and argued, "Search engines are not in a position to censor the entire Internet, deleting every mention of the existence of a site" (Walker 2011, 7). He also emphasized that search intermediaries cannot make problematic sites "unfindable" (Walker 2011, 7).

In many ways, Walker's statement is correct. It is difficult for search engines to block all search results relating to certain types of content, such as child pornography, or to de-index all infringing sites. However, Walker was not being entirely candid. Google already uses blacklists compiled by FCACP and the Internet Watch Foundation to block sites distributing child sex abuse images. The search macrointermediary also blocks searches for hundreds of search terms related to child sex abuse.

Technically, Google could apply its child-protection enforcement practices to intellectual property and block access to blacklisted infringing sites, cease indexing infringing sites for its search results, and block search results for search terms related to counterfeit goods and copyright-infringing content. These efforts would not be completely effective, since people could use alternative search terms to access infringing sites. Moreover, Google's web crawlers would mistakenly include some web pages linking infringing sites in its search index, or the infringing-sites blacklist could be incomplete or become outdated. As Katherine Oyama, senior policy counsel for Google, explained in her testimony before Congress in relation to SOPA and PIPA, "No intermediary will be able to prevent all abuse of its systems" (Oyama 2011, 7). Even if Google dramatically ramped up its enforcement efforts against infringing sites, search intermediaries can only make it more difficult to access such sites. "Filtering a website from search results won't remove it from the web," explains Adam Barea, a legal director at Google, "or block other websites that link to that website" (Barea 2013). As Walker says, those sites still remain "findable" (Walker 2011, 7).

One principal reason that Google resisted applying its anti-child-pornography measures to strengthen protection against intellectual property is that they are vastly different social problems. There is a strong moral (and legal) argument for enhancing state and private-sector enforcement efforts to protect children from sexual abuse. In contrast, Internet intermediaries typically argue that protecting intellectual property rights is largely the responsibility of the rights holder. In addition, child sexual abuse is arguably simpler to identify and less controversial to ban, since there are no legal exceptions to possessing or distributing child pornography. Trademark infringement, however, is more difficult to identify online. Merchants accused of selling counterfeit goods may argue that they have the right to manufacture, distribute, or advertise products bearing particular trademarks, or that such activity does not violate the trademarks in question. Simply put, battles over counterfeit goods are sometimes better characterized as commercial disputes. Rights holders, for example, may identify certain products as counterfeit, whereas a merchant may claim that the goods resulted from the unauthorized diversion of genuine trademarked goods from one market to another—an issue of parallel trade, not infringement.

More broadly, Google and other search intermediaries are generally resistant to any regulation that restricts the way they crawl the web and index search results. "Search results reflect the web and what's online," explains Barea, "the good and the bad" (Barea 2013). This statement underscores Google's argument that search engines are an objective representation of all information on the web. Despite these claims, search intermediaries routinely intervene to control the way that their web crawlers index content and modify how their algorithms prioritize search results. Detective Superintendent Bob Wishart of the City of London Police recalls how officials from his agency pointed out that Google could do more to regulate its search results in relation to infringing sites: "Google has said to us that they are massively reluctant to police the Internet, massively reluctant to do anything where they are perceived to be influencing peoples' choices or intrusively looking at what people are doing. Our argument is: 'You do that anyway. You do that from the commercial perspective'" (interview, Wishart 2012).

Scholars studying search engines have repeatedly shown how these intermediaries filter and control access to information through their search processes in ways that favor their own products over their competitors' or privilege certain search results over others (see Elkin-Koren 2001; Introna and Nissenbaum 2000; Kohl 2013). Search intermediaries, especially Google, as the dominant actor, should be understood as routinely and strategically shaping the indexing and presentation of search results to benefit their commercial interests. Google, like other intermediaries, does not want its services to be associated with illegal activity. However, Google's business model is oriented toward the mass accumulation and monetization of information, including its users' personal information. While Google modifies its search algorithms to serve its commercial interests, it is reluctant to impose rules that may constrain the way it acquires, indexes, or monetizes information.

Because of the death of the Stop Online Piracy Act in January 2012, search intermediaries do not have a statutory requirement in the United States to block access to infringing sites in their search results. While Congress was considering SOPA and PIPA, Victoria Espinel and the Office of the U.S. Intellectual Property Enforcement Coordinator brought together major intermediaries to incorporate elements from the bills into non-legally binding agreements. These negotiations, as discussed in chapter 3, led to informal agreements with payment and advertising intermediaries to choke revenue to infringing sites. Google joined the discussions in relation to its advertising business, but Espinel did not negotiate a specific nonbinding agreement for search intermediaries. Because these negotiations occurred in closed-door meetings, it is unclear why the agreements did not seek to regulate search results in a manner similar to efforts in the United Kingdom. One possible reason is that rights holders, particularly in the pharmaceutical industry, were more focused on pushing Google to prevent advertisements for illegal online pharmacies from showing up next to its search results. Certainly, the music and movie lobbies in the United States have pushed Google for years to stop URLs for infringing sites from appearing in its search results (see Motion Picture Association of America 2013). As a result, U.S. rights holders are without legislative or nonbinding agreements relating to intermediaries' regulation of search results linking to infringing sites.

As the next section discusses, U.K. rights holders were successful where their U.S. counterparts were not. Officials from the Department for Culture, Media and Sport, employing threats of legislation, pushed Google, Yahoo, and Bing to draft a nonbinding agreement to strengthen their enforcement efforts against infringing sites.

GOOGLE'S U.K. INFORMAL AGREEMENT

At the same time that the U.S. Congress was trying to pass SOPA and PIPA, and Espinel was strong-arming intermediaries to adopt informal agreements, similar discussions were occurring in the United Kingdom. The impetus for U.K. negotiations was a protracted argument between rights holders and Internet service providers like Virgin Media over a copyright law—the controversial Digital Economy Act. The government passed this law in 2010, but an important element—the three-strikes program—was stalled because rights holders and intermediaries disagreed about who should pay for passing on warnings of copyright infringement from rights holders to users and then terminating users' Internet access. Copyright-related trade associations, especially the Federation Against Copyright Theft, criticized the delay and lobbied the Department for Culture, Media and Sport to intervene and jump-start negotiations with intermediaries to find non-legally binding solutions.

The failure of the Digital Economy Act, or at least its three-strikes program, marked an opportunity for the U.K. government and rights holders to broaden enforcement efforts against infringing sites by shifting to non-legally binding enforcement agreements. It was also an opportunity to broaden enforcement efforts from Internet service providers to a wide range of intermediaries. The U.K. government's support for informal efforts to control unlawful online content was clear. Jeremy Hunt, secretary of state for culture, media and sport, stressed in a September 2011 speech: "We are working towards a consensus in the industry as to the best solution" (Hunt 2011). Hunt proposed that a "cross-industry body" should deal with infringement by bringing together advertising, payment, search, and web-hosting intermediaries (Hunt 2011).

This cross-industry group came into being in a series of roundtable meetings hosted by DCMS officials that brought together intermediaries, trade associations, and rights holders. One topic of negotiations was a new regulatory program to address advertising on infringing sites (explored in chapter 3). Participants at the roundtable meetings also negotiated a non-legally binding enforcement agreement to govern the U.K. operations of Google, Yahoo, and Bing.

U.K. Search Engine Code of Conduct

Negotiations over the search intermediaries' agreement highlight starkly differing views on the regulation of intellectual property, as well as on the degree of enforcement responsibility that intermediaries should bear for infringing sites. Instead of a single, collectively drafted informal agreement, two proposals emerged from the roundtable talks. Rights holders proposed a set of guidelines to shape the way that search engines index sites, allow users to search, and display search results. Search intermediaries rejected this proposal and drafted an alternative code that largely ignored rights holders' demands. These conflicting proposals underscore continuing tension between intermediaries and rights holders.

In contrast to the status of other informal agreements discussed in this book, the status of the search agreement is unclear. Neither the U.K. government nor the search intermediaries announced the agreement publicly. Since the roundtable discussions are largely off-limits to the public, it is unknown if negotiations are continuing in this area. Despite this uncertainty, the fact that search macrointermediaries collectively drafted a nonbinding enforcement agreement to address infringing sites is noteworthy. Further, the roundtable discussions usefully illustrate the tensions between rights holders and intermediaries and underline the importance of coercive government pressure—in the form of a threat of legislation—in the creation of nonbinding agreements.

Between 2011 and 2012, Ed Vaizey, on behalf of DCMS, chaired a series of meetings with search intermediaries, rights holders, and trade associations. Participants included the Federation Against Copyright Theft, British Phonographic Industry, and Motion Picture Association of America, along with representatives from Google, Yahoo, and Bing. No representatives from the trademark-related associations attended, such as the U.K. Anti-Counterfeiting Group, although they were aware of the meetings. The roundtable discussions focused exclusively on addressing copyright infringement. This is not surprising, since prominent copyright trade associations working on behalf of the music, movie, and software industries typically lead enforcement efforts, as explained earlier, and far more people access copyright-infringing content than purchase counterfeit goods. However, trade associations and rights holders concerned about counterfeit goods could later adopt the informal enforcement measures that emerged from the roundtable meetings.

The first milestone for the meetings came on November 15, 2011, when rights holders presented a nine-page proposal titled "Responsible Practices for Search Engines in Reducing Online Infringement: Proposal for a Code of Practice."[7] In this code, rights holders proposed five key areas where they wanted search intermediaries to revamp their enforcement processes:

- Demote repeatedly infringing sites in rankings of search results. This measure was intended to promote legitimate sources of content and encourage consumers to choose a top-ranked legitimate source instead of a lower-ranked infringing site.
- Prioritize sites certified by industry in search rankings. This was intended to boost the rankings of legitimate sources.
- Automatically remove any search results relating to sites subject to a court order. Sites blocked by court order in the United Kingdom, like the Pirate Bay, would be de-indexed from search results.
- Institute notice-and-takedown programs in which rights holders can take advantage of "automated tools" for the "rapid removal and disabling of infringing links."

- Limit "autocomplete" or "suggested" searches, which suggest search terms as users are typing, based on popular searches. This measure was intended to ensure consumers are not directed toward illegal content.

Minutes from this November meeting reveal, unsurprisingly, that Google, Yahoo, and Bing balked at adopting the code. Implementing rights holders' proposals would have entailed making significant changes to their search practices. For example, the intermediaries would have had to alter their search algorithms to prioritize rights-holder-certified sites in their search results while demoting the search results relating to sites that were the subjects of rights holders' complaints of infringement. Further, the search intermediaries would have had to amend their "suggested" search tools so that users would not be steered toward certain search terms and then access sites with infringing content.

After rights holders presented their proposal, search intermediaries gave their opinions. According to the meeting minutes, Hunt, after listening to the discussion, "stressed that the UK needed a functioning legal marketplace so that it could be a world leader" (Bradwell 2011). Hunt then warned the search intermediaries that the U.K. government preferred "industry to find a way forward" through self-regulatory frameworks, but stressed that the government was "willing" to legislate if there was no industry consensus (Bradwell 2011). To address the rift between rights holders and search intermediaries, Hunt directed the latter to create their own code of conduct in consultation with rights holders (Bradwell 2011).

On February 28, 2012, the search intermediaries released their code of conduct, a four-page document titled "UK Search: The Way Ahead."[8] Differences between the proposals by rights holders and search intermediaries are striking (see table 8). Overall, the differences illustrate the degree to which rights holders and search intermediaries have divergent ideas of intermediaries' responsibility for regulating infringing sites. In their code, the search intermediaries rejected most of the rights holders' demands. Specifically, the search intermediaries ignored rights holders' demands that they demote search results, prioritize certified sites, or de-index sites subject to court orders. The search intermediaries also disregarded rights holders' appeal to make changes to suggested-search functions.

The search intermediaries' code is organized into four broad sections: a preamble and three sets of principles. The preamble discusses the importance of the Internet economy and affirms the search interme-

TABLE 8   COMPARISON OF CODES OF CONDUCT FOR SEARCH INTERMEDIARIES

Rights Holders' Proposed Code of Conduct	Search Intermediaries' Code of Conduct
Demote repeatedly infringing sites	No demotion policy
Prioritize certified sites	No certified sites policy
Stop indexing sites subject to court orders	No such policy
"Improved" notice-and-takedown	"Expeditious" notice-and-takedown
Constrained suggested and related searches	No changes to suggested and related searches

diaries' support for the Department for Culture, Media and Sport's "multistakeholder" approach. In the preamble, the search intermediaries also emphasize that they are "not the source of infringing content," and that rights holders have "the primary responsibility for protecting their intellectual property" (Bradwell 2012). The first principle recommends that search intermediaries should have processes for undertaking "expeditious" processing of complaints through their existent notice-and-takedown programs and "eliminate inefficiencies" (Bradwell 2012).

The second set of principles proposes measures to guide rights holders in their complaints in relation to search results. Search intermediaries instruct rights holders to work with site operators before making complaints to search intermediaries. Intermediaries also note that any complaints must be narrowly targeted toward the removal of specific web pages. Further, they recommend that rights holders be "accountable for improper notices" served to search intermediaries, make their complaints publicly available, and agree to reasonable appeals processes (Bradwell 2012). The third set of principles pertains to search intermediaries' efforts as advertisers to address the placement of advertisements on infringing sites.

Predictably, rights holders and trade associations attending the February 2012 roundtable meeting expressed "disappointment" in the search intermediaries' code (Bradwell 2012). They noted that it "did not refer to or respond to the rights holders' own earlier paper," and that "it did not include any detail on influencing search rankings" (Bradwell 2012). Rights holders also argued that the search intermediaries' agreement "set out revisions to the notice and takedown procedure which would make it more difficult for rights holders" (Bradwell 2012). This last point refers to the search intermediaries' recommendations that rights holders deal first with site operators about search results linking to infringing sites, narrowly target their complaints to search intermediaries, institute an appeals process for site operators, and agree to be held accountable for wrongful takedowns.

Unlike the other informal agreements relating to payment, advertising, domain or marketplace intermediaries, negotiations with search intermediaries did not culminate in a public announcement of a new nonbinding agreement to address infringing sites. Instead, following the search intermediaries' release of their search code of conduct, Ed Vaizey directed them to continue working with rights holders in relation to search-demotion practices and emphasized that Secretary of State Jeremy Hunt wanted to see progress in this area (Bradwell 2012).

Roundtable discussions among intermediaries, rights holders, and DCMS officials continued at least until May 2013. In contrast to its previous practice, the DCMS publicly posted minutes of its May 15, 2013, meeting on the departmental website. At this meeting, no one referred to the search code of conduct. Instead Vaizey stated, "Government and Parliament wanted to see the search issue addressed with tangible results" (Department for Culture, Media and Sport 2013). He also argued that "related searches" listed alongside Google's search results still "pointed to illegal sites" (Department for Culture, Media and Sport 2013). Rights holders also continued to press Google for changes relating to Google's autocomplete function and search-demotion policies (Department for Culture, Media and Sport 2013). From these minutes, it is apparent that rights holders and departmental officials were still dissatisfied with search intermediaries' enforcement practices, especially those of Google.

CHALLENGES OF REGULATING SEARCH

Google has long resisted the idea that it should assume greater regulatory responsibility for policing its search results, particularly in relation to protecting trademarks and copyright. "Google is not, and should not become, the arbiter of what does and does not appear on the web," argued Rachel Whetstone, director of global communications and public affairs for Google. "That's for the courts and those elected to government to decide" (Whetstone 2007). Despite these claims, Google has made significant changes to its search practices, which is understandable given the considerable pressure the U.S. and U.K. governments have exerted on the search macrointermediary.

Between late 2011 and early 2012, Google brought its enforcement practices more in line with U.K. rights holders' proposed search code

TABLE 9   PROPOSED AND ACTUAL RULES FOR SEARCH INTERMEDIARIES

Rights Holders' Code	Search Intermediaries' Code	Google's Policies
Demote repeatedly infringing sites	No demotion policy	Demotion policy introduced in August 2012
Prioritize certified sites	No policy	No policy
Stop indexing sites subject to court orders	No policy	No policy
"Improved" notice-and-takedown	"Expeditious" notice-and-takedown	"Streamlined" notice-and-takedown in 2012
Constrained suggested and related searches	No policy	Changes to autocomplete feature introduced in January 2011

(see table 9). In 2010, Google announced that in January 2011 it would begin implementing changes to prevent "terms that are closely associated with piracy" from appearing in its autocomplete program (Walker 2010). In terms of search demotion, Google had argued for years that it would not alter its algorithms that index and rank its search results. However, it capitulated in August 2012, announcing that it would amend its search algorithms to consider the number of "valid copyright removal notices" against sites and then demote search results from sites with a "high" (but unspecified) number of removal notices (Singhal 2012). In 2012, Google also created the Trusted Copyright Removal Program to fast-track complaints from complainants with "a proven track record of submitting accurate notices" and "a consistent need to submit thousands of URLs each day" (Google 2013). Neither Bing nor Yahoo has made similar changes, but they are not subject to the same degree of governmental pressure as Google.

Google's changes to its enforcement policies made it easier for rights holders to submit massive numbers of complaints about problematic search results, and rights holders have done just that. Large rights holders, trade associations, and monitoring and investigative firms, like the multinational U.S.-based MarkMonitor, file thousands of complaints daily and submit tens of millions of takedown requests to Google annually. Automated tools make such mass policing possible and simplify the process for both the complainant and the intermediary. However, as discussed earlier in this chapter, these automated tools also raise serious questions about accuracy and accountability. While wrongful removal of lawful content is a problem, there is little data that indicates the scope of the problem: a 2014 study of takedown requests in relation to copyright infringement decries the "relative paucity" of research in this area (Seng 2014, 2). Google's amended enforcement practices, which streamlined its search-result takedown program, likely exacerbate the problem of wrongful takedowns as Google receives and processes ever-increasing number of complaints, which in 2016 will surpass the 558 million requests the company received in 2015 (Ernesto 2015).

Like Google's streamlined takedown program, changes to its search-demotion policies, too, may wrongfully target lawful content and legitimate sites. Google's search-demotion changes involve demoting search results relating to sites with a "high" number of complaints. Google does not publicly specify what constitutes a high number of complaints and fails to provide an appeal process for people with demoted sites.[9] Demoting search results based solely on accusations gives rights holders "one more bit of control over what we see, hear, and read" (Samuels and Stoltz 2012).

The goal of using search macrointermediaries to enact access chokepoints is to make it more difficult for people to find and access unlawful content. This assumes, of course, that search engines can act effectively as gatekeepers to deter people from seeking "inappropriate" information and instead steer them toward "appropriate" information. Search engines are relatively ineffective regulators of trademark or copyright infringement. As search intermediaries regularly point out, removing or blocking search results does not remove the problematic content from websites. Similarly, Google's change to its autocomplete tool limits the type of search terms suggested to users, but users can still type their full search queries into Google themselves. Google's down-ranking of search results linking to infringing sites may steer some people toward choosing genuine products and legitimate sources of content. People intent on accessing counterfeit goods, however, can scroll through search results until they find what they want. Overall, then, search intermediaries are relatively ineffectual regulators of infringing sites. However, despite this, government officials in the United States and Europe continue to pressure Google to reform its search practices to prevent results relating to copyright or trademark infringement in its search results page.

DOMAIN NAME SYSTEM

While governments and rights holders regularly publicly condemn Google's search practices and demand changes, GoDaddy has faced little equivalent pressure, at least publicly. In contrast to search engine or marketplace intermediaries, domain intermediaries are less well known as regulators, even to those within the brand-protection industry. Most people rely upon the domain name system with little understanding of how it operates or which entities provide services. This is not surprising given the technical complexity of the domain name system that operates as good infrastructure should—unobtrusively, effectively, and without requiring its users to comprehend its operations. Simply put, the domain name system operates much like a telephone book for the Internet, matching easy-to-remember domain names (e.g., www.nytimes.com) to their corresponding unique Internet protocol (IP) address (e.g., 170.149.168.130). Universality is a fundamental principle of the domain name system, in which anyone can reach the same website by entering its domain name.

When users type a domain name into a web browser, a series of transactions occur in the fraction of a second that it takes to load the domain name. Simplifying somewhat, the following process occurs. The translation, or "resolving," of a specific domain name to its IP address to reach a desired site is called "name resolution" or "DNS resolution." It involves an Internet service provider, like Verizon in the United States, sending a series of queries called "DNS queries" to different domain name servers. These are massive databases that map domain names to their Internet protocol addresses. The Internet service provider sends queries until the address is found, and then it loads the site in the user's browser.

Domain names are not sold outright: one must register them for fixed periods of time, and they can be automatically renewed. Registrars are companies or nonprofit organizations that manage and register domain names for people (called registrants) who want to operate websites. Registrars may offer retail-level services registering domain names to individuals and companies, wholesale-level services to companies that are resellers of domain names, or both. Domain names are organized into a complex global hierarchal system of different types of domain name extensions.

There are 250 unique country-code designations (country-code top-level domains), such as .us (United States), .ca (Canada), .uk (United Kingdom), and .jp (Japan). Beyond these, there are generic designations (generic top-level domains) of which .com, .net, and .org are commonly recognized. The .com designation is the most popular code for commercial sites. Codes that refer to specific agencies or institutions are called sponsored designations (sponsored top-level domains), such as the commonly used .edu (education) and .gov (U.S. government). As the Internet expands, there are an increasing number of new top-level domains, particularly in non-Latin characters, such as Chinese or Arabic.

Domain registrars work closely with another important intermediary—domain name registries. Some registries are public-sector institutions or nonprofit organizations, while others are for-profit commercial firms. Each registry has the responsibility of operating specific top-level domain names. The U.S.-based company Verisign, for example, is the authoritative registry for one of the most popular generic top-level domain names, the .com designation. This means that all registrars that want to issue .com domains must work with Verisign. Each registry also acts as a database for all domain names registered within a specific top-level domain and operates the infrastructure that converts IP addresses into domain names. Domain registries, therefore, are an indispensable part of the domain name system.

Each domain registrar may work with multiple registries depending on the types of domain names that each domain registrar offers. While all domain registrars that want to offer people .com domains must work with Verisign, those that want to offer .biz domains must work with the U.S.-based registry Neustar, which is in charge of the .biz designation. Large domain registrars typically work with multiple registrars to offer their customers a variety of domain options.

GoDaddy

There are many different domain registrars operating worldwide. From a regulatory perspective, the key player is GoDaddy, based in Phoenix, Arizona. Founded in 1997, GoDaddy is the world's largest domain registrar. It has a self-reported global market share of almost 13 million customers and over 57 million domains. GoDaddy has about 30 percent of the market worldwide (Cannon 2014) and the authority to register multiple generic top-level domains, including .com, .net, .org, .info, .biz, .travel, and .xxx. The company launched an initial public offering in March 2015 and is valued at nearly $4 billion (CNN Money 2015).

In addition to operating its domain registrar business, GoDaddy is also one of the world's largest web hosting companies, with about a 5 percent market share (Costa 2015). This means that it provides content storage or hosting services to individuals or companies who establish sites. From a regulatory standpoint, this is important because GoDaddy can seize any websites it hosts for violating its policies. Given its dominant position as the largest domain registrar, coupled with its web hosting services, the intermediary is a valuable regulator for governments and rights holders alike.

To understand how domain registrars regulate, imagine you want to set up a website. The first step is to check with a registrar to see if your desired name is available. You select a simple and catchy domain name and use the registrar's automated process to register your name. GoDaddy registers domain names "at a rate of more than one per second," explains Christine Jones, executive vice president and general counsel for GoDaddy in testimony before Congress in 2011 in relation to SOPA and PIPA (Jones 2011, 4).[10] This makes it "virtually impossible for a human being to verify the legitimate use of every domain name" (Jones 2011, 4).

GoDaddy approves your registration and issues the name to you for a specified period of time as long as you abide by the company's terms and conditions regarding your use of the domain name (see GoDaddy 2016). GoDaddy's rules are incorporated within its domain name registration agreement with the website operator.

DOMAIN INTERMEDIARIES' ENFORCEMENT POLICIES

Domain registrars, like other intermediaries, are subject to various national laws, which they incorporate into their contractual agreements with people who register domain names with them (termed "registrants"). To understand how domain registrars work and regulate their services, it is important to appreciate the important roles played by ICANN, the Internet Corporation for Assigned Names and Numbers, and domain registries like Verisign.

ICANN may be unfamiliar to the average Internet user, but it plays a critical role in the universality of the Internet by overseeing and coordinating the Internet's technical infrastructure, including the domain name system. It is a private, nonprofit institution based in California. Since its creation in 1998, ICANN has operated through a series of memoranda of understanding with the U.S. Department of Commerce. This relationship has frustrated civil-society groups and governments, especially the Russian government, which argue that the agreement gives the U.S. government undue influence over the current operation and future direction of the Internet (see e.g., Carr 2015; Mueller 2015). Since 2006, ICANN has been slowly transitioning toward a multistakeholder governance model that will enable input by governments, civil society, academia, and industry. Skeptics, however, question the degree to which a multistakeholder model will diffuse power, and they contend that this model may actually concentrate power in ways that favor the U.S. government and its commercial interests (see Carr 2015).

As part of its duties governing the domain name system, ICANN sets out the responsibilities of registrants, registrars, and registries, which are then echoed in the contractual agreements that these parties have with one another. For example, ICANN sets out policies that each registry must adopt or institute in its agreements with registrars. ICANN also has the authority to suspend or terminate registrars that violate its policies by, for example, permitting illegal activity or failing to comply with court orders (Internet Corporation for Assigned Names and Numbers 2013).

ICANN also accredits registrars, although not all choose accreditation. ICANN accreditation is necessary for registrars that want to offer the .com, .net, and .name designations. Two of ICANN's policies are particularly relevant to the online regulation of intellectual property. First, registrants must attest that neither the registration of the domain name nor its use "directly or indirectly infringes the legal rights of any third party" (Internet Corporation for Assigned Names and Numbers 2013, 15). Second, as of July 2013, ICANN stipulates that each contractual agreement among registries, registrars, and registrants must explicitly prohibit registrants from, among other things, engaging in trademark or copyright infringement, or counterfeiting (Internet Corporation for Assigned Names and Numbers 2013).

Domain registries institute all of ICANN's policies in contract with each of the registrars with which they work, under the Registry-Registrar Agreement. Each registry may work with hundreds of registrars, and each registrar may work with multiple registries. GoDaddy, for example, has multiple contracts with Verisign pertaining to the .com, .net, and .name domains, and also with the U.S.-based Neustar registry for the .biz domain. In addition to instituting all of ICANN's policies, registries also reserve the right to control any domain names registered by any of their contracted registrars. For example, Verisign requires each of its registrars (e.g., GoDaddy) to stipulate in the Registrar-Registrant Agreements that Verisign can deny, suspend, cancel, or transfer any domain name (Internet Corporation for Assigned Names and Numbers 2012, 2.7a).

Domain registrars, then, are bound by agreements with multiple registries and must also abide by ICANN's policies and accreditation

TABLE 10 DOMAIN INTERMEDIARIES' ENFORCEMENT MEASURES

Technique	Result
Change domain name registrant	Registrant loses domain name
Prevent transfer of domain name	No change or modification of name
Transfer to different registrar	Transfer to new registrar
Cancel domain name	Domain returns to common pool
Suspend DNS resolution (seize-and-takedown)	No resolution (e.g., error message or site-not-found message)
Redirect DNS resolution (seize-and-post notice)	Redirection to warning page

agreement. Registrars may also stipulate their own rules for registrants. GoDaddy, for example, prohibits users of any of its services from involvement with malware, spam, hacking, the promotion of terrorism, or the distribution of child sexual abuse images (GoDaddy 2016). According to its terms-of-use agreement, GoDaddy also prohibits its users from promoting, selling, or distributing prescription medication to a buyer who lacks a valid prescription, and from infringing on any entity's intellectual property rights (GoDaddy 2016). GoDaddy may terminate its services to repeat offenders and then may remove and destroy any of the offender's data stored on its servers (GoDaddy 2016).

Domain Seizures and Takedowns

Given the complexity of the domain name system, registrars have multiple methods with which to regulate the use of domain names that they register (see table 10). In 2012, David Piscitello, vice president of security and ICT communications at ICANN, published a guide called "Thought Paper on Domain Seizures and Takedowns" (see Piscitello 2012). The document usefully explains the technical measures that domain intermediaries can take in response to illegal or objectionable conduct on their platforms. According to Piscitello, the document is intended to offer "guidance" and "help preparers of legal or regulatory actions understand what information . . . registries and registrars will need to respond promptly and effectively to a legal or regulatory order or action" (Piscitello 2012, 1). Domain intermediaries may take these measures upon receiving court orders. Intermediaries can also "voluntarily cooperate with law enforcement agents and the private sector" (Piscitello 2012, 2) or take action independently in response to a registrant's violation of the intermediaries' policies.

The guide outlines six technical measures. First, registrars can reregister the account in the name of the party who made the complaint of wrongdoing. Courts have ordered registrars to transfer domain names from site operators selling counterfeit goods to the authorized owners of the trademarks in question. In consequence, site operators lose the domain names. Second, registrars can prevent the transfer of a domain name during an investigation or court proceeding. This means site operators under investigation by the registrar or law enforcement cannot transfer the frozen domain name to another registrar. Third, registrars can transfer domain names to a different registrar. For example, a court may order all domain names pertaining to a case be transferred to a specific registrar pending the court's decision in the case. Fourth, registrars can cancel domain names. This action returns the names back to the pool of available domain names that anyone may register.

Registrars also have two more powerful technical measures: domain seizures and takedowns. In a "seize and takedown" action, registrars suspend proper DNS resolution for the targeted domain name. As a result, the domain name will not resolve to its proper site and will instead show an error message. David Lipkus, an associate with the Toronto law firm Kestenberg, Siegal, and Lipkus, explains that if someone types into a browser a domain name that is subject to a seize-and-takedown order, such as "ChanelCheapFakes.com," then "it won't take you anywhere. It will just say, 'This website page cannot connect'" (interview, Lipkus 2012).

The sixth measure registrars can take is called "seize and post notice," and it involves registrars redirecting domain resolution so that the domain name will not properly resolve and the user will instead be directed to another web page. Law enforcement agencies, for example, work with registrars to seize the domains of websites involved in child pornography and then redirect users wanting to access that domain instead to a web page warning that the site in question is under investigation for the distribution of child pornography.

These measures are different from a notice-and-termination action undertaken by payment or advertising intermediaries, because the domain intermediary does not terminate its services to the targeted domain names. Instead, the registrar seizes and controls the domain names, thereby preventing the sites' operators from using their sites. The goal, however, is the same as notice-and-termination programs. Seize-and-takedown actions and seize-and-post-notice actions are intended to disable sites' functionality and disrupt their commercial operations.

Rights holders employ seize-and-post-notice measures. U.S. courts have ordered registrars to use seize-and-post-notice measures in relation to sites selling counterfeit goods, in which users are redirected to web pages with banners warning against the purchase of counterfeit goods. Some rights holders seek court orders to "point the domain name to their authorized website, so even if you are looking for 'Brandfakes.com' you'll end up at the authorized site for that product" (interview, Lipkus 2012).

Domain takedowns, seizures, and redirection raise serious due-process concerns. From rights holders' perspective, the seizures prevent site operators from shifting their operations to other service providers and also stop the continued sale of counterfeit goods. In cases where counterfeit goods may pose health and safety risks, such action could protect consumers. However, registrars redirect users of the sites to warning banners before court decisions are handed down. In cases where domain intermediaries work voluntarily with rights holders, they redirect anyone attempting to access the domain names to warning banners or to rights holders' authorized sites based simply on rights holders' allegations of wrongdoing.

Because the technical measures outlined above are complex, an example of registrars' enforcement efforts can usefully clarify domain intermediaries' regulatory capacity. Christine Jones, GoDaddy executive vice president and general counsel, provided a valuable, but rare, glimpse into domain registrars' enforcement processes in her testimony to the Subcommittee on Intellectual Property, Competition and the Internet in 2011. Jones explained that when GoDaddy receives a complaint of illegal content associated with a domain name, such as controlled drugs that are being sold without prescriptions, it conducts an investigation. As part of that investigation, GoDaddy determines whether the registrant in question has "other domains resolving to that site and whether there are other sites in that registrant's account" (Jones 2011, 5).

Once GoDaddy determines evidence of illegal content, the registrar designates the site as a "ParaSite." Then "we suspend all the ParaSites associated with the customer's account, not just the ones about which we receive a complaint or notification" (Jones 2011, 6). GoDaddy may also redirect would-be users of the site to a warning notice. If GoDaddy also provides the web hosting services to the targeted site, then in addition to seizing the targeted domain names GoDaddy can also seize the websites to prevent anyone from accessing the them. GoDaddy's capacity to seize domain names and websites demonstrates its considerable regulatory capacity as a commercially dominant registrar and web host.

DOMAIN REGISTRARS AS REGULATORS

GoDaddy, like the payment and advertising macrointermediaries discussed earlier, has a history of voluntary enforcement actions against child pornography. In testimony to Congress, GoDaddy representatives emphasized the company's commitment to good corporate citizenship. Christine Jones told members of Congress that GoDaddy "always has and always will support both government and private industry efforts to identify and disable all types of ParaSites on the Internet" (Jones 2011, 7). Alongside PayPal, MasterCard, Google, and Microsoft, GoDaddy is a member of the Financial Coalition Against Child Pornography and the U.K.-based Internet Watch Foundation. GoDaddy agrees to block access to sites that these organizations blacklist for containing child sexual abuse images. GoDaddy is also a member of another voluntary initiative, the Anti-Phishing Working Group, which is a nonprofit coalition of law enforcement agencies and industry actors working together to crack down on and raise awareness about cybercrime worldwide.

Operation In Our Sites

As early as 2010, domain intermediaries have worked with law enforcement agencies in the United States to crack down on the online sale of counterfeit goods. The focus of these efforts is the much-publicized Operation In Our Sites, which began in June 2010. The National Intellectual Property Rights Coordination Center (NIPRC Center), which is housed in the Department of Homeland Security, launched the project to dismantle sites selling counterfeit goods and copyright-infringing content. The NIPRC Center is a multiagency organization that brings together law enforcement and regulatory agencies to investigate intellectual property rights crime. Among its partners, the NIPRC Center works with the Federal Bureau of Investigation, the Food and Drug Administration's Office of Criminal Investigations, the U.S. Customs and Border Protection, as well as Interpol and Europol. The breadth of the NIPRC Center's enforcement partnerships illustrates the importance that the U.S. government accords to the protection of intellectual property rights.

Operation In Our Sites is the NIPRC Center's flagship enforcement project to disrupt the online sale of counterfeit and copyright-infringing goods. The operation targets a wide range of counterfeit goods, from luxury goods, sporting products, and apparel to pharmaceuticals. In the project, rights holders submit to NIPRC Center officers the lists of sites that they contend are violating their trademarks. "We've found better success if the industry chooses sites," explains a senior NIPRC Center official, because rights holders have usually done some work on the sites to make sure that they are active sites and target U.S. consumers (interview, NIPRC Center official 2012). The NIPRC Center officers purchase sample products from the targeted sites, and then "we send the product to the rights holder and they verify the infringement" (interview, NIPRC Center official 2012). For sites that appear to be involved in both illicit and legitimate activities, the case becomes more complicated. "Is it 90 percent counterfeit stuff and 10 percent legitimate stuff?" If the site has both illicit and legitimate products, "we'll send it to a field office for more of a workup" (interview, NIPRC Center official 2012).

Once the NIPRC Center is satisfied that the site operators are involved in the sale of counterfeit goods, the agency seeks a federal court order (called a "seizure warrant") to seize the targeted site's domain name(s) (Immigration and Customs Enforcement 2014). The NIPRC Center officers work closely with the U.S.-based Verisign when investigating any infringing sites that use .com and .net domains, since Verisign is the authoritative registry for those domains. The agency works only with U.S. registries and registrars, because it wants to work with companies "that will honor a U.S. seizure court order." Domain intermediaries based outside the United States are not compelled to honor U.S. court orders (interview, NIPRC Center official 2012). Verisign then seizes the targeted domain name, which prevents the site operators' registrar or the site operators from accessing the domain name. As part of the seizure order, Verisign redirects any traffic attempting to access the seized domain name to a warning banner. The banner, bearing the seals of the NIPRC Center, Department of Justice, and Homeland Security Investigations, states that the domain name for that site has been seized under the authority of a U.S. district court in relation to copyright infringement or counterfeit goods.

This brief overview of Operation In Our Sites illustrates that the U.S. government regards domain intermediaries as valuable partners in enforcement efforts to disable sites selling counterfeit goods and copyright-infringing content. It also demonstrates the regulatory capacity of registries like Verisign, which can seize domains linked to any of the top-level domain designations that they operate (such as .com), regardless of the location of the domain registrar. By working with U.S.-based registries, the U.S. government can reach globally to target any sites using domain names governed by those registries. Operation In Our Sites is an industry-driven enforcement project (right holders identify the targeted sites) that functions by using federal court orders served to U.S.-based domain intermediaries.

SOPA and PIPA

Legislators who drafted the Stop Online Piracy Act and Protect Intellectual Property Act also recognized the regulatory power of intermediaries, including domain registrars. Under these bills, domain intermediaries would have been responsible for removing their services from sites distributing counterfeit goods or copyright-infringing content, thereby forcing site operators to seek domain services from other providers. In contrast to Operation In Our Sites, however, SOPA and PIPA would have granted domain intermediaries the right to act voluntarily, instead of requiring their action in response to federal court orders. Under these bills, domain intermediaries could have acted voluntarily against sites that endangered public health by advertising and distributing pharmaceuticals to U.S. consumers in violation of U.S. federal and state laws. Although SOPA and PIPA never made it out of Congress, their provisions related to voluntary enforcement by intermediaries against unauthorized pharmacies live on in the form of a non-legally binding agreement. As a result, instead of a voluntary right of action granted by legislation—and subject to judicial and legislative scrutiny—intermediaries work through secretly negotiated, informal handshake agreements officially endorsed by the U.S. government, with no official court oversight.

Center for Safe Internet Pharmacies

While Congress was hearing testimony concerning PIPA, GoDaddy was quietly meeting with Victoria Espinel at IPEC, along with payment and advertising intermediaries. The goal of the discussions was a non-legally binding enforcement program to address what Espinel referred to as "illegal fake online 'pharmacies'—criminals masquerading as legitimate pharmacies" (Espinel 2012). In December 2010, Espinel announced an industry-focused initiative to address the unauthorized distribution of pharmaceuticals on the Internet. In July 2012, GoDaddy and Google led a group of intermediaries in officially launching the program under the auspices of a newly registered nonprofit organization called the Center for Safe Internet Pharmacies (CSIP). Signatories to the CSIP agreement are domain registrars (GoDaddy and eNom), search intermediaries (Google, Yahoo, and Bing), and payment providers (Visa, PayPal, MasterCard, and American Express). The Washington State–based eNom is a domain name wholesaler, which resells domain names—including the .co, .net, .com, and .uk top-level domains—to registrars.[11]

Promoting public health and safety is a laudable goal and is especially important in relation to prescription medication. It is difficult to estimate the number of unlawfully operating online pharmacies, as is the case with any illicit market. LegitScript, a pharmacy-monitoring company and ex-officio member of CSIP, estimates that thirty thousand to thirty-five thousand illegal online pharmacies are active globally (LegitScript 2016, 2). Counterfeit pharmaceuticals may contain incorrect medicinal ingredients, insufficient medicinal ingredients, or be adulterated with toxic chemicals (Tusikov 2006).[12] The medication's appearance and its packaging may be visibly different from the genuine product, or the pharmaceutical packaging and the medication may be exactly replicated (Tusikov 2006). Counterfeit medicines can result in unexpected side effects, incorrect dosages, dangerous drug interactions, allergic reactions, or the worsening of medical conditions (Tusikov 2006). Consumers may not receive proper information on correct use, dosages, drug interactions, or side effects. An additional public health concern is that manufacturers may disregard regulatory standards for the production, distribution, and storage of medication.

In light of the serious health and safety problems that can result from counterfeit, substandard, or poorly regulated medicine, CSIP's purpose is twofold. It concentrates on raising public awareness about unauthorized online pharmacies and encouraging consumers to purchase medication from licensed, accredited pharmacies. More unusual in a nonprofit, nongovernmental organization, CSIP takes enforcement action against online pharmacies that violate U.S. law regarding the online sale and distribution of pharmaceuticals. Marjorie Clifton, CSIP's executive director, describes the center as providing the "first-ever private sector solution" to the problem of unauthorized online pharmacies (Clifton 2012). GoDaddy's Christine Jones described CSIP members as working "to eviscerate the online sale of counterfeit and otherwise illegal prescription drugs" (Berkens 2011, 3).

CSIP sets out intermediaries' roles and responsibilities in a March 2014 document titled "Principles of Participation for Members." In the document, CSIP requests that its members agree to participate in sharing data about online pharmacies, and that all enforcement action taken against "illegitimate sites is voluntary and subject to individual company guidelines" (Center for Safe Internet Pharmacies 2014, 8). As members of CSIP, domain registrars are asked to "immediately lock and suspend the domain names from use or resolution in the domain name system if a hosted website is determined to be operated by an illegitimate online pharmacy" (Center for Safe Internet Pharmacies 2014, 10). The CSIP agreement differs from the other nonbinding enforcement agreements discussed in this book because it involves a coalition of domain, payment, and advertising/search macrointermediaries working in a coordinated fashion to disable sites designated as illegal online pharmacies. Search intermediaries remove search results relating to unauthorized pharmacies, while companies operating advertising platforms remove advertisements relating to these sites and payment providers cancel the sites' merchant accounts.

In addition to a membership of powerful macrointermediaries, CSIP has two ex-officio members with close ties to the pharmaceutical industry. One member is the Alliance for Safe Online Pharmacies, a nonprofit advocacy group whose membership is largely composed of pharmaceutical companies and pharmacies, including Eli Lilly, Johnson & Johnson, and the National Association of Chain Drug Stores. The alliance describes its work as advocacy, education, and outreach to patients, health care providers, and governments in relation to the safe distribution of medication (Alliance for Safe Online Pharmacies n.d.). In addition to these efforts, the alliance also supports "legal voluntary actions by Internet intermediaries," including "terminating service, [and] locking domain names" (Alliance for Safe Online Pharmacies n.d.a).

CSIP's other ex-officio member is the Oregon-based company LegitScript, which investigates and certifies online pharmacies. The company sells monitoring and enforcement services to pharmaceutical companies, including threat assessments that inform companies how their businesses are negatively affected by illegal online pharmacies. LegitScript also certifies pharmacies' online operations on behalf of the U.S. National Association of Boards of Pharmacy, accrediting those operating in compliance with U.S. laws.[13] The company also identifies pharmacies that operate in violation of U.S. laws and, as part of its work with CSIP, alerts CSIP members so they can take enforcement action against those pharmacies. Based on LegitScript's information, the payment, advertising, and domain intermediaries remove their services from and disable the pharmacies.

No Safe Haven for Illegal Pharmacies

Like the other nonbinding agreements, CSIP releases little information publicly regarding its members' enforcement efforts. It is possible, however, to gain insight into CSIP's activities from other sources. The organization's members are involved in the Operation Pangea, Interpol's annual, weeklong, international enforcement project that dismantles unlawfully operating online pharmacies worldwide. For Operation Pangea, GoDaddy, Google, and other intermediaries, like PayPal, work with law enforcement agencies worldwide and with regulatory agencies, including the U.S. Food and Drug Administration. In 2013, Operation Pangea shut down over 13,700 sites selling pharmaceuticals, and in 2014 it closed another 10,600 sites (Interpol 2013). In 2015, Operation Pangea took down only 2,414 sites but reported seizing more than twice the amount of medication as compared with the 2013 operation (Interpol 2015). These figures give an indication of the scale of macrointermediaries' efforts against illegal online pharmacies.

Domain registrars may be active in enforcement efforts against online pharmacies, but the U.S. Government Accountability Office concludes that they are relatively ineffective regulators. It is important to remember that unless the registrar also operates as the web host, registrars cannot remove a site's content, which remains online. In its review of measures to regulate illegal online pharmacies, the GAO found that unlawfully operating pharmacies may "keep domain names in reserve so that they can redirect traffic to new websites" (Government Accountability Office 2013, 27). As a result, targeting sites' domain names is "disruptive" at most, a fact acknowledged by U.S. government officials (Government Accountability Office 2013, 27) and confirmed in recent scholarly studies of illegal online pharmacies (e.g., Liu et al. 2011).

The domain industry's regulatory practices, such as ICANN's accreditation of registrars, and domain registrars' withdrawal of services from noncompliant site operators appear effective in shifting bad actors to a small number of less-scrupulous registrars. According to industry estimates, few domain registrars knowingly facilitate infringement. John

Horton, president of LegitScript, testified before the Subcommittee on Courts, Intellectual Property, and the Internet in the U.S. House of Representatives that the vast majority of registrars have effective policies (Horton 2015). Horton explains that unscrupulous site operators "cluster at a handful of domain name companies," which he calls "rogue registrars" for their inadequate regulation of their registrants' activities (*PR Newswire* 2013). A senior officer from the NIPRC Center made a similar observation in relation to Operation In Our Sites: seizing domain names is "not going to push bad guys out of the system. . . . What we're doing is shrinking the pool of people that we have to focus on" (interview, NIPRC Center official 2012).

Referring to the public health problems posed by illegal online pharmacies, Libby Baney, executive director of the Alliance for Safe Online Pharmacies, called on all intermediaries to ensure that they do not "serve as a safe-haven or facilitator for criminal activity. . . . Especially when lives are at stake, responsible voluntary actions," Baney emphasized, "should be the norm" (Baney 2015). Regulating pharmacies that may pose threats to public health is an important policy goal. Enforcement efforts through CSIP, however, are troublingly opaque and raise potential problems in relation to due process.

Consider the following scenario. Under CSIP's auspices, a company (LegitScript) alleges wrongdoing and independently judges an online pharmacy to be operating in violation of U.S. federal and state laws, and then calls upon other companies (like GoDaddy) to impose sanctions on the targeted pharmacy. Intermediaries take action in the absence of any judicial or law enforcement processes as they act based on the authority of their terms-of-service agreements with the site operators. It is unclear if there is an appeal processes for site operators, or if any independent third party reviews enforcement actions on pharmacies designated as "illegal."

Further, LegitScript and the pharmaceutical industry have a financial conflict of interest in regulating online pharmacies. LegitScript contends that it does not refer noncompliant pharmacies to intermediaries "as a paid service" to any pharmaceutical company (LegitScript n.d.). However, LegitScript's business principally sells its monitoring and enforcement services to pharmaceutical companies. While LegitScript may not receive direct payment for this service, its efforts in regulating online pharmacies benefit pharmaceutical companies, which in turn, have financial interests in controlling the ways in which pharmaceuticals are priced and distributed to U.S. consumers. Pharmaceutical companies have shaped laws in the United States and internationally in favor of their business models and financial interests for decades (see Drahos and Braithwaite 2002). The pricing structure set by U.S. pharmaceutical companies means that medications are typically more expensive in the United States than other countries. As a result, some consumers seek medication from online pharmacies that may not be licensed for operation in the United States. Consumers may be unfairly caught in a situation between legally accessible, less-affordable medication and (some) unauthorized pharmacies that provide safe, affordable medication.

WRONGFUL TAKEDOWNS AND OVERBLOCKING

The two informal agreements examined in this chapter—the agreement that created the Center for Safe Internet Pharmacies and the search intermediaries' code of conduct—illustrate a component of the transnational anticounterfeiting regime aimed at throttling access to infringing sites. Victoria Espinel, head of IPEC, and Jeremy Hunt and Ed Vaizey from the Department for Culture, Media and Sport, played central roles in the regime, since they secured macrointermediaries' participation in negotiations with rights holders and facilitated the creation of the agreements. Coercive pressure from the U.S. and U.K. governments was instrumental in the creation of this regime, because rights holders alone did not have the requisite authority to bring together all the macrointermediaries involved in CSIP or to direct Google, Yahoo, and Bing to draft a nonbinding code of conduct. By compelling Google and GoDaddy—through threats of legislation and legal action—to enter talks, IPEC and the DCMS legitimized rights holders' demands that macrointermediaries assume greater regulatory responsibility for online infringement.

Google and GoDaddy, the dominant firms in their industry sectors, are technologically sophisticated regulators with a capacity for mass policing: each year, Google removes hundreds of millions of search results and GoDaddy cancels the domain names of thousands of sites. But because they only impair access to targeted sites, and do not remove content from them,[14] they are prolific but not particularly effective regulators.

The goal of using search macrointermediaries to enact access chokepoints is to make it more difficult for people to find and access unlawful content. This assumes, of course, that search intermediaries can effectively set up roadblocks to deter people from seeking "inappropriate" information and to steer them toward "appropriate" information. Google's changes to its autocomplete tool and down-ranking of search results linking to infringing sites may steer some people toward choosing genuine products and legitimate sources of content. However, people can still type their full search queries into Google themselves, scroll down through search results until they find the links they want, or locate infringing sites from other sources, such as advertisements or links on social media.

The shift to mass, automated notice-and-takedown efforts that are directed at Google's search results has exacerbated the problem of wrongful and even abusive enforcement practices. Studies of takedown requests that Google receives reveal serious problems with inaccurate complaints that result in Google wrongfully removing legitimate, non-infringing content (see Seng 2014; Urban et al. 2016). In a random sample of 108 million takedown complaints, most of which relate to Google searches, Urban et al. (2016) found that just over 28 percent of complaints were of questionable validity. This study underlines the challenge of regulation through automation, which has become necessary because the volume of complaints—Google receives thousands of complaints a minute—makes human review impossible. Google reports that it acts in response to 97 percent of the takedown complaints it receives (Google 2013), which means that the company errs on the side of removing links rather than refusing requests. Given the shift toward automation, which increases the speed and volume of complaints, and Google's high response rate, links to lawful content will continue to be removed.

Similar problems are evident in relation to domain macrointermediaries' enforcement practices. Regulatory policies, such as ICANN's accreditation of registrars, and domain intermediaries' transfer or seizure of domain names from noncompliant site operators, are effectively shifting bad actors to a small number of less-scrupulous registrars. However, the practice of seizing—and redirecting—domain names raises serious concerns, as explained earlier in the chapter. Industry-led enforcement actions undertaken in the absence of a judicial or independent hearing raise the risk of overblocking domains or subdomains for websites that are not engaged in wrongdoing, since domain seizures can affect all subdomains. Further, redirecting users attempting to access seized domain names to warning banners can wrongly label legitimate site operators as criminals. In contrast with the U.S.-government-run Operation In Our Sites, which functioned through federal court orders, intermediaries working on behalf of CSIP operate through their privately drafted terms-of-service agreements. Because neither CSIP nor the intermediaries are forthcoming about their enforcement efforts, it is unclear how—if at all—domain intermediaries handle appeals from site operators or ensure that their regulatory actions do not unfairly block lawfully operating subdomains.

5

Marketplace Chokepoints

Online marketplaces have fundamentally transformed the way individuals and businesses buy and sell goods and services. The U.S.-based eBay and the Chinese Taobao marketplaces are the largest online marketplaces globally. Taobao is part of the massive Alibaba Group, which operates several online marketplaces, including the Alibaba marketplace, which caters to wholesale buyers. Since the early days of eBay and Amazon, which were the first major marketplaces of this type, people have tried to sell illicit, dangerous, fraudulent, or outright bizarre goods. eBay's early years were marked by people's attempts to sell items including magic amulets, souls, cadavers, children, and virginity (Kravets 2009). Beginning in the early twenty-first century, with the growth of online shopping, rights holders began to complain of the sale of counterfeit goods through online marketplaces, especially eBay. Rights holders demanded that marketplaces remove these "infringing" sales listings for counterfeit goods and sanction the sellers.

U.S. and European rights holders currently focus much of their enforcement efforts regarding marketplaces on eBay and Taobao. "We focus on Alibaba and Taobao because that's where we found the volume of violations that affect our clients," explains Allan Watson, director of global operations of Gamble Investigations International in London. "They are two of the biggest ones" (interview, Watson 2012). The sale of counterfeit goods online is "a massive problem on a global scale," says Bob Barchiesi, president of the International Anti-Counterfeiting Coalition (CNBC 2014). "The Chinese copycat culture, combined with the insatiable appetite of U.S. consumers looking for a bargain, creates this perfect storm across the Internet," Barchiesi notes (CNBC 2014).

eBay and Taobao represent a different dimension of the private transnational anticounterfeiting regime. These marketplaces are legally operating trading platforms on which some individuals sell counterfeit goods in violation of the marketplaces' policies. In contrast, other elements of the anticounterfeiting regime are directed at websites that are involved in selling counterfeit goods, and that may have few, if any, legitimate activities. eBay and Taobao facilitate a massive volume of trade involving hundreds of millions of users worldwide. Given the scope of these marketplaces, rights holders are concerned that the marketplaces' users could mistakenly or willingly purchase counterfeit versions of their products instead of legitimate products. "The stand-alone site [a self-contained website operated by an individual or a company, not a marketplace like eBay] is a lower priority than taking action on the trading platform," explains Tim Waring, director of Intelligence Technologies, a U.K.-based brand-monitoring firm, "because the trade platform has a much higher visibility than a stand-alone site" (interview, Waring 2012). By focusing on illicit sales through eBay and Taobao, rights holders hope to throttle the sale of counterfeit goods on the most popular trading platforms.

Like other intermediaries, eBay and Taobao have faced years of pressure from governments and rights holders to crack down on the sale of counterfeit goods on their platforms. In 2011, eBay and Taobao yielded, and each signed non-legally binding enforcement agreements. eBay accepted a deal that the European Commission crafted on behalf of European rights holders to regulate the distribution of counterfeit goods through European marketplaces, while the Office of the U.S. Trade Representative played a key role in coercing Taobao into cooperating with the International Anti-Counterfeiting Coalition on behalf of its U.S. and European rights-holder members. eBay and Taobao amended their enforcement efforts to make their practices more rapid, streamlined, and proactive than their previous measures. The European Commission approvingly refers to the marketplaces' new enforcement approach as a "beyond-compliance" regulation (European Commission 2013, 5–6).

Following the pattern described in chapters 3 and 4, the nonbinding agreements are rooted in the United States and the European Union and stretch globally. Marketplaces in China are a particular concern to U.S.

and European rights holders, because the country is a major location for the manufacture of counterfeit goods. Moreover, these rights holders want to expand their access to China's burgeoning population of online shoppers and ensure that those consumers purchase authentic trademarked products, not counterfeit goods.

Shared and Divergent Interests

Rights holders, marketplaces, and consumers have shared interests in a secure, effectively functioning e-commerce environment. Consumers also benefit from programs that remove fraudulent, shoddy, or unsafe products from the marketplace. Like Google, with its preference for minimally regulated search results, marketplaces have an interest in facilitating the sale of a diverse array of goods at a range of different prices, and in granting their merchants latitude to set prices and sell legitimate goods and services. eBay emphasizes this point when it describes its platform as operating "under the pillars of trust, value, and selection" in order to provide "the best prices for genuine products" (Brewer-Hay 2010). Marketplaces' preference for a varied selection of listings and a large stable of sellers is a financial consideration, since sellers' sales listings and fees provide revenue to platforms.

The popularity of eBay and Taobao demonstrates that people want the ability to buy and sell a wide variety of new and secondhand goods at varying prices. These marketplaces enable people to supplement their incomes by selling goods online, and they allow businesses to capitalize on the trading platforms to serve new and existing markets. Marketplaces increasingly use automated enforcement tools to detect suspicious sales listings, as do many rights holders and their brand-protection firms. These tools target sales listings based on indicators, not proof, of suspicious activities and can result in wrongful takedown of sales listings for legal goods.

Marketplaces have an interest in ensuring that legitimate sellers are not inaccurately or unfairly penalized or wrongly characterized as criminals. However, enforcement practices that prioritize streamlined, proactive mass enforcement often sacrifice precision for speed. Such practices can harm small-scale merchants who have few resources to challenge the removal of their sales listings or to launch appeals after being sanctioned by the marketplaces. An "automated notice and takedown system leaves little room for traders to appeal," argues Monica Horten, an intellectual-property scholar in the United Kingdom, who notes that such a system makes it more difficult for "people who genuinely sell second-hand goods or old stock" (Horten 2011), since listings for these types of goods are more likely to be wrongly identified as suspicious and then removed.

Consumers are the missing voice in regard to informal anticounterfeiting agreements, especially in relation to eBay. The European Commission, along with the rights holders, trade associations, and marketplaces involved in the European agreement, stresses that a primary goal is to protect consumers from unsafe or deceptively marketed goods (European Commission 2013). The European Commission identifies consumers as one of its main stakeholder groups, yet no consumer protection organizations participated in or appear to have been consulted in the negotiation of the European Union's nonbinding agreements. Further, the informal agreements generally lack safeguards to ensure that small-scale traders are not unfairly swept up in enforcement dragnets.

As noted in chapters 3 and 4, there is tension between marketplace intermediaries and rights holders, which are backed by powerful governmental actors in the United States and Europe. Rights holders, especially those with luxury brands, have demonstrated an interest in expanding their control over the online distribution and pricing of their products. As legal battles between eBay and U.S. and European rights holders show, some luxury-brand rights holders are using their concerns about counterfeit goods as a pretext to argue that marketplaces should not be permitted to sell their luxury goods. This battle highlights larger questions about the consequences when large corporate interests, supported by powerful state actors, set rules that may unfairly constrain how people access and exchange goods and services online.

Before turning to the eBay and Taobao case studies and further discussing the ideas raised above, it is important to give a brief overview of how online marketplaces operate and regulate their users in relation to the sale of counterfeit goods.

ONLINE MARKETPLACES

Marketplaces like eBay offer a broad diversity of newly manufactured and secondhand goods to meet consumers' desire for multiple types of products at a range of prices. These platforms also allow people to trade in secondary-market goods, such as secondhand clothing, books, and electronics, and nostalgia items like vintage toys and jewelry.

Marketplaces vary in the way that they sell goods and generate revenue. Business-to-business marketplaces, like the Alibaba marketplace, largely facilitate transactions among businesses involving wholesale quantities of goods. Others, like Amazon, provide businesses with a platform to sell goods to consumers; this is termed a business-to-consumer marketplace. eBay and Taobao operate both as business-to-consumer and consumer-to-consumer marketplaces, because they enable businesses to sell to individuals, and consumers to sell to one another. Taobao is China's biggest consumer-to-consumer marketplace but also has storefronts through which merchants sell directly to consumers. The variety of different marketplaces allows people to purchase large quantities of goods from a wholesale-level market like Alibaba and resell them in a consumer-oriented marketplace like eBay or Taobao. "There are a lot of sites in China where people tend to buy in bulk" and then "maybe sell it on eBay," points out Damian Croker, CEO of Brand-Strike Limited, a London-based brand-monitoring firm (interview, Croker 2012).

While online marketplaces share some similarities with their offline counterparts, they differ in several key aspects. Unlike a retailer such as Walmart, these marketplaces do not handle or sell the goods themselves, nor do they verify products' quality, legality, or authenticity. Instead, they claim only to facilitate commercial transactions between parties by providing the interface to support the transactions. eBay underlines this distinction in its user agreement. "You acknowledge that we are not a traditional auctioneer. Instead, our sites are venues to allow users to offer, sell, and buy just about anything, at any time, from anywhere, in a variety of pricing formats and locations" (eBay 2014).

Online marketplaces make their money in a number of ways. One of the most common ways is through fees charged to sellers (buyers generally are able to register for free). eBay, for example, charges sellers fees for listing their products and upon the conclusion of sales.[1] It also makes money by charging sellers for seminars and marketing advice to increase sales. Taobao, in contrast, does not charge sellers for transactions, but instead charges fees for marketing, shipping, and advertising services, and for export-related services such as customs clearance, logistics, and cargo insurance. Marketplaces also generate significant revenue by charging transactional fees for the use of their proprietary payment systems. The Alibaba Group controls Alipay, a payment processor with about 50 percent of the online payment-industry market share in China (Jackson 2014). eBay owned PayPal from 2002 until 2015, when it separated PayPal and made it into an independent, publicly traded company. Although the two companies are now separate, eBay users can still use PayPal to pay for their shopping.

eBay and Taobao

eBay was one of the first online marketplaces, and it remains the most well-known and most popular worldwide, outside of China. In 1995, Pierre Omidyar, a computer programmer in San Jose, California, launched an online marketplace that he first called AuctionWeb before renaming it eBay in 1997. eBay has platforms around the world, such as eBay.se in Sweden and eBay.co.uk in the United Kingdom. In 2015, eBay had 160 million active users and 800 million listings globally, and it generated $81.7 billion in gross merchandise volume (the total value of all merchandise sold), with $7.2 billion in revenue (eBay 2015). Beyond its namesake marketplace, eBay also operates other popular online marketplaces, such as Gumtree and Kijiji, which are popular in Canada; Marktplaats.nl in the Netherlands; and mobile.de in Germany.

Four years after eBay's launch, entrepreneur Jack Ma launched the Alibaba marketplace, in 1999, from his apartment in Hangzhou, China, with a group of eighteen other people. Alibaba was one of the first business-to-business marketplaces in China and the beginning of what would become the Alibaba Group, a massive e-commerce conglomerate. Ma, who is currently the executive chair of the Alibaba Group, says he first realized the necessity of an online marketplace in the 1990s when he typed "Chinese beer" into a search engine and received no results (*The Economist* 2010).

Until the Alibaba Group filed its much-anticipated and highly publicized initial public offering in the United States in September 2014, few people outside China had even heard of the company. This lack of attention, which changed quickly when the company's U.S. initial public offering generated a record-breaking $25 billion, belies its size and importance. Far from being an upstart, the Alibaba Group is the largest Internet company in China and one of the largest globally in terms of the number of its users and the business generated by its marketplaces. A good way to understand the Alibaba Group is to consider it "a mix of Amazon, eBay and PayPal, with a dash of Google thrown in" (Osawa 2014). The company runs several marketplaces (Alibaba, Taobao, and Tmall), cloud storage businesses (AliCloud), and a search engine (Aliyun). The Alibaba Group also provides financial services through an independent subsidiary, Ant Financial Services Group (an ant being the Alibaba Group's mascot). Through Ant Financial Services, Alibaba operates an online bank as well as Alipay, China's most popular online payment service.

Following the creation of the business-to-business Alibaba marketplace, which has a Chinese-language platform for Chinese businesses and an English-language international platform, the Alibaba Group set its sights on establishing a consumer-to-consumer trading platform that could challenge eBay's attempts to expand into China. In 2003, the Alibaba Group created Taobao, a name that translates as "hunting for treasure." The clash between eBay and Taobao was brief, but fierce. Within three years of its creation, Taobao displaced eBay and claimed 67 percent of the consumer-to-consumer market in China (Mitchell 2010). Jack Ma remarked of the eBay-Taobao rivalry: "eBay may be a shark in the ocean, but I am a crocodile in the Yangtze River. If we fight in the ocean, we lose—but if we fight in the river, we win" (Wang 2010). Yahoo recognized the Alibaba Group's potential in 2005, when it acquired a 40 percent stake in the company—one of the few things that the company has done right in the twenty-first century. Both companies shared a common interest in thwarting eBay's advance into China.[2]

The vast majority of Taobao's sales are in China, where it reports 231 million active buyers annually (Alibaba Group 2014). For 2015, the Alibaba Group reported $394 billion in gross merchandise volume and $12.3 billion in total revenue (Alibaba Group 2015). The Alibaba Group announced plans in 2014 to launch versions of its marketplaces in other languages, including English, but it has not yet provided a timeline for this expansion. The Alibaba Group's Tmall, formerly known as Taobao Mall, is comparable to Amazon. Created in 2008, Tmall was spun out from Taobao. It is China's top business-to-consumer site, with approximately 40 percent to 50 percent of the market share in China, compared to Amazon at less than 5 percent (Millward 2013). Tmall sells more than seventy thousand multinational brands and Chinese brands (Spelich 2012).

Many U.S. and European rights holders, especially those selling luxury goods, are eager to enter, or expand their presence in, China. Given Tmall's dominant market share, U.S. and European rights holders regard Tmall as an entry point into the Chinese marketplace and a way to access hundreds of millions of shoppers. Before they establish partnerships with Tmall to sell their products, however, rights holders want to ensure that Tmall—and the Alibaba Group generally—have enforcement policies and programs in place to combat the sale of counterfeit goods.

MARKETPLACES' ENFORCEMENT POLICIES

Before the introduction of their respective nonbinding agreements in 2011, discussed below, both eBay and Taobao had enforcement procedures in place to deal with complaints of counterfeit goods and copyright-infringing content. eBay introduced its anticounterfeiting policies in 1998, while Taobao (created in 2003) started to strengthen its nascent enforcement practices after the Office of the U.S. Trade Representative blacklisted it as a notorious market in 2008. Like the other Internet companies examined in chapters 3 and 4, marketplaces operate within a web of national laws and company-specific rules regarding the sale of goods across their platforms. Marketplaces incorporate state laws and industry- or company-specific rules within the contractual terms-of-service agreements that they have with individuals and businesses who buy and sell goods through the marketplaces.

Marketplaces that operate in multiple countries are subject to varying national laws that affect the types of goods and services that can be sold. The U.S. version of eBay, eBay.com, prohibits the sale of most tobacco products to U.S. consumers but allows sales on its platforms that serve other countries. Similarly, Taobao prohibits the sale of chewing gum in Singapore in accordance with that country's laws, which also forbid the sale of processed eggs, laser pointers, and seditious material. In addition to national laws, marketplaces may institute company-specific rules that regulate transactions. eBay prohibits the sale of items that glorify or promote hate, such as Nazi memorabilia and U.S. Confederate flags, on all its country-specific platforms. The intermediary's policy on prohibited and restricted items states that the company "may also base our policies on input from our members and our own discretion, especially for dangerous or sensitive items" (eBay n.d.).

In addition to their lists of prohibited items, eBay and Taobao both have policies in their terms-of-service agreements that specifically forbid the sale of copyright-infringing content and counterfeit goods. eBay also prohibits its users from encouraging or enabling others to infringe the intellectual property rights of a third party, or claiming certain items are authentic or believed authentic when they are not. Taobao prohibits listing or selling counterfeit goods or unlicensed replica items.

Notice-and-Takedown Programs

Both eBay and Taobao use notice-and-takedown programs to address the sale of counterfeit goods on their platforms. Marketplaces operating in the United States, such as eBay, target copyright-infringing goods, using the U.S. Digital Millennium Copyright Act. To address the sale of counterfeit goods, U.S. marketplaces employ notice-and-takedown programs similar to the DMCA, although there is no statutory requirement in the United States for them to do so. In 1998, the same year the DMCA was signed into law, eBay created the first notice-and-takedown program specifically for counterfeit goods, which it calls the Verified Rights Owner (VeRO) Program.

Marketplaces' notice-and-takedown programs are relatively straightforward. Rights holders (or their authorized third parties, such as attorneys or investigative firms) submit notices of infringement, proof of ownership of the trademark(s) in question, references to specific listings, and a sworn statement. In the words of eBay, these statements must attest that the complainants have a "good faith belief" that listings "are not authorized by the IP Owner, its agent, or the law."[3]

Marketplaces operating in the European Union, meanwhile, are subject to the European Commission's 2000 Electronic Commerce Directive, as implemented in member states' laws. eBay's European platforms are subject to the E-Commerce Directive. Like the DMCA, the E-Commerce Directive considers marketplaces to be hosting intermediaries; in contrast to the DMCA, it addresses both copyright and trademark infringement. Notice-and-takedown regimes under the E-Commerce Directive are similar to those prescribed by the DMCA.

Marketplaces operating in China are subject to legislation similar to that in Europe and the United States. In 2010, China revised article 36 of the Tort Liability Law of the People's Republic of China, which sets out the conditions under which Internet intermediaries are liable for the infringement of intellectual property rights. In particular, article 36 allows rights holders to require intermediaries to remove, block, or disable access to infringing material, and its notice-and-takedown regime resembles the DMCA and E-Commerce Directive (Ferrante 2014, 4).

Regulating through Technology

Automated monitoring and enforcement tools are an important component of the nonbinding enforcement agreements and, indeed, a central element of marketplaces' daily operations and regulatory practices. Marketplace intermediaries, like the intermediaries described in other chapters, use sophisticated automated systems that enable marketplaces to respond to violations of their policies and proactively identify potential wrongdoers or suspicious activities. Companies are reluctant to describe their internal security measures publicly. "We're never going to give tons of detail," said a representative from the Alibaba Group, "because that would help fraudsters get around it" (Erickson 2011).

eBay and Taobao both report using proprietary software programs to gather valuable commercial data by tracking their customers' transactions, consumer behavior, and purchasing patterns, as well as to detect anomalies among transactions. The marketplaces also automatically scan sales listings for terms that may indicate the sale of counterfeit goods, such as *knockoff* or *replica,* and they search sellers' trading histories to identify those who have a suspicious pattern of selling particular items or brands. As part of its campaign to persuade the Office of the United States Trade Representative to remove Taobao from its notorious-markets blacklist, which it did in 2012, the Alibaba Group strengthened its enforcement practices and expanded its regulatory capabilities. This included dedicating over twenty-three hundred employees to detecting counterfeit goods on its marketplaces and enlisting around fifty-four hundred volunteers to undertake "daily online surveillance" of sales listings (Alibaba Group 2015a). To undertake this monitoring, Taobao uses data-mining tools to analyze and track transactions of counterfeit and copyright-infringing products, as well as to identify hotspots in sales and distribution patterns (Alibaba Group 2015a).

Other prominent regulatory actors that use technology to police marketplaces are the brand-protection companies. These firms, part of the broad private-security industry, provide an important and increasingly popular service for rights holders by scanning the web for indicators of the sale of counterfeit goods or copyright-infringing content. For example, these companies send Google mass takedown notices for search results that link to copyright-infringing web pages, as described in chapter 4. Brand-protection companies play an even more prominent enforcement role in regulating marketplaces on behalf of rights holders concerned about counterfeit versions of their products.

Brand-protection companies that target the online trade in counterfeit products observe "a range of compliance" in relation to online marketplaces, explains Tim Waring, director of Intelligence Technologies, a

U.K. monitoring firm. "But generally we find all the platforms are responsive to some degree. The larger and more established the platform, the easier it is to deal with" (interview, Waring 2012). Rights holders' strategy in relation to the sale of counterfeit goods is to "get them off the bigger auction sites," says Kieron Sharp, director general of the Federation Against Copyright Theft, a U.K. trade association. In doing so, rights holders seek to reduce the opportunity of consumers "looking to find that kind of thing" (interview, Sharp 2012).

To rid the major marketplaces of counterfeit goods, brand-protection companies monitor specific key words, logos, symbols, images, and other indicators in a variety of languages, and they track multiple marketplaces worldwide. They use software with photo-detection and graphics-recognition tools to compare rights holders' copyrighted photographs and logos with those posted by sellers in sales listings. The companies may extract geo-locational data to plot sellers' physical locations and then link the profiles of multiple sellers on different platforms by matching telephone numbers, mailing addresses, and Internet protocol addresses. These techniques enable monitoring companies to identify possible targets for civil or criminal action, since "brand owners are looking to identify big bulk sellers," explains James Ramm, director of Commercial Security International, an investigative firm in London (interview, Ramm 2012).

Many monitoring firms have established cooperative working relationships with marketplaces in order to facilitate the firms' detection of counterfeit versions of their clients' products, removal of infringing listings, and sanctioning of sellers. Some marketplaces even permit certain brand-monitoring firms a direct portal into the marketplace through an application programing interface. APIs specify how software programs should interact with one another through a specific interface. The eBay and Alibaba marketplaces allow certain monitoring firms to use APIs to submit infringement notices directly to the marketplace, automate the process of listing and monitoring auctions, and extract user information for investigations.

eBay "looked at our code, and they've agreed to give us a link into their database," says Ramm (interview, Ramm 2012). By using APIs, brand-protection firms can submit thousands of complaints for the removal of sales listings on behalf of their clients, monitor multiple trading platforms simultaneously, and track individuals as they target different marketplaces. "We can automate a cease-and-desist," notes Ramm, and send an "instant removal request" to the marketplaces (interview, Ramm 2012). Similarly, an investigative firm operating in London that wishes to remain unnamed has "direct access" to the Alibaba marketplace and can "take hundreds if not thousands of [sales] advertisements down in one hit" from the marketplace (interview, director, private security firm 2012).

Regulation through automated and semiautomated tools raises serious challenges in terms of precision, accountability, and adherence to due-process measures. "Lots of brand owners, I think, hope that there is some magic computer program that you can just put the brand name in, and [then] everything is off the Internet," says Duncan Mee, director and co-owner of Cerberus Investigations in London (interview, Mee 2012). The reality, of course, is much more complex. Underlying the use of automated tools—and, indeed, prominent in brand-protection firms' marketing literature promoting their use—is an assumption that the trade in counterfeit goods can be detected with a strong degree of accuracy. Rights holders, marketplaces, and monitoring firms have all wrongly identified secondhand goods, parallel-trade goods, and even authentic trademarked goods as counterfeit products. Rights holders, for example, have ordered multiple eBay sellers to stop offering secondhand Coach purses (Masnick 2011).

One way to strengthen the accuracy of removals is to make test purchases of suspected goods in order to examine products physically to determine whether they are counterfeit or genuine. Operation In Our Sites, undertaken by the U.S. National Intellectual Property Rights Coordination Center and described in chapter 4, routinely performs test purchases before its officials seek warrants to seize targeted sites' domain names. Rights holders, however, have an interest in determining infringement quickly, broadly, and at minimal cost. Test purchases can be "tricky if you've got a site selling very expensive goods," notes Siân Croxon, a partner with the law firm DLA Piper in London (interview, Croxon 2012).

Rights holders' attempts to persuade eBay and Taobao to strengthen their enforcement practices voluntarily were largely unsuccessful. As the following sections describe, U.S. and European rights holders targeted eBay with a series of lawsuits, alleging that the marketplace facilitated the sale of counterfeit goods on its platform. Because these lawsuits provided only partial victory for rights holders, the latter persuaded the European Commission in 2009 to intervene and compel eBay to adopt a nonbinding enforcement agreement in May 2011. State coercion was successful where rights holders' legal efforts had fallen short. The European Commission took a carrot-and-stick approach. The incentive was a moratorium on litigation for signatories that would calm the adversarial environment. The stick was a threat of legislation if industry could not come up with a voluntary agreement. The Alibaba Group, likewise, resisted making wholesale changes to Taobao's enforcement practices, until the USTR blacklisted both Alibaba and Taobao as notorious markets from 2008 to 2012 as part of its Special 301 Process. Taobao's nonbinding agreements with the International Anti-Counterfeiting Coalition illustrates the degree to which corporate actors, especially from the United States, set standards in relation to intellectual property, even in China.

EBAY AS A REGULATOR

Since the early twenty-first century, eBay has depended on its VeRO Program to deal with complaints about the sale of counterfeit goods on its platform. Created in 1998, the VeRO Program is the earliest and most well-established enforcement program among marketplaces. The marketplace intermediary has investigative teams based in North America, Europe, and the Asia-Pacific region to work with and support law enforcement investigations (Dougherty 2011). The VeRO Program sets out policies and procedures for rights holders to make complaints about, and to police, the sales of their brands on eBay. Approximately forty thousand rights holders participate in the program, each of which owns one to several hundred brands (eBay 2013). The VeRO Program, like those of most marketplaces, allows complainants to submit notifications of infringement electronically. eBay accepts complaints of infringement in relation to counterfeit goods, as well as complaints of copyright and patent infringement.

In response to infringement complaints, eBay generally deletes the targeted listings within a few hours. Once the listings are removed, eBay notifies any bidders, cancels the bid or calls for any outstanding transactions not to be completed, and advises the seller of the reason for the cancellation. Sellers repeatedly found to be in violation of eBay's policies may be suspended from the marketplace without a refund of their fees. eBay also monitors its platform in case suspended account holders attempt to regain access to its services (Dougherty 2011).

In addition to its VeRO Program, eBay has several educational initiatives to raise awareness among its users about intellectual property rights. The marketplace intermediary created interactive tutorials to teach users about eBay's policies, about applicable national laws, and how to ensure that their listings comply with these laws and policies in relation to intellectual property rights (Dougherty 2011). Following eBay's detection of a user selling counterfeit or copyright-infringing goods, it may require the user to complete a tutorial successfully before reinstating the user's account. eBay also permits rights holders, trade associations, law enforcement and regulatory agencies, and consumer protection organizations to educate eBay users on various issues by creating an "About Me" page on eBay (Dougherty 2011).

eBay's Battles with Tiffany

For rights holders, litigation and threats of legal action can be useful tools to persuade intermediaries to strengthen their enforcement practices. That said, rights holders' capacity to make a credible threat of litigation varies widely. There "aren't many rights holders with the interest and the resources and, I suppose, the commercial interest to bring significant cases to court," observes Jeremy Newman, a partner with the law firm Rouse Legal in London (interview, Newman 2012). There are also significant drawbacks to litigation. "It's slow. It's expensive," notes Newman.

Since its creation, eBay has faced considerable pressure from rights holders to crack down on the sale of counterfeit goods. Rights holders and attorneys specializing in intellectual property rights even take credit for convincing eBay to create its VeRO enforcement program. "They had to be pulled kicking and screaming into doing it," recalls Siân Croxon, a partner with the law firm DLA Piper in London (interview, Croxon 2012). At a 2004 conference on counterfeiting and copyright infringement hosted by Fordham University in New York City, a panel of attorneys and a representative of the International Anti-Counterfeiting Coalition made a similar claim. "It took many years to get there, by threatening to sue [eBay] under the doctrines of contributory and vicarious infringement," said Barbara Kolsun, general counsel for the luxury firm Kate Spade (Kolsun, McDonald, and Pogoda 2004).

eBay's legal battles with U.S. and European rights holders between 2004 and 2010 in relation to counterfeit goods resulted in starkly different judgments from U.S. and European courts. These cases, discussed below—especially eBay's epic, years-long battle with the New York City–based luxury jeweler Tiffany & Company in relation to counterfeit goods—aptly illustrate the tension between marketplaces and rights holders over the division of enforcement responsibilities. While rights holders and eBay were locked in seemingly endless litigation, European rights holders appealed to the European Commission for assistance. Between 2009 and 2011, as these court cases progressed in the United States and France, the European Commission negotiated talks among rights holders, their trade associations, and marketplaces, especially eBay, and announced a nonbinding enforcement agreement in May 2011.

Tiffany's case against eBay began in 2003, when Tiffany's lawyers made multiple complaints to eBay about the sale of counterfeit Tiffany-branded jewelry.[4] The companies began working cooperatively in 2004 to detect and remove listings for counterfeit products, but their partnership soon crumbled as Tiffany accused eBay of failing to crack down on merchants selling counterfeit Tiffany products. In response, Tiffany in 2004 launched one of the first infringement lawsuits against eBay (Tiffany, Inc., v. eBay, Inc. 2008). Tiffany claimed that eBay was facilitating trademark infringement by allowing the sale of counterfeit Tiffany products and turning a blind eye to bad actors. In the court case, Tiffany characterized eBay as "a pirate bazaar, a 'flea-market,' and a seller of fakes and counterfeits" (Rimmer 2011, 134).

The case is influential because, in July 2008, a New York district judge found in eBay's favor and ruled that rights holders, not intermediaries, bear the responsibility to police and protect their trademarks. Tiffany appealed the decision, but in April 2010 an appeals court, too, ruled in eBay's favor. In the 2008 ruling, the judge found that eBay removed problematic listings promptly once alerted by Tiffany and suspended repeat offenders. Importantly for eBay, the judge concluded that the "burden of policing the Tiffany mark appropriately rests with Tiffany" (Tiffany, Inc., v. eBay, Inc. 2008, 57).

eBay was jubilant with the 2008 and 2010 court decisions.[5] Dan Dougherty, global head of intellectual property at eBay, contended the case "broadly endorsed eBay's anti-counterfeiting efforts" (Dougherty 2011, 1). One key point of contention in the case was the degree to which eBay is responsible for monitoring its platform proactively in the absence of specific complaints from rights holders. The district court found that eBay developed enforcement measures that were not legally required: eBay "consistently took steps to improve its technology and develop anti-fraud measures as such measures became technologically feasible and reasonably available" (Tiffany, Inc., v. eBay, Inc. 2008, 57). eBay was not legally required to implement these measures, because the court found marketplaces have "no affirmative duty to ferret out potential infringement" (Tiffany, Inc., v. eBay, Inc. 2008, 52).

These court rulings vindicated eBay's enforcement processes. The marketplace interpreted the decisions as findings that it "exceeds all legal requirements in the fight against counterfeits," said Rob Chesnut, senior vice president and legal counsel at eBay (Brewer-Hay 2008). eBay's measures included software to detect patterns of fraudulent activity, search tools to detect sales listing for counterfeit goods, and programs to identify "potentially problematic sellers" (Dougherty 2011, 3). eBay's decision to exceed its legal requirements can be explained as an attempt to mitigate the risk of (further) legal action by rights holders. eBay's actions are, in part, efforts to secure some measure of regulatory certainty.

eBay's Battles with European Rights Holders

While Tiffany lost against eBay in the United States, European luxury brands were triumphant in European courts. The lawsuits against eBay in Europe are complex, but two cases are especially important to understand, because the courts' rulings usefully illustrate why eBay—and other marketplace intermediaries—face an uncertain legal landscape. In the first case, the conglomerate Louis Vuitton Moët Hennessy (LVMH), which owns the French luxury brands Louis Vuitton, Christian Dior, and Givenchy, brought legal action against eBay. In a decision siding with LVMH, the French court ruled in SA Louis Vuitton Malletier v. eBay, Inc. (2008) that eBay's enforcement efforts were insufficient to control the sale of counterfeits.

The French court's ruling went beyond dealing with counterfeit versions of LVMH's brands. One of the claims made by LVMH was that eBay had violated commercial distribution agreements by allowing unlicensed parties to sell luxury goods over the objections of rights holders. In essence, LVMH contended that eBay sellers were not authorized to sell its products through the marketplace. In response, the French court found that eBay was guilty of practicing unlawful sales in allowing perfumes belonging to Christian Dior, Givenchy, and others to be sold outside the companies' network of distributors (Rimmer 2011, 147). In what is known as parallel trade, rights holders may use licensing agreements to authorize certain parties to distribute their products in specific geographical areas, and may set different prices for the same products in different regions.

The French court in the second case made a similar ruling against eBay but also went further, requiring eBay to assume greater responsibility for goods sold on its platform. In this second case, in a suit brought by the French company L'Oréal, which supplies perfumes and cosmetics, the French court ruled that eBay did not take appropriate steps to address the sale of counterfeits (L'Oréal, SA, v. eBay France, SA, 2009; see Rimmer 2011).

In 2011, L'Oréal's complaint against eBay was again before the courts (L'Oréal, SA, and Others v. eBay International, AG, and Others, 2011). This time the European Court of Justice issued a ruling that considered larger questions raised in L'Oréal's action against eBay. The European Court of Justice found that goods might be considered infringing if parties sell them outside channels authorized by rights holders (Rimmer 2011, 154). This means that the European Court of Justice adopted a broad interpretation of counterfeit goods based on where the goods are sold. If eBay sells products outside the European Union that European rights holders authorize for sale only within the European Union, a European court may hold eBay liable for trademark infringement.

The ruling by the European Court of Justice essentially conflates two separate concepts (counterfeit goods and parallel trade goods). For rights holders intent on exerting greater control over the pricing and distribution of their goods, the European Court of Justice grants them the latitude to do so in the European Union. As a result, the ruling also imposes greater responsibilities on eBay to police its platform for certain European goods sold outside authorized European Union markets. In response to the ruling, eBay officials condemned the "attempt to use the ruling to confuse the separate issues of counterfeit and restrictive sales" and suggested "that counterfeit suits are being used by certain brand owners as a stalking-horse issue to reinforce their control over the market" (Brewer-Hay 2008a).

A second finding from the European Court of Justice in relation to L'Oréal's action against eBay was also important to the creation of the anticounterfeiting agreements. The court ruled that intermediaries might be liable for facilitating infringement if the intermediaries "should have realised that the offers for sale in question were unlawful" and "failed to act expeditiously" (L'Oréal, SA, and Others v. eBay International, AG, and Others 2011, 145). Simply put, marketplaces may be responsible for infringement by their users if they have prior knowledge of wrongdoing. According to this ruling, then, intermediaries must consider taking a more proactive role in detecting, addressing, and preventing infringement. The European Court of Justice's ruling that marketplaces have some responsibility for monitoring their platforms proactively sharply diverges from U.S. court rulings that find marketplaces do not have a general obligation to monitor their platforms.

Looking for Regulatory Certainty

As eBay's legal battles with U.S. and European rights holders indicate, eBay was motivated to accept the European Commission's nonbinding agreement in order to establish a degree of regulatory certainty regarding its enforcement responsibilities and to avoid legislation threatened by the European Commission. Marketplace intermediaries, especially those stretching globally, operate in an uncertain regulatory environment, where the nature and degree of their responsibility for users who sell counterfeit goods on their platforms tend to be uncertain.

Lawsuits by luxury-brand rights holders against eBay reveal that U.S. and European courts have differing interpretations of eBay's regulatory responsibilities (see Mac Síthigh 2013; Rimmer 2011). Joe McNamee, advocacy coordinator at the European Digital Rights group, underlines this regulatory uncertainty when he points out that intermediaries like eBay "will not be held liable in cases where they unknowingly host illegal material, provided they act in an (undefined) expeditious way after having received (undefined) actual knowledge of the infringement" (McNamee 2011, 18). This uncertainty has significant implications for regulation on the Internet, because it means that intermediaries are more inclined to remove content (or disable services) when rights holders make complaints of infringement. Marketplaces thus operate in a regulatory environment where the rules are largely in flux, which makes it difficult to mitigate the risk of lawsuits by rights holders.

EUROPEAN COMMISSION'S MEMORANDUM OF UNDERSTANDING

In 2009, at the same time that eBay was battling lawsuits in the United States and Europe over counterfeit goods, it, along with a group of rights holders and their trade associations, entered closed-door negotiations with the Directorate General Internal Market and Services at the European Commission. After two years of negotiations, the European Commission quietly published a nonbinding agreement relating to marketplace intermediaries in May 2011 called the "Memorandum of Understanding on the Sale of Counterfeit Goods via the Internet" on its website (European Commission 2011). Curiously, although the agreement was released on the commission's website, it was titled only "Memorandum of Understanding" and did not contain the European Commission's logo.

The agreement, which covers the European Economic Area,[6] applies only to counterfeit and copyright-infringing goods and excludes any disputes over parallel trade. Signatories include an array of trade associations and rights holders from the pharmaceutical, consumer electronics, sporting goods, software, apparel, and toys industries. Participants include Proctor & Gamble, Adidas, Nokia, Louis Vuitton, Microsoft, Burberry, and Nike, as well as the massive consumer care conglomerate Unilever, which owns dozens of well-known brands, including Best Foods, Dove, Lipton, and Sunlight.[7] The agreement covers thirty-nine online marketplaces, including country-specific versions of eBay and Amazon that operate across Europe, such as those in France, Belgium, the United Kingdom, and Poland. Other marketplaces operating throughout Europe, like Ricardo, Tuktuk, and Allegro, also participate.

As with the other nonbinding agreements discussed in previous chapters, coercive state pressure was central to the creation of the European agreement. The European Commission persuaded marketplaces to join the agreement by warning that "if voluntary arrangements cannot be agreed [upon]," the commission would "need to consider legislative solutions" (European Commission 2009). The commission argued that voluntary arrangements aimed at counterfeiting could give industry stakeholders "the flexibility to adapt quickly to new technological developments" (European Commission 2009, 10).

Although the European Commission used threats of legislation, it also offered signatories some relief from litigation, since participants agree "not to initiate any new litigation against each other" while the agreement remains in force (European Commission 2013, 4). eBay, like most corporate actors, candidly acknowledges its preference for avoiding litigation. "We continue to support cooperation, rather than litigation, as the best way to address these issues in everyone's best interests," says Michael R. Jacobson, eBay general counsel (Brewer-Hay 2010). The litigation moratorium promises a measure of legal certainty and a possibility of signatories working cooperatively instead of being stuck in an endless, expensive cycle of legal battles.

TABLE 11   KEY PROVISIONS IN EUROPEAN COMMISSION'S AGREEMENT

Measures	Nonbinding Principles
Notice-and-takedown programs	Marketplaces agree to institute streamlined, simplified programs to remove infringing listings more rapidly and effectively
Proactive measures	Marketplaces and rights holders agree to monitor sales listings to prevent sales of counterfeit goods
Penalties	Marketplaces agree to increase sanctions against repeat offenders

Proactive and Preventive Measures

Like the other nonbinding agreements, the European Commission's memorandum is based upon broadly worded general principles. The commission recognizes that marketplaces are reluctant to adopt uniform standards and processes, particularly given the differences among their business models and existing enforcement measures (European Commission 2013). One of the agreement's principal goals is to push marketplaces, in the words of the European Commission, "to move beyond mere compliance with legislation" (European Commission 2013, 5–6).

Beyond-compliance measures are evident in two areas. First, the agreement sets out general principles to streamline notice-and-takedown programs and speed up the removal of problematic sales listings (see table 11). In particular, marketplaces agree to institute notice-and-takedown programs that are "not excessively burdensome and simple to subscribe to, complete and process" and that deal with complaints "in an efficient and comprehensive manner" (European Commission 2011, 4, 5). In turn, marketplaces urge rights holders to target their complaints narrowly instead of submitting notifications that are incomplete or too general, or that target "whole catalogues of products" (European Commission 2013, 9). The modified notice-and-takedown programs would be more streamlined than marketplaces' previous measures.

The agreement also introduces what the European Commission refers to in the memorandum as "preventive" and "proactive" anticounterfeiting measures. Industry participants agree that reactive enforcement measures alone, like notice-and-takedown programs, are "insufficient to address the issue of counterfeit sales on online marketplaces (European

Commission 2013, 10). In response, rights holders agree to monitor marketplaces for infringing versions of their products, while marketplaces endeavor to work proactively to identify and prevent the sale of counterfeit goods.

This measure is significant: marketplaces agreed to move from reactive enforcement in response to complaints to monitoring their platforms independently for suspicious activities. Rights holders and their trade associations have campaigned since the early twenty-first century to push eBay "to take a bit of proactive enforcement," explains Ruth Orchard, director of the Anti-Counterfeiting Group, a prominent British trade association (interview, Orchard 2012). It took the threat of legislation from the European Commission to persuade eBay to strengthen its proactive enforcement practices. According to the memorandum, signatories may conduct monitoring through technical means, such as through automated software, manually through human analysis, or through a combination of these measures.

In addition to strengthening reactive and proactive enforcement practices, the agreement contains measures relating to repeat offenders. Marketplaces agree to disclose to rights holders the identity and contact details of alleged infringers (where permitted by law) and to sanction repeat infringers, including "the suspension (temporary or permanent) or restriction of accounts or sellers" (European Commission 2011, 6–7). Marketplaces may consider a number of variables when determining sanctions against sellers of counterfeit goods. Intermediaries may weigh the number of alleged infringements, the scale of legitimate business, and the efforts to avoid detection to determine the severity of the penalty against the seller of counterfeit goods (European Commission 2013, 11).

"More Proactive Cooperation"

The goal underlying the European memorandum is to push marketplaces to institute streamlined, rapid, and proactive enforcement measures, which the European Commission praises as a "beyond-compliance" enforcement strategy. In general, rights holders have been largely successful in this objective. According to two European Commission studies of enforcement efforts, conducted in the first two years of the agreement, rights holders are generally satisfied with the agreement. Participants say that the agreement "increased a sense of trust and confidence between parties" and has been "instrumental in opening avenues to more in-depth dialogues and exchanges of information" (European Commission

2012a). Rights holders say that they have "experienced more pro-active cooperation" among participants in addressing counterfeit goods, especially since marketplaces seldom reject rights holders' removal requests (European Commission 2012a, 1; European Commission 2013). Marketplaces have also increased their sanctions of repeat offenders, and rights holders have observed fewer repeat offenders (European Commission 2013).

Those familiar with eBay's work in relation to the European agreement offer somewhat more mixed views on eBay's performance. "I think on the whole we've had a very good experience with eBay," says Alastair Gray, head of the London branch of Cerberus Investigations (interview, Gray 2012). Others highlight areas for further improvement. eBay is "very good," remarks Susie Winter, director general of the Alliance for Intellectual Property, a U.K. trade association, but she criticizes the marketplace for allowing those kicked off the platform for selling counterfeit goods to register again (interview, Winter 2012). "eBay has certainly tried a bit," argues Siân Croxon, a partner at DLA Piper. "It is just the sheer scale of the criminality that is still going on. It seems to me that you have to still question whether it's enough" (interview, Croxon 2012). Gavin Hyde-Blake, director of research and investigation at the U.K.-based investigative firm Eccora, argues that eBay could "be more proactive," but he acknowledges that it's difficult for marketplaces to distinguish genuine from counterfeit goods (interview, Hyde-Blake 2012).

In its memorandum, the European Commission recognizes the problem of wrongful removals of lawful sales listings and commits rights holders to "avoid[ing] unjustified, unfounded and abusive notifications" (European Commission 2011, 4). The agreement also sets out provisions for marketplaces to deny or restrict rights holders' access to their notice-and-takedown programs, and to reimburse sellers in cases of unfounded or abusive notifications. While these are useful measures, the commission provides little information on how or if these provisions are used. The commission's reviews of the enforcement efforts relating to the agreement, too, are silent as to whether marketplaces have sanctioned rights holders for incorrect claims of infringement or for abusive behavior. Because the majority of intermediaries' efforts in relation to the agreement involve proactive enforcement, measures governing notice-and-takedown programs (reactive responses) do not apply.

The European Commission stated that it took on "a novel function as facilitator" to coordinate negotiations among intermediaries, rights holders, and their trade associations (European Commission 2013, 6).

In doing so, the commission said, it provided administrative and logistical support in addition to "safeguarding, where necessary, a fair balance between all the different interests at stake, including the legitimate rights and expectations of EU citizens" (European Commission 2009, 10). Despite its commitment to safeguarding all interests, no consumer organizations or civil-society groups were involved or consulted in the drafting of the agreement, nor were negotiations open to the general public. Further, the agreement came as a "surprise" to those who study the online regulation of intellectual property in Europe, as intellectual property scholar Monica Horten noted in her blog post about the agreement (Horten 2011).

TAOBAO AS A REGULATOR

Nearly a decade younger than eBay, Taobao has a shorter history of dealing with counterfeit goods, but its experiences have been similar to those of its North American counterpart. U.S. and European rights holders are generally less interested in pursuing litigation in China than against intermediaries in the United States or Europe. Chinese courts historically have been reluctant to hold online marketplaces liable for trademark infringement (Woo 2010, 51). In addition, rights holders complain that the Chinese judicial system presents certain challenges. A Hong Kong–based lawyer interviewed for this research, who wished to remain anonymous, said that litigating intellectual property cases in the Chinese legal system is difficult. The lawyer explained this is because the judiciary is inadequately trained and the lack of separation between government and the judiciary results in politically motivated decision-making (interview, lawyer, Hong Kong law firm, 2012).

There are several important court cases in China that consider Taobao's responsibility for addressing the distribution of counterfeit goods on its platform. In 2010, for example, in a case brought by a Shanghai company, E-Land International Fashion, the court found that it was not sufficient for Taobao simply to remove sales listings for counterfeit goods once alerted by rights holders (Ferrante 2014, 5). It ruled that Taobao should have taken additional measures to address the sale of counterfeit goods. According to the court, such activities could include restricting sellers' activities on Taobao, downgrading their merchant rating, or even banning sellers from the marketplace (Ferrante 2014, 5). These cases show that Chinese courts, like those in the United States and Europe, are weighing intermediaries' regulatory responsibilities in relation to counterfeit goods, a response that challenges intermediaries to determine how they can best meet those duties.

Pressure from U.S. Rights Holders

Taobao attracted the attention of U.S. and European rights holders around 2007—four years after its creation—with its rapid growth, huge population of users, and perceived growing involvement in counterfeit goods. These rights holders, especially those with well-known luxury brands, wanted to expand their markets in China and ensure that the growing population of Chinese shoppers would purchase genuine trademarked products. When Taobao resisted changing its enforcement practices to tackle counterfeit goods, rights holders enlisted a powerful ally, the U.S. government. U.S. rights holders and trade associations successfully petitioned the Office of the U.S. Trade Representative to designate Taobao as a "notorious market" in the USTR's influential *Out-of-Cycle Review of Notorious Markets*.

Taobao Becomes a Notorious Market

The *Out-of-Cycle Review of Notorious Markets* is part of the USTR's *Special 301 Report*, which was discussed in chapter 2. As part of the Special 301 Process, the USTR pressures blacklisted markets to make specific changes to their enforcement policies as demanded by U.S. industry; it also threatens to impose sanctions against countries in which the notorious markets are based. The *Review of Notorious Markets* is a powerful tool for rights holders because it offers a way to pressure companies (and countries) to strengthen their protection of intellectual property rights that is backed by the economic leverage of the U.S. market. By working with the USTR, U.S. rights holders and trade associations gain an international reach in protecting their trademarks and shaping rules governing the sale of goods online.

One of the key players in the campaign to reform Taobao's anticounterfeiting enforcement practices was the International Anti-Counterfeiting Coalition, a prominent trade association based in Washington, D.C. On behalf of its members, the IACC operates a payment-termination program that disables infringing sites, which was explored in chapter 3. Beginning in 2007, the IACC submitted complaints about Taobao's sales of counterfeit goods to the USTR. In 2008, the USTR designated Taobao and the Alibaba business-to-business marketplace as notorious markets, along with Baidu, China's largest search engine. Following the blacklisting of some of China's biggest e-commerce firms, the U.S. government likely exerted coercive pressure on the blacklisted firms and the Chinese government, since this pattern has been evident in cases of other markets and countries that the USTR has blacklisted. Taobao would remain on the notorious-markets list for four years, until the USTR removed it in December 2012 (the USTR dropped the Alibaba marketplace from the list in 2011).

Complaints against Taobao continued even while the marketplace was blacklisted. In 2011, for example, the IACC argued that Taobao was "believed to function as a virtual, and 24-hour, 'trade exhibition' for counterfeiters and pirates seeking sources for illicit goods" (International Anti-Counterfeiting Coalition 2011a, 20). Based on its members' comments, the IACC repeatedly condemned Taobao's enforcement measures and urged the USTR to continue listing the company as a notorious market, citing "Taobao's continued resistance to taking down larger quantities of listings on a timely basis, inconsistent handling of complaints and documentary requirements, [and] reluctance to focus more attention on repeat offenders and other, similar concerns" (International Anti-Counterfeiting Coalition 2012a, 17).

The Special 301 Process can be an effective tool in pressuring countries and notorious markets to amend their practices regarding intellectual property protection. This is particularly the case if those states and markets want to gain or maintain access to the U.S. market. Unlike the Pirate Bay, which has no ambitions to become a legitimate enterprise and is indifferent to its designation as a notorious market, the Alibaba Group has an interest in expanding outside of China. This was a strong economic incentive to rehabilitate Taobao's image as a notorious market. While the USTR was blacklisting Taobao, the Alibaba Group was planning to issue an initial public offering.

Initially, the company chose Hong Kong, but after a protracted disagreement with the stock exchange authorities and regulators over the company's governance structure, the Alibaba Group planned an initial public offering in the United States. The Alibaba Group was motivated to convince the U.S. financial industry and securities regulator that it takes seriously the problem of counterfeit goods and protects intellectual property rights. Taobao's removal from the USTR blacklist eliminated a significant barrier to its plans: in September 2014 the Alibaba Group issued a record-breaking $25 billion initial public offering that made its founder, Jack Ma, the richest man in China.

The USTR removed Taobao's notorious-market designation in December 2012, after the marketplace instituted the changes that rights holders demanded. These included permanently banning individuals who repeatedly sell counterfeit goods, removing infringing listings more quickly, and monitoring its platform for violations of its policies. In light of these changes, U.S. ambassador Ron Kirk, head of the USTR, praised Taobao's "notable efforts" to "clean up its site" (Erickson 2012). The USTR also warned Taobao that its removal from the notorious-markets list was conditional. USTR officials urged Taobao "to further streamline procedures" for dealing with counterfeit goods, speed up its removal processes, and continue working toward "a satisfactory outcome with U.S. rights holders and industry associations" (Erickson 2012). John Spelich, vice president of international corporate affairs at the Alibaba Group, acknowledged Taobao's removal by saying that protecting intellectual property "is a long march in China; this is a milestone and it is only the beginning" (Erickson 2012).

Taobao's Enforcement Policies

In contrast with U.S.-based macrointermediaries, Taobao had offered little information publicly on its enforcement processes, especially written in English, before the USTR's blacklisting of Taobao. As part of the Alibaba Group's efforts to free Taobao from the notorious-markets list, however, the Alibaba Group detailed the changes it made to Taobao's enforcement policies and programs. John Spelich wrote to senior USTR officials in September 2012 and outlined changes to Taobao's policies (see Spelich 2012). The public version of this letter and the accompanying twenty-nine-page report, which were posted on the USTR's website, provide a fascinating and detailed window into Taobao's enforcement practices.

To rehabilitate Taobao's practice, the company conducted "extensive consultations with U.S. stakeholders" to identify ways to strengthen the platforms' enforcement processes and "eliminate bottlenecks" in processing and removing listings (Spelich 2012, 3). Following these consultations, the Alibaba Group instituted what Spelich describes as "broad-based measures and severe penalties to prevent the sale of infringing goods" and to "cleanse" the platform of problems (Spelich 2012, 1). Unsurprisingly, given the IACC's prominent role in pressuring Taobao, the marketplace's enforcement changes closely resemble the demands made by the IACC's members. Taobao made several significant changes to its enforcement practices with the following amendments:

- "significantly upgrading" its notice-and-takedown program, including adding measures for complaints to be made in English;
- "substantially reducing" the time frame for removing problematic sales listings; and
- toughening penalties for repeat offenders. (Spelich 2012, 3–7)

Taobao's notice-and-takedown system, which, by 2013, thirty-six thousand rights holders had registered to use (Liang 2014), closely resembles that of eBay. The complaint program is in Chinese, but Taobao provides English instructions for navigating the system.[8] Rights holders must submit proof of identity; proof of ownership of the intellectual property in question, including country of registration and validity period; and hyperlinks to the allegedly infringing listings (Spelich 2012). Taobao also requires rights holders to provide details of the complaint—including whether it involves a listing or storefront and why the rights holder alleges infringement—and to submit any supporting documentation, such as comparison charts or analytical reports (Spelich 2012).

Once Taobao receives a notification of infringement, it informs the seller and discloses details of the complaint. If the seller fails to contest the complaint, Taobao removes the listing. In contrast to eBay, which removes infringing listings within hours, Alibaba and Taobao take approximately two to three working days to process complaints. During that time, Taobao allows sellers accused of selling counterfeit goods an opportunity "to refute the allegation and provide evidence of the authenticity of the product" (Alibaba Group 2015a). However, for complainants with "an established track record of submitting accurate and complete takedown notices" Taobao reports that it undertakes removals more rapidly, usually within hours or a day (Taobao n.d.).

Taobao has two systems of escalating penalties for individual sellers and operators of storefronts, which operate as a "points deduction" system. Each registered member on Taobao gets a certain number of points every calendar year, and Taobao deducts points from sellers found to violate its policies on intellectual property (Liang 2014). If a seller loses all points, Taobao removes the individual from its platform. In 2013, Taobao introduced a four-strikes program to strengthen enforcement against repeat offenders, who are removed after the fourth strike (Liang 2014). As part of this system, Taobao may remove storefronts from the marketplace's search results, which means that the store or its products will not appear in a user's search results (Spelich 2012).

Taobao may also temporarily or permanently ban sellers from operating a storefront and, for Tmall storefront operators, confiscate the operator's consumer protection security deposit (Alibaba Group 2015a). Taobao can force sellers to reimburse buyers who complained about receiving counterfeit goods (Alibaba Group 2015a). Taobao also uses shame to sanction repeat infringers by publicly publishing a blacklist of merchants that Taobao has penalized for selling counterfeit or substandard products on its platform (Erickson 2012a).

Many of Taobao's enforcement practices likewise are highly similar to those of eBay. For example, the Alibaba Group's amendments to Taobao streamlined the marketplace's notice-and-takedown program, shifted it toward more proactive enforcement activities, and toughened sanctions for repeat offenders. This regulatory convergence between the U.S. and Chinese marketplaces in terms of their enforcement policies is the result of prominent U.S. and European rights holders and their trade associations pressuring both marketplaces to address the sale of counterfeit and copyright-infringing goods on their platforms. By working through the USTR, U.S. rights holders and trade associations globally exported U.S.-style rules and standards to protect their trademarks and copyrights. This was fundamentally a coercive process, since U.S. rights holders' demands for Taobao to transform its enforcement practices were backed up by the power of the U.S. government.

State coercion alone does not fully explain Taobao's overhaul of its enforcement practices to address counterfeit goods. The Alibaba Group had a strategic economic interest in convincing the USTR to remove Taobao from the notorious-markets list. At the time Taobao was blacklisted, the Alibaba Group planned to expand its operations outside of China. The company also wanted to persuade more U.S. and European rights holders to sell their brands through Alibaba's popular Tmall marketplace to meet Chinese consumers' growing demand for foreign luxury brands. The Alibaba Group's campaign to rehabilitate Taobao's image—and, more broadly, that of the Alibaba Group—also entailed demonstrating to the U.S. financial industry that the company had solid financial and regulatory foundations.

Memoranda of Understanding

As part of its campaign to be removed from the USTR's notorious-markets list, Taobao signed multiple informal enforcement agreements with prominent trade associations, including the IACC, and rights holders.

These agreements are intended to strengthen existing enforcement standards, enhance cooperation between Taobao and rights holders, and improve efficiency in regulatory efforts. None of these non-legally binding agreements have been publicly released, but details are available through press releases.

Taobao's nonbinding agreement with the International Anti-Counterfeiting Coalition is the most high-profile and wide-ranging of its informal agreements with rights holders. Taobao initiated the agreement with the IACC: Taobao personnel approached IACC officials in the summer of 2012 with an "interest in partnering" with the trade association to address the sale of counterfeit goods (International Anti-Counterfeiting Coalition 2012). Taobao and the IACC signed an agreement in September 2012. This agreement is important because the IACC represents multiple multinational rights holders, including Nike, Proctor & Gamble, and Adidas. These companies also participate in the European Commission's agreement with eBay.[9]

According to the IACC, the goal of the agreement with Taobao is to "leverage available technologies to ensure a streamlined and efficient system for the identification and reporting of illicit sales through the platform" and to "identify the worst offenders" (International Anti-Counterfeiting Coalition 2012b). This is the same approach the IACC takes with payment providers, as discussed in chapter 3.

An important element of the IACC-Taobao agreement is the shift of greater enforcement responsibility to the marketplace. "Every legitimate business has a shared interest, and a shared responsibility, in making sure that the online marketplace continues to develop as a trusted commercial platform," explains IACC president Bob Barchiesi (*PR Newswire* 2012). John Spelich, a senior executive with the Alibaba Group, said in his announcement of the company's support of the agreement: "Our goal at Taobao is to be synonymous in consumers' minds with trust and value" (International Anti-Counterfeiting Coalition 2013).

In the same month that Taobao signed its agreement with the IACC, the intermediaries also signed a memorandum of understanding with the Motion Picture Association (MPA), the international arm of the powerful Motion Picture Association of America, which represents the interests of the film industry. For Taobao's part, the agreement committed the company to requiring all its shops to hold "valid and active" publication licenses in order to sell audiovisual content, and it entailed Taobao adopting "more transparency criteria" to sanction repeat offenders (Motion Picture Association 2012). Taobao also agreed to work with the MPA "to efficiently and effectively identify and remove listings" of counterfeit or copyright-infringing copies of MPA member-company products and to partner with law enforcement to "pursue serial offenders" (Motion Picture Association 2012). In its press release, the MPA stated that both parties "reached a common understanding regarding the importance of strengthening existing standards, mechanisms, and mutual responsibilities" relating to the protection of intellectual property (Motion Picture Association 2012).

Alongside its agreements with the IACC and MPA, Taobao is establishing cooperative enforcement relationships with rights holders, and it reports collaborating with over one thousand Chinese and international brands (Liang 2014). For example, Taobao has signed memoranda of understanding with two U.S.-based rights holders, Samsonite, manufacturers of luggage, and Coach, a luxury apparel brand, as well as the Paris-based Louis Vuitton. These agreements typically establish joint regulatory standards between the companies and Taobao and may involve targeted enforcement campaigns in which Taobao officials scrutinize all sales listings and merchant activities for indicators that merchants may be selling counterfeit versions of the brands in question.

Taobao's informal agreements with the IACC, MPA, and various well-known rights holders illustrate the degree to which U.S. and European companies, backed by the power of the U.S. government, are exporting their preferred rules and standards globally to influence the operation of Chinese marketplaces. As part of their non-legally binding agreements with Taobao, these rights holders persuaded Taobao to exceed its legal responsibilities and conduct brand-specific enforcement sweeps for counterfeit goods. In order to secure Taobao's removal from the USTR's notorious-markets blacklist, the Alibaba Group significantly revised Taobao's enforcement policies and practices in light of demands from U.S. industry, especially the influential International Anti-Counterfeiting Coalition. Taobao's regulatory practices are more streamlined, coordinated, rapid, and efficient than its previous measures, and it has adopted a tougher approach to sanctioning repeat offenders who sell counterfeit goods. Taobao's enforcement practices exceed the marketplace's legal responsibilities under Chinese law.

MOVING BEYOND COMPLIANCE

The two nonbinding agreements examined in this chapter illustrate a part of the transnational anticounterfeiting regime that is rooted in the

United States and the European Union and which extends across the European Economic Area and China. As with the informal agreements discussed in chapters 3 and 4, coercive state pressure underpins the informal agreements that were adopted by the marketplace intermediaries, eBay and Taobao. Pressure from the European Commission and the USTR provided rights holders with the coercive force that they could not achieve themselves through legal action or pressuring the marketplaces. Because U.S. and European rights holders pressured both eBay and Taobao, there are strong similarities between the marketplaces' enforcement measures. As these marketplaces show, standards relating to intellectual property enforcement tend to reflect the interests and preferences of prominent U.S. (and European) rights holders.

The marketplaces' agreements are also structurally similar to those with the payment, advertising, search, and domain macrointermediaries. Through their private agreements, eBay and, especially, Taobao significantly strengthened their enforcement practices in order to crack down on the sale of counterfeit goods on their platforms. Their enforcement efforts are more rapid, streamlined, and proactive than their previous enforcement measures. The goal behind these agreements, as expressed by the European Commission, is to implement "beyond-compliance" regulatory strategies (European Commission 2013, 5–6). To do so, both eBay and Taobao agreed to undertake proactive monitoring and policing of their platforms, which generally exceeds their legal responsibilities for addressing the infringement of intellectual property on their platforms.

Marketplaces' shift to prioritizing streamlined, proactive mass enforcement, which the nonbinding agreements encourage, sacrifices precision for speed. It is often difficult to determine the legality of products through marketplaces' sales listings. Marketplaces do not have the requisite brand-specific knowledge to distinguish counterfeit goods across hundreds or thousands of brands. Test purchases would improve the accuracy of rights holders' efforts to police marketplaces for counterfeit goods. The European agreement, however, does not have a test-purchase requirement because rights holders complained about the time and expense involved in these programs, and no test-purchase measures are evident in the Taobao agreement.

State and industry pressure on marketplaces to shift their enforcement efforts from largely reactive to increasingly proactive activities can negatively affect the types of goods that users are permitted to buy and sell. Automated enforcement programs can mistakenly target people legally selling secondhand goods or misidentify the sale of parallel trade goods as counterfeit products. Heavy-handed enforcement practices, by marketplaces or rights holders, can unfairly stifle merchants engaged in legitimate trade. Further, users can be caught in skirmishes between marketplaces and rights holders, especially in cases where rights holders want to limit the sale of their brands to authorized distributors. eBay and the Alibaba Group both complain that rights holders are using the protection of intellectual property rights as a pretext, in the words of an eBay executive, "to exact ever greater control over e-commerce" (Brewer-Hay 2008a; see also Liang 2014, 6). In these battles between big corporate actors—multinational rights holders and marketplace macrointermediaries—the interests of users and small-scale merchants are largely overlooked.

6

Changing the Enforcement Paradigm

The nonbinding enforcement agreements discussed in the previous chapters have transformed the regulation of intellectual property online and recast Internet firms as global regulators for multinational rights holders. Those within the anticounterfeiting regime quietly drafted a series of handshake deals that effectively implemented measures from the defeated Stop Online Piracy Act and the Protect Intellectual Property Act.

These case studies illustrate a complex regulatory regime that stretches globally to regulate intellectual property through advertising, payment, search, domain name, and marketplace macrointermediaries. While the parts of this overall regime, discussed in their separate chapters, are distinctive, they share key similarities. The first portion of this chapter considers the regime as a whole, highlighting the key actors and the regime's essential characteristics: compliance-plus regulation, corporate-state interdependence, and the importance of secrecy, flexibility, and extraterritoriality. It also considers the key role of state coercion in creating and maintaining this regime. This chapter then briefly considers the question of whether these agreements are effective in delivering what they promise.

Nonbinding agreements offer corporate actors (both intermediaries and rights holders) certain advantages. Chiefly, these agreements offer regulators both considerable latitude in the determination of infringement and flexibility to decide what enforcement measures to undertake. Underlying this flexibility, however, and belying the rhetoric of "voluntary" regulation, is state coercion. As this chapter highlights, each nonbinding agreement resulted from varying degrees of state coercion, from soft pressure and the U.S. government using its market leverage, to threats of legislation and legal action.

In the final part of the chapter, I turn to the key policy question of the problems posed by informal agreements that are designed to enable more streamlined regulation, oriented toward mass policing. While this regime provides a clear benefit for rights holders, these agreements share many of the same flaws critics identified in SOPA. Most serious are problems with wrongful targeting of legal content and lawful behavior; a heavy reliance on technology, especially through automated enforcement tools; a near lack of transparency; and weak due-process measures. Further, although public safety is often cited as a driving force behind the shift toward informal regulation, consumers were largely absent from the negotiations and are unaware of the enforcement campaigns.

MAPPING THE ANTICOUNTERFEITING REGIME

Considered as a whole, these nonbinding enforcement agreements are a novel development in the online regulation of intellectual property. They accord rights holders—largely prominent multinational corporations based in the United States and Europe—access to a powerful regulatory capacity in the form of major, globally operating U.S.-based Internet firms and payment providers. Until now, the regulatory capacity enjoyed by macrointermediaries was largely available only to powerful state actors, like the U.S. and U.K. governments and the European Commission, and, in relation to criminal offenses, was used primarily to address social problems such as commercial child pornography, illegal gambling, and political extremism. Rights holders' successful push for nonbinding enforcement agreements, backed by state coercion, has added infringement of intellectual property to the social problems the intermediaries are now responsible for regulating. By tapping into macrointermediaries' global regulatory capacity, rights holders have dramatically expanded the scope and scale at which they can police their trademarks and copyrights.

As each case study shows, the private anticounterfeiting regime is rooted in the United States and Europe, particularly the United Kingdom. The U.S. and U.K. governments, along with the European Commission, have a strong history of supporting self-regulation and nonbinding regulation in regard to controlling certain types of illegal online content, as well as content deemed "inappropriate." These state actors also share strong support for increased protection for intellectual property rights. As discussed in chapter 2, this support extends back to the 1970s with the rise of industry campaigns to strengthen intellectual property rights.

The anticounterfeiting regime grew out of earlier efforts in the United States and the United Kingdom to address the online distribution of counterfeit and copyright-infringing content. In the United Kingdom, the City of London Police first established nonbinding arrangements with payment intermediaries to shut down unauthorized downloads of music. The U.K. Department for Culture, Media and Sport later expanded those efforts to include search and advertising intermediaries. The Office of the U.S. Intellectual Property Enforcement Coordinator—influenced by U.K. efforts and Operation In Our Sites, in which U.S. Immigration and Customs Enforcement uses court orders to shut down infringing sites—created a series of nonbinding agreements with macro-intermediaries.

The regime has a distinct Global North-South configuration in which rules and standards are set in the United States and Europe and then exported worldwide. In terms of online marketplaces, much of rights holders' attention is directed to China. China is of particular concern to rights holders because it is a major source of counterfeit goods that are exported to North America and Europe. Rights holders want to ensure that consumers in these massive markets purchase authentic trade-marked goods, not counterfeit products.

China is also important because U.S. and European rights holders want to expand sales of legitimate versions of their brands to China's burgeoning population of online shoppers. To do so, rights holders want to ensure that the Alibaba Group's marketplaces, especially Tmall and Taobao, which are dominant e-commerce platforms in China, have appropriately tough (that is, "U.S.-style") enforcement measures in place. Taobao's policies and enforcement measures now align generally with standards set by U.S. and European rights holders.

Key State and Nonstate Actors

Although the regime represents a wide range of rights holders and encompasses diverse Internet sectors, from advertising to marketplaces, there is a core of key actors. Small groups of government officials and powerful multinational corporate actors drove negotiations on the non-binding agreements. In the United States, IPEC and the Office of the U.S. Trade Representative compelled intermediaries to adopt nonbinding enforcement agreements. Victoria Espinel at IPEC was a singular force coordinating multiple agreements among payment, search, advertising, and domain name macrointermediaries. In the United Kingdom, Ed Vaizey and Jeremy Hunt at the Department for Culture, Media and Sport pushed forward agreements covering search intermediaries and the digital advertising industry. In Europe, meanwhile, the Directorate General Internal Market and Services at the European Commission facilitated the creation of nonbinding agreements for marketplace intermediaries. These state actors largely operated from the shadows, strategically underplaying their role as architects of the regime by emphasizing the voluntary nature of the agreements.

In terms of industry participants, several prominent trade associations played a major role in pushing forward the informal agreements. These include the International Anti-Counterfeiting Coalition, which established a nonbinding agreement with Taobao and operates a payment-termination program on behalf of rights holders. In the United Kingdom, influential copyright associations, particularly the Federation Against Copyright Theft and the British Phonographic Industry, lobbied the U.K. government to push ahead nonbinding regulatory programs with advertising and search intermediaries. Multiple trade associations helped craft the European Commission's marketplace agreement, including the U.K. Anti-Counterfeiting Group, the Business Action to Stop Counterfeiting and Piracy, and the Motion Picture Association. Many of these trade associations have been active in pushing for strengthened protection of intellectual property rights since the 1970s.

The involvement of individual rights holders in the informal agreements is more difficult to identify, in contrast to the high-profile advocacy of their trade associations. Signatories to the European Commission's agreement represent a wide range of industry sectors and include Adidas, Burberry, Louis Vuitton, Microsoft, Nike, Nokia, Proctor & Gamble, and Unilever. Other participating rights holders can be determined by examining the membership roster of trade associations, such as the IACC, whose members include Chanel, Calvin Klein, Nike, Proctor & Gamble, and Colgate Palmolive.

With the exception of the Chinese Alibaba Group, the macrointermediaries involved in the anticounterfeiting agreements are headquartered in the United States, with operations in multiple countries worldwide.

Most of these macrointermediaries dominate their respective industry sectors. These macrointermediaries, by virtue of their global operations and technologically sophisticated enforcement systems, are attractive enforcement partners for rights holders, especially since they set and enforce rules using their contractual terms-of-service agreements.

REGIME CHARACTERISTICS

These nonbinding agreements share important commonalities, especially in regard to pushing intermediaries to exceed their regulatory responsibilities and disable entire sites, instead of simply targeting unlawful content. These agreements have expanded the types of intermediaries involved in regulating intellectual property. Traditionally, search intermediaries, web hosts, and online marketplace intermediaries were primarily involved in addressing counterfeit goods. Under the nonbinding agreements, payment providers, domain intermediaries, and advertising intermediaries have expanded and strengthened their enforcement efforts against infringing sites. Macrointermediaries that are signatories to the nonbinding agreements—payment, search, advertising, and domain— are the same ones that the Stop Online Piracy Act proposed to make responsible for targeting infringing sites. With the European Commission's marketplace agreement, however, the nonbinding agreements go beyond SOPA, because that bill did not include marketplaces.

Compliance-Plus Regulation

Since the implementation of the nonbinding agreements, not only have more intermediaries assumed responsibility for policing intellectual property, but they also have ramped up their enforcement measures. All the intermediaries discussed in this book have amended or expanded their enforcement practices to regulate counterfeit goods and copyright-infringing content in a more rapid, streamlined, and comprehensive manner. Intermediaries are also taking a tougher approach to repeat offenders, such as temporarily or permanently banning them from using their services. Further, these agreements are intended to push intermediaries to exceed their legal responsibilities voluntarily, in the absence of legislation and court orders, in the form of compliance-plus regulation.

Compliance-plus regulation in the anticounterfeiting regime occurs in two ways: the removal of infringing content and the withdrawal of services from infringing sites. Content removal, now often undertaken using automated tools, is a traditional enforcement tactic for dealing with infringement of intellectual property that stems from the 1990s. Intermediaries, based on rights holders' complaints or their own proactive efforts, remove sales listings for counterfeit goods (eBay and Taobao), search results linking to web pages that infringe intellectual property rights (largely Google), and so-called bad advertisements for counterfeit goods (largely Google). Automated programs make it easier and faster for rights holders to submit massive numbers of complaints and for intermediaries to process complaints more quickly.

Another similarity among the nonbinding agreements is an emphasis on disabling sites through intermediaries' withdrawal of important services. This tactic involves attacking websites directly. The goal is to render the targeted websites commercially nonviable by impeding the sites' proper functioning. Rights holders want to make it more difficult for potential customers to find and access such sites and to push website operators away from mainstream intermediaries toward less-reputable service providers.

This practice of disabling sites essentially enacts controversial provisions from SOPA. Compared to the targeted removal of specific problematic content, the practice of disabling entire sites is a disproportionate enforcement response. Further, as intermediaries act in the absence of any independent oversight mechanisms, there is the problem of wrongful targeting of lawfully operating sites, which is explored later in the chapter.

Another fundamental development in online enforcement is intermediaries' increased proactive regulatory efforts. From the first notice-and-takedown programs in the 1990s, intermediaries were responsible for acting promptly once they received a complaint. Under the nonbinding agreements, however, intermediaries are increasingly responsible for proactively policing their platforms for infringement. They remove content and withdraw services from targeted sites on their own. Rights holders' emphasis on proactive enforcement, supported by the U.S. and U.K. governments and the European Commission, marks an important shift in intermediaries' regulatory responsibilities, since intermediaries generally are not legally responsible for independently policing their platforms.

Coercion Underlying "Voluntary" Agreements

Prominent U.S. and European rights holders and trade associations have had considerable success since the late 1970s in shaping the creation of rules and standards domestically and internationally (Drahos and Braithwaite 2002; Sell 2003). In their campaigns, they have emphasized the significant economic revenue they generate through their multibillion-dollar brands, which is coupled with a compelling narrative of the harmfulness of counterfeit goods to public safety and economic integrity. Rights holders' arsenal of tactics includes high-powered pressure, shaming, granting or withholding business deals, making credible threats of legal action, and, where resources and opportunity permit, litigation. These tactics, when employed by wealthy, multinational rights holders or trade associations, can be relatively effective in compelling other private parties to adapt or adopt regulatory measures.

Corporate actors, however, have a finite array of sticks and carrots with which to convince others. These actors' authority may also be limited if their demands exceed their ability to apply a corresponding level of threat to persuade others to comply. There is a significant difference, for example, in Visa agreeing to process a handful of merchant account-terminations voluntarily and its adoption of a privately negotiated non-legally binding agreement to terminate thousands of accounts on behalf of rights holders in the absence of legislation or court orders requiring such action.

If actors are loath to expend greater resources in solo campaigns to persuade actors, or find that their authority is limited in this regard, they can seek assistance from the state. The degree of direct state involvement varies according to whether the topic of regulation is a matter of concern to the state or is seen by state officials to align with its interests. The state may endorse a particular strategy or set of rules, or it may mandate specific action in ways that favor one group over another. In each of the case studies, government coercion was necessary to persuade the likes of Google, Yahoo, Visa, PayPal, eBay, and GoDaddy to come together and negotiate industry-specific informal agreements. The government agencies involved in the regime directed negotiations among industry stakeholders. In doing so, they legitimated the concept of nonbinding private agreements and, more broadly, of rights holders' authority to set and enforce rules and standards to protect intellectual property on the Internet.

Bargaining in the Shadow of Law

Intermediaries, particularly those with global operations, operate within an uncertain regulatory landscape because of shifts in the political, technological, and legal environments. Rights holders are intent on shifting greater responsibility for policing online infringement to intermediaries and have used litigation to accomplish this goal. Following lawsuits by prominent rights holders in the United States and Europe, there are divergent legal rulings on eBay's responsibilities for policing its platform for counterfeit goods. This means that there is a lack of harmonization internationally on the degree to which intermediaries are liable for trademark infringement occurring on their platforms (see Rimmer 2011). For globally operating intermediaries, like eBay, different regulatory responsibilities among countries can pose challenges, since their business models tend to try to minimize differences among their country-specific platforms.

More broadly, given these divergent legal rulings and continued pressure from rights holders on intermediaries, there is also a lack of clarity on what represents an appropriate notification of infringement from rights holders (McNamee 2011). How quickly intermediaries must respond to rights holders' complaints of infringement, the nature of complaints they must accept, and the degree to which they should act independently and proactively are open questions. Simply put, compliance is a moving target. As a result, intermediaries are highly motivated to police their platforms for any suspicious behavior or content and are more inclined to remove content and terminate services quickly than to undertake an investigation to determine wrongdoing.

Alongside an uncertain legal environment, one of the major downsides of the flexibility and informality of nonbinding agreements for intermediaries is a lack of legal protection from liability. Integral to the Digital Millennium Copyright Act and the European Commission's E-Commerce Directive are provisions that shield certain intermediaries from liability for infringement on their platforms if they respond promptly to complaints and remove the specified content. The informal agreements contain no such provisions because they are handshake deals, not legal contracts. Those working in intellectual property protection acknowledge that the threat of litigation impedes cooperative partnerships between rights holders and intermediaries. "If you're in a litigious environment, then poor old Google would be mad to be saying anything except 'It's not our fault,'" says Jeremy Newman, a partner with Rouse Legal in London (interview, Newman 2012).

The European Commission recognized the adversarial legal environment between rights holders and macrointermediaries and, in response, placed an embargo on signatories engaging in litigation against one another, because "cooperation is better than litigation" (European Commission 2013, 4–5). The European agreement is the only one of the agreements studied that places a limitation on litigation.

Those participating in the anticounterfeiting regime candidly acknowledge the coercive nature of the informal "voluntary" agreements. A representative from the Motion Picture Association of America observes that in these agreements, "parties are always bargaining in the shadow of the law" (Sheffner 2013, 2). The threat of future legal proceedings against intermediaries for liability is "the pressure that gets everyone to agree to the arrangements," explains Robert Guthrie, an associate at the law firm S.J. Berwin in London (interview, Guthrie 2012).

An intermediary's decision to participate in informal agreements thus depends "on what it perceives to be the legal consequence (or lack thereof) of continuing its current course of action, and not committing to any voluntary agreement" (Sheffner 2013, 2). As a result, intermediaries' adoption of the informal agreements should be considered "defensive" (Lindenbaum and Ewen 2012), a way to reduce their risk of being sued by rights holders or targeted by states for legal action.

Soft Pressure

Each of the private agreements relies upon direct pressure from governments in the United States, United Kingdom, and European Union, although the degree of coercion varies. At the softer end of the spectrum, government officials facilitated negotiations between intermediaries and rights holders. A senior policy advisor from IPEC observes that government can "open the lines of communication" among industry actors and stimulate industry cooperation because the "White House" can be "an important endorsement" (interview, government official, IPEC 2012). As IPEC did, the European Commission and Department for Culture, Media and Sport facilitated industry negotiations so that rights holders and intermediaries could reach a consensus on how to police intellectual property online.

Government actors can also directly prod industry actors to change their policies. Victoria Espinel, for example, urged payment providers to ramp up their regulatory efforts against infringement voluntarily. "We know you're at the table being proactive, but you need to do more," Julie Bainbridge, senior brand protection manager at PayPal, recalls Espinel saying to PayPal (interview, Bainbridge 2012). Although the state's representatives involved tended to downplay their roles, representing themselves as mere facilitators, they compelled actors to negotiate and played a vital role in coordinating discussions.

Threats of Legislation and Legal Action

In addition to urging cooperation and industry consensus, the states involved in the regime also employed more coercive tactics. Negotiations for all the nonbinding agreements occurred in the shadow of legislation. In the United States, IPEC representatives facilitated discussions with macrointermediaries while Congress was considering several intellectual property bills, including SOPA, that would have imposed new enforcement requirements upon these Internet firms. Similarly, officials at the European Commission and Department for Culture, Media and Sport expressed willingness to "consider legislative solutions" if informal arrangements were not forthcoming (European Commission 2009, 11).

Alongside the specter of legislation, government actors used the threat of legal action to motivate intermediaries' compliance. The City of London Police first secured the "voluntary" cooperation of Visa and MasterCard by warning them that they could face criminal charges for laundering proceeds of crime unless they took action against the sites voluntarily (interview, Wishart 2012). U.S. officials employed the same practice. Google forfeited $500 million and changed its advertising practices in 2011 to settle a federal investigation into its acceptance of advertisements from illegal online pharmacies.

By employing threats of criminal charges and legislation against intermediaries, government officials in the United States and Europe demonstrated the importance they place on intellectual property rights. Further, these efforts to compel intermediaries to enter into negotiations with rights holders reveals close ties between rights holders and the regime's state actors. This finding accords with other research that highlights overlapping state-corporate interests in relation to the ever-increasing protection of intellectual property rights (see Drahos and Braithwaite 2002; Sell 2011).

Power of Market Leverage

As the Taobao case demonstrates, U.S. rights holders have an additional weapon in their arsenal with which to push for the export of their desired standards globally and to shape policy making by corporations and countries: the leverage of the massive U.S. market. By working with the Office of the U.S. Trade Representative through the Special 301 Process, U.S. rights holders can get the USTR to blacklist problematic companies or websites as "notorious markets" and pressure them to amend their enforcement policies in line with rights holders' demands. To do so, the USTR may impose, or threaten to impose, sanctions against countries that fail to take action against designated notorious markets. The case of Taobao aptly illustrates the USTR's power and reveals the closely intertwined relationship between U.S. rights holders and the U.S. government. Taobao was dropped from the list after bringing its enforcement practices in line with rights holders' demands.

The Special 301 Process is particularly effective when the blacklisted market is interested in operating legitimately. The Pirate Bay, for instance, has no interest in offering music and movies in compliance with copyright laws and defiantly resists rights holders' continued efforts to shut it down. The Alibaba Group, in contrast, operates a massive e-commerce conglomerate and wants to expand outside of China as well as sell more U.S. and European brands through its Chinese marketplaces. The Alibaba Group was motivated to remove Taobao from the notorious-market list because it planned to issue an initial public offering and needed to reassure the U.S. financial industry and securities regulator that it employed sound enforcement practices. The strategy worked. In September 2014, the Alibaba Group issued a record-breaking initial public offering in the United States.

As a result of these actions, there is a noticeable convergence of Taobao's enforcement policies and eBay's measures, which is the result of U.S. and European rights holders pressuring both marketplace intermediaries at different points in time. This distinct pattern, in which rules set in the U.S. and Europe diffuse globally, is a key feature of the anticounterfeiting regime.

Interdependence of Corporate and State Interests

Corporate and government actors within the anticounterfeiting regime have common interests in addressing online infringement and, more broadly, in exerting greater control over the global flow of information on the Internet. Within the regime, states and markets mutually constitute interests, policy preferences, and regulatory strategies (Underhill 2003). This means that political processes help constitute the market, and that market actors, especially certain influential corporate actors, partly construct the state's policy preferences (Underhill 2003). Governments involved in the regime arbitrate among competing corporate interests. The degree to which corporate actors can influence state policy making depends on their organizational capacities, their power, and the persuasiveness of their claims (Underhill 2003, 765). In the anticounterfeiting regime, as with the information-industrial complex, the policies and regulatory strategies largely privilege Western legal, economic, and political preferences (Powers and Jablonski 2015). The regime broadly favors large multinational rights holders, major intermediaries with global platforms, and states intent on expanding their economic and security interests on the Internet.

The United States and European Union assign significant political and economic importance to intellectual property rights because the ownership of such rights is integral to economic dominance. Politically, the U.S. interest in strong intellectual property dates from the late 1970s, when rights holders conceptually linked intellectual property with international trade and economic success (see Braithwaite and Drahos 2000; Halbert 1997). Economically, companies in the United States and Europe own the greatest proportion of intellectual property rights, including trademarks. This means that benefits from the informal anticounterfeiting agreements disproportionately flow to Western commercial interests, particularly to large multinational rights holders. This Global North-South revenue flow replicates patterns found in other studies of intellectual property rights (see Drahos and Braithwaite 2002; Sell 2003).

For rights holders with problems of counterfeited products, lobbying governments and pressuring intermediaries for tougher enforcement efforts is a rational response. Rights holders have a strong economic interest in protecting their trademarks from counterfeiting and safeguarding their valuable brands. They are also interested in preventing their customers from being deceived into purchasing counterfeit goods or harmed by counterfeit products that pose health and safety risks. Because enforcement programs can be costly, particularly for multinational rights holders with popular brands attractive to counterfeiters, rights holders strategically seek to shift the enforcement burden to government or other private actors, especially Internet intermediaries. The nonbinding agreements are merely the latest installment—although a very ambitious one—of rights holders' efforts to shift the burden for policing intellectual property to others. The degree to which these nonbinding agreements are effective in curbing the trade in counterfeit goods is explored later in this chapter.

Like rights holders, intermediaries are concerned with maintaining and promoting their valuable brands and fear a loss of reputation—and a risk of liability—if their brands are associated with the sale of counterfeit goods. They also have an economic interest in adopting measures that elicit greater consumer trust and confidence in their respective industries. eBay, for example, admits that if its business were associated with counterfeit goods, even inaccurately, it would "damage our reputation, lower the price our sellers receive for their items and damage our business" (eBay 2013, 9). Intermediaries are also motivated to adopt measures that elicit greater consumer trust and confidence in their respective industries while not alienating customers through unduly aggressive or unfair enforcement efforts.

Secrecy, Flexibility, and Extraterritoriality

For states, nonbinding measures offer additional benefits, such as the flexibility to sidestep controversial, stalled, or failed legislation and achieve similar or even enhanced regulatory outcomes. Avoiding the sometimes-fractious public debates relating to legislation by drafting measures in secret can be seen as a valuable feature for scandal-weary leaders. Negotiating informal agreements quietly also offers government officials an avenue by which to avoid "being SOPA-ed" (Goldman 2012) by massive, unpredictable protests that can torpedo intellectual-property policies. The U.S. and U.K. governments, facing unpopular, flawed legislation and delays in implementing legislation, intensified their support for nonbinding private measures. Secrecy can also be useful to coax reluctant industry actors into negotiations that they may otherwise be hesitant to participate in publicly.

Nonbinding agreements can give state officials more flexibility in disclosing publicly the state's often politically contentious role in the regulatory arrangement. States may choose to publicly endorse the regulatory activities or reveal state officials' roles in shaping or approving the goals or measures related to the regulatory program. State officials can also strategically downplay the state's role by emphasizing the role of corporate actors. Officials from IPEC, the European Commission, and the Department for Culture, Media and Sport each emphasized its role as a facilitator in coordinating, not directing, negotiations among macrointermediaries, rights holders, and trade associations.

By claiming merely to facilitate industry negotiations, government actors can "avoid having to defend, question, interrogate or widely consult on the proposals" (Bradwell 2011). All responsibility for designing and using nonbinding agreements thereby falls upon corporate actors, not the participating government agencies. Governments can also sidestep complaints or protests from the public by arguing that companies, not the state, undertook the enforcement efforts.

Non-legally binding agreements can also offer corporate and state actors greater flexibility than legislation or litigation. New intermediaries or rights holders can easily join, and the agreements can be expanded to include other types of intermediaries, such as social media platforms like Twitter and Facebook. Unlike legislation, which can be difficult or time-consuming to amend, those participating in informal agreements can adapt them more quickly to changes in technology, to the nature the problem in question, or to new demands from rights holders. The European Commission, for example, argued that nonbinding agreements can give industry stakeholders "the flexibility to adapt quickly to new technological developments" (European Commission 2009, 10).

Agreements based upon nonbinding measures may also offer corporate actors greater flexibility and less onerous conditions than legislation or court-imposed requirements. SOPA's section 102, for example, would have imposed strict five-day time frames on payment providers for responding to rights holders' complaints. Such "artificial deadline[s]," argues Linda Kirkpatrick, senior executive at MasterCard, "may present impossible compliance challenges in some circumstances" (Kirkpatrick 2011, 11). In testimony before Congress in relation to SOPA and PIPA, Google, MasterCard, and GoDaddy all expressed support for some form of voluntary regulation, instead of legislation, that would give them the flexibility to address infringement in their own way (for MasterCard, see Kirkpatrick 2011).

Informal agreements, especially those with globally operating actors, enable states and corporations to extend their enforcement reach. Victoria Espinel argues that informal, intermediary-facilitated regulation of intellectual property enables governments to have an "impact on websites that are beyond the reach of U.S. law enforcement agencies" (Bason 2012).

Rights holders have a clear economic interest in tapping into macrointermediaries' global regulatory capacity to police their brands across marketplaces and sites worldwide. Macrointermediaries, too, may benefit. Informal agreements can minimize or eliminate regulatory variations among countries, which can serve corporate actors that desire a "global initiative," not "different laws in different countries" (interview, Kotecha 2012).

EFFECTIVENESS OF THE ANTICOUNTERFEITING REGIME

While this book does not focus on evaluating the effectiveness of the anticounterfeiting regime in combating the trade in counterfeit goods, it is important to consider broadly the utility of macrointermediaries as global regulators of intellectual property. Regime participants recognize the futility of trying to stop copyright and trademark infringement entirely. Instead, the regime aims both to make it more difficult for infringing site operators to market their wares and to dissuade average Internet users from accessing copyright-infringing content and counterfeit products.

Macrointermediaries, which have vast platforms and command dominant market shares in their respective industry sectors, are a special type of Internet intermediary with considerable regulatory capabilities. With their global scope and technologically sophisticated surveillance and enforcement programs, these companies have capabilities that outstrip those of traditional physical-world gatekeepers such as banks. As global regulators of counterfeit goods, however, their regulatory effectiveness varies widely.

Firms with direct, contractual relationships with operators of infringing sites and the capacity to remove hard-to-replace services have greater regulatory effectiveness than those without such relationships. Sites that lose the services of major payment providers—PayPal, Visa, and MasterCard—are commercially unviable until they secure alternative payment-processing services, because they cannot generate revenue through sales or donations. This finding is corroborated by studies of illegal online pharmacies that conclude that payment providers are more difficult to replace than other online services, such as domain names (see McCoy et al. 2012).

Intermediaries that offer easy-to-replace services or lack a direct contractual relationship with site operators have a lesser capacity to control infringing sites. Like payment providers, advertising intermediaries, too, can terminate revenue to targeted sites. This strategy would be effective in starving sites of funds in cases where infringing sites rely upon revenue from mainstream advertisements. But research on infringing sites, particularly those offering unauthorized downloads, has found that these sites tend not to reply upon mainstream advertising.[1] If infringing sites host ads, they tend to be for less-reputable market sectors, like the sex industry or gambling (see Watters 2013, 2014). Of course, ads for "escort services and high-interest lenders" do not pay as much as "the Chevys and Coca-Colas of the world" (Healey 2013).

GoDaddy has contractual relationships with all site operators to which it issues domain names, and it is the largest domain name provider worldwide. Domain intermediaries can transfer infringing sites' domain names to other parties, prevent sites from resolving correctly (seize-and-takedown), or redirect users to a warning banner (seize-and-post notice). However, domain names are easy and inexpensive to replace. Unlike losing a major payment provider, losing a domain name is generally only a temporary inconvenience as long as site operators can alert users to the new domain name.

In contrast to the other intermediaries, search and marketplace intermediaries generally only remove problematic content rather than disable sites. Search intermediaries remove search results that hyperlink to infringing web pages but do not affect the content of those web pages, which may then be found by means of other search engines or ads on social media platforms. Marketplace intermediaries remove infringing sales listings, but individuals can relist items, set up another merchant profile on the marketplace, or move to another trading platform. Overall, except for the work of payment macrointermediaries, the anticounterfeiting regime's enforcement efforts are relatively ineffective.

Bad Sites, Bulk Sellers, and Average Users

If most intermediaries are relatively ineffective regulators of intellectual property, what is the purpose of the anticounterfeiting regime? The regime is not directed at eliminating the trade in counterfeit goods. Rights holders and those in the brand-protection business recognize that this is an impossible goal. "If you're a popular brand of anything or you're an innovative technology, you can't prevent people from trying to steal it or counterfeit it," explains Vincent Volpi, CEO of PICA Corporation, an Ohio-based security firm (interview, Volpi 2012). Further, the existence of counterfeit versions of your products is an unmistakable sign of popularity, because people only counterfeit goods that they can entice or deceive people into purchasing. The regime's focus is threefold: to reduce the population of intermediaries who service infringing sites, to target bulk sellers of counterfeit goods, and to discourage "average" users from seeking or purchasing counterfeit goods or copyright-infringing content.

By working with macrointermediaries, rights holders want to steer operators of infringing sites away from legitimate, mainstream intermediaries toward less-reputable service providers. Once macrointermediaries institute tougher rules or amend their enforcement practices to protect intellectual property, other intermediaries in that sector may follow their lead. For example, once the IACC secured the cooperation of Visa, MasterCard, PayPal, and American Express for its payment-termination program, other payment providers followed, including Discover, Diners Club, MoneyGram, and Western Union (see International Anti-Counterfeiting Coalition 2012).

Enforcement efforts are also directed at bulk sellers of counterfeit goods, particularly those operating on popular marketplaces like eBay, Amazon, and Taobao. Those platforms have "much higher visibility than a stand-alone site," says Tim Waring, director of Intelligence Technologies, a U.K.-based brand-monitoring firm (interview, Waring 2012). In addition to potentially reaching a large customer base, individuals selling goods on legitimate trading platforms may also deceive consumers seeking genuine trademarked products into purchasing counterfeit goods. Rights holders fear these deceived consumers may lose confidence in their brands, especially if the counterfeit products are shoddily made or pose safety problems.

Finally, the anticounterfeiting regime seeks to make it more difficult for average people to locate and purchase counterfeit goods online. Rights holders recognize that some individuals will continue to purchase counterfeit goods or download copyright-infringing content regardless of enforcement programs or sanctions. This is where the regime's work on access chokepoints comes into play. By removing search results and sales listings and seizing infringing sites' domain names, rights holders want to make it more difficult for average users to access counterfeit goods or copyright-infringing content. In doing so, regime participants aim to steer users toward authentic trademarked products and lawfully operating sites.

FLAWS AND PROBLEMS

The creation of a global regulatory regime based on a series of secretly negotiated, non-legally binding agreements is a monumental achievement for advocates of tougher enforcement measures in the effort to protect intellectual property. This accomplishment is more noteworthy given the regime's goal to push macrointermediaries to exceed voluntarily their legal responsibilities, a form of state-backed compliance-plus regulation. For these advocates, as already noted, there are many benefits to the rapid, flexible, and highly discrete enforcement measures that extend globally. There are also serious shortcomings to the nonbinding agreements, as noted earlier in this chapter, given the regime's lack of oversight, troubled due-process measures, and problem of wrongfully targeting legal content and lawful behavior.

Forum Shifting to the Underground

One of the principal problems with the nonbinding agreements is that proponents of stronger online regulation of intellectual property rights deliberately created them in backroom deals instead of through legislation in the public realm. As a result, the nonbinding agreements studied in this book represent a pernicious type of forum shifting. In relation to intellectual property, *forum shifting* commonly refers to instances where proponents of stronger standards strategically move vertically and horizontally to advance their interests (see Braithwaite and Drahos 2000; Sell 2011). Actors shift horizontally and work among different multilateral or international institutions, such as the World Trade Organization. They also strategically shift forums vertically, pursuing their agendas by setting rules and influencing norms at the local, bilateral, plurilateral, and multilateral levels, especially through trade agreements (see Sell 2011). Because of this shifting among different fora, "some negotiations are never really over" (Drahos 2007, 5). The goal is to establish new baselines that subsequent efforts continually "ratchet up," thereby resulting in ever-increasing standards of enforcement (Sell 2010).

In the nonbinding anticounterfeiting agreements, there is a shift away from legally binding rulemaking through formal institutions—democratic, legislative processes in states and international agreements like TRIPS—to informal, closed-door regulation by powerful multinational corporate actors backed by powerful states. This shift, therefore, is twofold: from the mostly public realm to the secretive, industry-only negotiations, and from legally binding rules to handshake agreements. In other cases of forum shifting, rights holders successfully negotiated new regulatory baselines that exceeded previous efforts, resulting in standards described as "DMCA-plus" (Bridy 2015a) and "TRIPS-plus" (Sell 2011).

The goal for the nonbinding agreements is compliance-plus enforcement, in which intermediaries exceed their legal responsibilities and undertake regulatory duties in the absence of legislation or court orders. In fact, those advocating informal agreements want to fundamentally change the online regulatory environment. Victoria Espinel endorsed this aim in testimony before the U.S. House of Representatives Subcommittee on Intellectual Property, Competition, and the Internet, when she argued, "Private sector voluntary actions can dramatically reduce online infringement and change the enforcement paradigm" (Espinel 2011a, 6). Similarly, the intent of the European Commission's nonbinding memorandum with marketplace intermediaries is to push intermediaries to take a "beyond-compliance" regulatory approach (European Commission 2013, 5–6).

In many cases of forum shifting, interested parties can generally observe the movement from one forum or institution to another, even if they are not privy to the content of discussions. In the anticounterfeiting agreements, however, rights holders and officials from the U.S. and U.K. governments, along with the European Commission, strategically shifted their negotiations from the visible public realm to closed-door meetings that excluded civil-society and consumer organizations. Most SOPA critics likely have little idea that some of the bill's provisions live on in a series of informal agreements among powerful U.S.-based corporations, since these enforcement agreements are relatively unknown. They have attracted little scholarly attention or media coverage outside specialized technology and intellectual-property websites.

In retrospect, despite the many problems with SOPA and PIPA, the bills would have been preferable to the nonbinding anticounterfeiting agreements, because elected officials drafted and publicly debated SOPA and PIPA, and stakeholders gave their opinions in testimony before Congress.[2] These bills also would have been subject to legislative oversight and to judicial interpretation of concepts like "infringing websites." As has been the case with the U.K. Digital Economy Act, those affected by the bills could have taken legal action in regard to legislation to clarify (or challenge) their enforcement responsibilities and related costs. In contrast, regime participants created the anticounterfeiting agreements in the absence of judicial and legislative safeguards with correspondingly weak oversight and due-process mechanisms.

Politics Shaping Technology

Technology is a core element of the anticounterfeiting regime because it enables powerful states and corporate actors to export standards, rules, and norms that favor their interests. In the anticounterfeiting regime, actors use technology as a regulatory instrument to govern users across multiple platforms and services, which is a form of techno-regulation. The regime's goal is twofold: to deter people from seeking counterfeit goods by removing search engine results, sales listings, and advertisements, and to make it more difficult for counterfeiters to advertise and sell counterfeit goods. With this goal in mind, intermediaries target and remove problematic content, withdraw their services from targeted sites, and impose sanctions on those selling or advertising counterfeit goods.

The technology underlying the anticounterfeiting regime did not, of course, simply evolve into being or suddenly materialize. Similarly, intermediaries are not "natural" gatekeepers. Intermediaries' primary role is to facilitate the hosting or sharing of information and to provide services that enable the sale of goods and services, as well as interactions or exchanges, among individuals online. With the rapid growth in some intermediaries' services and market share, coupled with their technologically sophisticated capabilities, intermediaries have become more attractive as regulators. Governments have increasingly designated more types of intermediaries as regulators with responsibilities for dealing with a growing array of types of third-party wrongdoing on their platforms.

Technology in the anticounterfeiting regime is partly socially constructed. This means technology should be understood as something that both performs specific tasks and is imbued with certain norms, ideas, and cultural values (Brey 2005; Leenes 2011).

Pressure from rights holders and, more importantly, from governments has shaped intermediaries' technological processes in certain ways and for specific outcomes. Government officials, acting on behalf of rights holders, directed intermediaries to make specific technical changes to their enforcement practices. For example, the European Commission's agreement pushed marketplace intermediaries to implement "preventive and proactive" anticounterfeiting measures (European Commission 2011). To comply, marketplace intermediaries instituted measures to monitor their platforms proactively for counterfeit goods through technical means (e.g., software), human analysis, or a combination of the two. Although the E-Commerce Directive does not impose a general obligation on intermediaries to monitor their platforms for third-party infringement,[3] the European Commission essentially imposes such an obligation on marketplace intermediaries, albeit through a non-legally binding agreement. Similarly, rights holders' demands on Taobao resulted in the company significantly overhauling its notice-and-takedown program, toughening its sanctions against offenders, and introducing proactive monitoring measures in order to be removed from the USTR's notorious-market blacklist (see Spelich 2012).

The most significant changes are evident in Google's policies. After years of governmental pressure and rights holders' demands that it alter its autocomplete and search-ranking processes, Google conceded. Between 2011 and 2012, Google made changes to its autocomplete practices to prevent "terms that are closely associated with piracy" from appearing (Walker 2010) and announced a search-demotion policy. The latter practice involves Google reconfiguring its web-page-indexing and -ranking processes to deprioritize sites that rights holders designate as "infringing" and to thereby elevate "legitimate" sites. Google's changes cannot be linked specifically to any government or nonbinding agreement, although Jeremy Hunt, secretary of state for culture, media and sport, made demands for similar changes by search intermediaries during the roundtable meetings. Google's changes, which came after years of concerted pressure by governments and rights holders, clearly illustrate politics shaping the development and use of technology.

In addition to demanding specific technological changes, government officials in the United States, United Kingdom, and European Union set the parameters for the informal agreements. Following the announcement of the ad networks' best practices in July 2013, Victoria Espinel praised the agreement. She stressed that all enforcement must be consistent with "the Administration's broader Internet policy principles emphasizing privacy, free speech, fair process, and competition" (Espinel 2013). The European Commission and U.K. Department for Culture, Media and Sport made similar statements. While these principles are laudable, the nonbinding agreements fall far short of achieving them.

Government officials could have required intermediaries to adhere to due-process measures and implement effective internal or third-party oversight processes. They could have insisted upon measures to protect users' privacy and safeguard free expression online. Instead, the officials created conditions favorable to expanding corporate control online by pushing for streamlined, proactive enforcement measures alongside stricter sanctions for offenders. Common throughout all the agreements are measures that simplify notice-and-takedown measures, promote the withdrawal of services, institute more punitive sanctions against repeat offenders, and facilitate mass automated monitoring and policing.

Techno-Regulation: Sacrificing Precision for Speed

The case studies examined in this book raise serious concerns due to rights holders' practices of regulating through technology and, especially, using intermediaries as regulators to police intellectual property. In part this is because the agreements were designed to sidestep the difficulties of drafting and passing legislation and to prevent a repeat of the protests that accompanied SOPA and the Digital Economy Act. Further, problems with oversight, accuracy, and due process are not surprising, since the agreements were intended to give corporate actors the significant latitude necessary to target infringement and the ability to do so in relative secrecy.

Automated enforcement tools present particular challenges because they can fundamentally change how regulation occurs. Using these tools, regulators can detect and target problems globally in ways that were previously unaffordable or technological unfeasible. The shift toward rapid automated enforcement, however, is generally incompatible with principles of due process and accountability. Precision is often sacrificed for speed and scale.

Automated processes enable rights holders to submit enormous numbers of complaints to intermediaries, which in turn can use automated programs to remove targeted content. For instance, large brand-protection firms send complaints to eBay regarding tens of thousands of sales listings on behalf of their clients, listings that eBay then removes in hours. Several major brand-protection firms also have a specialized portal with eBay and Alibaba—an application-programing interface—that enables these firms to automate their takedown requests (interview, Ramm 2012). At an exponentially larger scale, Google receives one hundred thousand takedown notices per hour (Ernesto 2016a) and over half a billion requests annually in regard to search results linking to infringing sites.

Given this volume of complaints and intermediaries' rapid enforcement response, intermediaries do not have adequate time to review or investigate the allegations. These systems can also result in the wrongful identification and targeting of legitimate content and legally operating sites. There is little data on the size of the problem of wrongful take-downs. This is because intermediaries do not publicly disclose (or, in most cases, track) the number of mistaken complaints relating to legal content or goods. Technology sites like *Techdirt* have identified multiple cases of rights holders or intermediaries wrongly targeting people who are legally trying to sell secondhand goods, not counterfeit products (see Masnick 2011). In some cases, the takedown notices are mistakes, but in other cases rights holders appear to be using trademark law to stifle sales of secondhand products.[4]

Intermediaries recognize that wrongful takedowns are a problem. Theo Bertram, Google's public policy manager in the United Kingdom, told the U.K. government's industry roundtable on intellectual property that search intermediaries' notice-and-takedown programs were subject to errors and abusive, bad-faith claims, including businesses sending complaints to remove lawful content concerning their competitors (Bradwell 2012; see also Seng 2014). Legitimate sites, particularly those run by small businesses and individuals, and small-scale merchants operating on eBay and Taobao, are poorly equipped to defend them-selves against heavy-handed enforcement practices. Civil-advocacy groups point out that few complainants are held liable for bad-faith accusations in relation to erroneous complaints of copyright or trade-mark infringement (Samuels and Stoltz 2012). Without repercussions for bad regulatory practices, rights holders have little motivation to alter unduly aggressive or poorly targeted mass-policing practices.

Automated regulation also poses risks to users' privacy. In relation to marketplaces, rights holders and their brand-protection firms tend to focus on trying to identify "big bulk sellers" of counterfeit goods (inter-view, Ramm 2012). They do so by collecting and mining personal data from marketplaces, including geo-locational data to plot sellers' physi-cal locations, and sellers' telephone numbers, mailing addresses, and Internet protocol addresses, as well as sellers' profiles from multiple dif-ferent trading platforms and social media networks (interview, Ramm 2012). In the process of trying to identify bulk sellers of counterfeit goods, brand-protection firms also collect data on individuals who are lawfully selling new or secondhand goods. In addition, regulators may mistake parallel trade goods for counterfeit products. "There are a lot more gray areas than brand owners will assume," comments Sherwin Siy of Public Knowledge, a digital-rights group based in Washington, D.C. (interview, Siy 2012). Here Siy is referring to the complexity of global supply and distribution chains, in which there may be many resellers of legitimate goods in parallel trade markets. Rights holders often oppose this practice, because they may price goods differently in different markets.

Enforcement programs based on the mass accumulation of personal information, particularly those facilitated by automated tools, are generating an increase in public and political scrutiny. People have started to become aware that the programs have labeled them, sometimes inaccurately, as risky, undesirable, or criminal individuals, which could negatively affect their ability to access services, gain or retain employment, or obtain credit (see Pasquale 2015). In relation to intellectual property, people inaccurately accused of selling counterfeit goods on marketplaces like eBay or Taobao may have their access to the platforms temporarily or permanently revoked, thus impeding their ability to generate an income. Since sellers in these marketplaces depend upon favorable reviews, inaccurate accusations of wrongdoing can damage their reputations. Payment providers like PayPal have authority under their terms-of-service agreements to freeze funds in individuals' accounts for violations of their policies, including the sale of counterfeit goods, and terminate users' accounts.

In addition to losing access to marketplaces and having their funds frozen, people wrongly accused of selling counterfeit goods may find themselves on industry blacklists. As discussed in chapter 3, the U.K. digital advertising industry, along with large advertising firms like 24/7 Media in the United States, uses blacklists to prevent the misplacement of advertising on infringing sites. Individuals may learn that their sites are blacklisted only when they are no longer able to place advertising on their sites, and it can be difficult to remove oneself from a blacklist. Site operators placed on blacklists could suffer reputational damage, lose business, or find it difficult to obtain credit.

Weak Oversight and Due-Process Measures

In addition to the inaccurate targeting of lawful content and behavior, the nonbinding agreements suffer from weak oversight and due-process measures. A key problem is that enforcement is based on rights holders' allegations, not proof of infringement. The practice of acting in response to rights holders' complaints is enshrined within copyright enforcement, particularly the Digital Millennium Copyright Act. Critics rightly point out that takedown requests are "nothing more than accusations of copyright infringement" (Samuels and Stoltz 2012). There is no judicial or independent review of complaints before intermediaries take action. In relation to counterfeit goods, intermediaries follow the copyright standard of acting in response to accusations of infringement. To take action against a site alleged to be facilitating the sale of counterfeit goods, intermediaries typically require only a sworn good-faith statement from rights holders, proof of ownership of the trademark(s) in question, and the web page(s) of the alleged infringement. To deter wrongful complaints, the DMCA has provisions that hold complainants liable for bad-faith accusations, whereas the nonbinding agreements have no similar safeguard.

Rights holders have an interest in determining infringement quickly, broadly, and with minimal cost. Intermediaries have an interest in enforcement processes that protect their businesses from liability, operate simply and effectively, impose as few costs on their business as possible, and do not unduly or unfairly target their customers. Given the anticounterfeiting regime's emphasis on streamlined, mass enforcement, there is, unsurprisingly, little emphasis on measures to strengthen accountability or oversight. Under programs oriented toward mass policing, "it becomes much harder for the private businesses involved to offer anything approximating due process, because it just becomes all that more resource-intensive," explains David Sohn, general counsel for the Center for Democracy and Technology, based in Washington, D.C., a civil-advocacy group (interview, Sohn 2012). In these situations, there is "tension," Sohn observes, between "a process that is more streamlined, and coming up with a process that's really fair to everybody" (interview, Sohn 2012).

In such cases where corporate actors find it difficult—or undesirable—to strive for regulatory fairness, it is understandable that they may turn to the state. A key shortcoming related to due process here is that the government officials involved in the nonbinding agreements do not require accountability or review mechanisms for intermediaries' enforcement efforts. In fact, a senior official at IPEC frankly admitted that the office did not want to stipulate oversight provisions in the agreements, which would "add layers of difficulty that might drive participants away" (interview, government official, IPEC 2012). The U.K. government, too, was disinclined to institute oversight measures or demand accountability from industry actors. According to the Open Rights Group, the U.K. government officials stated that the roundtable meetings were "focused on industry-led measures," and that information stemming from the meetings was not intended "to establish the validity, consequences or relevance of these measures" (Bradwell 2011). Simply put, the roundtable meetings existed to persuade intermediaries to strengthen their enforcement practices against online infringement, and did not consider the issue of whether the claims of harm or solutions proposed were valid or relevant. Similarly, the European Commission declined to require rights holders to make test purchases of suspicious products, which is generally a more reliable, albeit slower and costlier, way of identifying counterfeit goods than making decisions based on indicators within sales listings.

The lack of governmental interest in requiring regime participants to institute measures to improve regulatory accountability and oversight is particularly problematic alongside the rise of intermediaries' proactive enforcement efforts. Rights holders' and government officials' efforts to pressure intermediaries to expand their proactive enforcement measures is based on the assumption that counterfeit goods can be easily identified and targeted, and that intermediaries can differentiate legality from illegality. However, intermediaries candidly admit that they do not have the requisite knowledge to identify the infringement of intellectual property online with any degree of certainty. Denise Yee, senior trademark counsel at Visa, acknowledges that the company is "not well positioned" to identify infringement. Where "legality is not clear, we have no authority to decide what is lawful," Yee says. "We are then forced into the precarious position of either agreeing with the IP owner or the merchant" (Yee 2011, 13).

As discussed earlier in this chapter, intermediaries are motivated to respond to rights holders' complaints in order to mitigate the risk of legal action by states or rights holders. Joe McNamee, executive director of the European Digital Rights group, contends that legal uncertainty pushes intermediaries into "defensive policing roles" (McNamee 2011, 10). From this defensive position, intermediaries are inclined to remove problematic content or withdraw services from targeted sites promptly. The resulting regulation is rapid and sweeping but "also much less procedurally fair than civil judicial process" (Bridy 2015, 1560).

The nonbinding agreements generally provide some form of an appeals process for individuals to challenge sanctions. The U.S. ad networks' agreement, for example, stipulates that the networks "may consider any credible evidence provided by the accused site in defense of the site" in response to a complaint of infringement (Ad Networks 2013).

Similarly, the payment providers' agreement reports that payment intermediaries have a process to allow a "prompt review" if merchants dispute the allegations.

However, appeal measures are generally available only after sanctions have been imposed on individuals, not at the time allegations are made. Further, both payment and advertising intermediaries demand that the accused merchants provide "credible evidence" that they are not engaged in illegal conduct. This requirement places the onus on merchants to defend themselves from allegations of infringement. As a result, there is a clear—and troubling—reversal of the traditional burden in civil suits on the complainant to provide proof against the accused (Bridy 2015, 1560).

Lack of Transparency

In addition to the issues related to the wrongful targeting of lawfully behaving site owners, and to weak due-process measures, the nonbinding agreements suffer from a near-total lack of transparency, both in the processes in which actors negotiate the enforcement guidelines and in the subsequent enforcement campaigns. Despite government officials' and rights holders' emphasis on protecting consumers from counterfeit goods, there was virtually no participation by civil-society or consumer organizations.

The exception was the U.K. roundtable discussions, which began with a degree of openness. At the outset of those meetings, officials at the Department for Culture, Media and Sport committed themselves to meeting regularly with consumer and digital-rights organizations and publishing meeting minutes publicly. In this spirit of openness, the DCMS invited several civil-society groups to participate in the discussion, including the Open Rights Group. After one civil-society advocate tweeted comments on the discussions during the meeting, industry participants at that meeting questioned whether "the exposure brought through live blogging was appropriate" (Firth 2011). As a result, civil-society groups were not invited to subsequent meetings. The Open Rights Group was forced to obtain copies of the meeting minutes and informal agreements relating to search intermediaries through freedom-of-information requests; it then posted this information on its website (see Bradwell 2012).[5]

Little transparency was evident in meetings coordinated by European or U.S. government officials. No civil-society organizations participated

TABLE 12 TRANSPARENCY AND NONBINDING AGREEMENTS

Nonbinding Agreement	Available Publicly
Agreement with payment providers (IPEC)	No (on file with author; IPEC negotiated agreements, IACC used them)
Payment-termination program (IACC)	
Ad networks' statement of best practices (IPEC)	Yes, posted online
Center for Safe Internet Pharmacies (targets unlawful distribution of medication) (IPEC)	No
Memorandum of understanding to remove counterfeit goods from Taobao marketplace (USTR)	No
Memorandum of understanding to remove counterfeit goods from eBay marketplace (European Commission)	Yes, posted online
Digital Trading Standards Group (advertising)	Yes, posted online
Search intermediaries code of conduct	Yes, through Open Rights Group

in the negotiations that Victoria Espinel coordinated. Further, the U.S. Office of Management and Budget, which operates IPEC, denied a freedom-of-information request for information pertaining to the payment providers' nonbinding agreements, citing trade secrets or privileged or confidential information (Masnick 2014).[6] Similarly, intellectual property scholars and activists reacted with "surprise" to the existence of the European Commission's agreement when it was quietly posted online, since there had been no public hearings (Horten 2011).

Four of the eight nonbinding agreements studied in the book are publicly available (see table 12). The U.S. ad networks and the U.K. digital advertising industry posted their agreements publicly online. Advertising intermediaries have a strong economic interest in emphasizing the safety of digital advertising in order to position themselves as trustworthy intermediaries for rights holders' advertisements.

The U.K. search agreement (along with the rejected agreement drafted by rights holders for search intermediaries) is publicly available on the Open Rights Group's website, not the U.K. government's. The agreements relating to payment providers, the Center for Safe Internet Pharmacies, and Taobao are not publicly available. Given the emphasis on protecting consumers from dangerous counterfeit goods, the absence of public consultation in the creation of the anticounterfeiting regime and the regulation of infringing sites is troubling.

Missing Consumers and "Stranded Citizens"

In considering the effects of the anticounterfeiting regime on consumers, it is important to recall, as argued in chapter 1, that counterfeiting is not a simple issue. Rights holders' claims of economic losses are difficult to verify given their poor data and weak methodologies. Consumers may willingly purchase counterfeit goods because of the lower price or as a substitution for a trademarked product. Further, despite rights holders' linkage of counterfeit goods with poor-quality, unsafe products, some counterfeits are virtually indistinguishable from authentic trademarked goods. Consumers—and the public in general—did not have seats at the negotiating tables that created the anticounterfeiting regime. As a result, while there is considerable overlap between the interests of rights holders and of consumers in targeting counterfeit goods, it is important to emphasize that consumers also have interests distinct from those of rights holders.

Rights holders and government officials, in drafting the nonbinding agreements with macrointermediaries, often cited the importance of consumer protection. Two of the agreements specifically underline the importance of consumer protection. The European Commission cited the education and protection of consumers as being among its primary reasons for tackling the online sale of counterfeit goods (European Commission 2013). The commission also stated that it played a role in "safeguarding" the rights of European Union citizens (European Commission 2013, 5–6). The ad networks' agreement commits participants, including Google and Yahoo, to an "ongoing dialogue" with stakeholders, including "consumer organizations, and free speech advocates" (Ad Networks 2013). It is unknown whether these discussions with civil-society and consumer groups have taken place, since there are no public indications of any discussions having occurred.

In terms of common interests, the public benefits from enforcement campaigns targeting counterfeit goods that pose health and safety risks. This includes counterfeit food and consumer care products, pharmaceuticals and medication, medical devices like pacemakers and insulin pumps, and industrial products like vehicle brake pads and aircraft parts. Consumers also benefit when regulators crack down on merchants trying to deceive people seeking genuine trademarked products into buying counterfeit goods. Sellers of counterfeit goods sometimes create sites identical to rights holders' legitimate sites to trick people into buying counterfeit goods.

The anticounterfeiting regime, however, does not prioritize the removal of dangerous counterfeit goods or deceptively marketed counterfeit products. Instead, the nonbinding agreements allow rights holders (and intermediaries) the flexibility to determine which trademarks or products to focus on. While individual rights holders may focus on dangerous counterfeit goods, there is no indication that public safety and protection of consumers are driving forces in the nonbinding agreements.

Similar problems are evident in regard to the Center for Safe Internet Pharmacies discussed in chapter 4. Consumers have an interest in accessing safe, affordable medicine, and they benefit from enforcement that targets dangerous, misbranded, or adulterated medication, or unsafe and unlicensed pharmacies. Consumers are also interested in seeking lower-cost medication through different suppliers, including licensed online pharmacies. This is particularly a problem in the United States, where millions of people lack access to affordable medication and may seek alternative sources, including unlicensed and unlawfully operating online pharmacies. While CSIP's mission of targeting illegal online pharmacies is laudable, its regulatory practices are troublingly opaque.

A case in point: because CSIP lacks an independent review of the processes in which pharmacies are determined to be illegal and then disabled, legitimate, legally operating pharmacies may be mistakenly targeted. An equally serious concern is that the pharmaceutical industry may push CSIP to restrict online pharmacies' involvement in certain practices, such as the sale of generic medication, that may be contrary to the pharmaceutical industry's economic interest but may benefit the public.

Marketplaces are another area where the interests of consumers and multinational corporations are not always aligned. In terms of online shopping, individuals have an interest in buying and selling a wide range of products, including secondhand goods, at differing prices. Marketplaces like eBay and Taobao enable people to earn income as small-scale merchants. However, the sale of secondhand and overstock goods, and the resale of wholesale quantities of goods, can be points of contention for some rights holders. Rights holders may wish to control the online distribution of their products or discourage the sale of secondhand products because of fears that these sales may damage their brands' reputations or cut into their customer bases.

Enforcement practices that enable rights holders to determine the legitimacy of products without physical evidence (that is, a test purchase) are prone to error. Further, small-scale merchants are vulnerable to being swept up in enforcement dragnets, especially given marketplace intermediaries' shift to proactive, increasingly automated anticounterfeiting efforts. As eBay and Taobao expand their proactive enforcement capacities, legitimate merchants will continue to be mistakenly targeted, with little recourse to appeal the allegations against them.

The public also has an interest in regulatory practices that adhere to the rule of law. These include effective oversight measures and avenues through which the accused may challenge or appeal enforcement actions. Website operators, and consumers more broadly, are ill served by mass-policing-oriented practices that remove content or withdraw services based only on allegations of wrongdoing. The increasingly common strategy of disabling sites by terminating their commercial and technical services can throttle legitimate activities alongside unwanted or illicit behavior. As a result, wrongly targeted legitimate merchants and site operators may become "stranded citizens" (Brown and Marsden 2013, 183), who typically do not have the resources or knowledge to challenge allegations of infringement, particularly when accused by large, multinational rights holders. Following intermediaries' transformation into regulators, they have more often treated their customers as "the enemy," whose activities must be "blocked, logged, spied upon, restricted and subjected to sanctions imposed by the intermediaries, who fear legal liability for the actions of their clients" (McNamee 2011, 8–9).

Constant corporate surveillance is now an integral, effectively inescapable, aspect of the online environment. Further, in contrast to state-operated surveillance systems, private regulatory regimes are typically unable—or even unwilling—to institute measures to deliver the procedural fairness and protection of due process that one expects from the judicial process (McNamee 2011). As evident from the case studies in this book, corporate actors do not uphold the fundamental rights of privacy and freedom of expression as core elements of their regulatory efforts. More troublingly, however, is the complete abdication of responsibility by the state actors whose coercive pressure created the anticounterfeiting regime.

Intermediaries' regulation of intellectual property through quietly drafted, non-legally binding agreements raises serious questions about how global flows of information, including personal data, can and should be regulated, by whom, and with what safeguards to prevent abuse by state and nonstate actors. Further, how can we establish a degree of balance between online regulation and the protection of fundamental digital rights, especially freedom of expression and privacy? An important first step is transparency from the state and corporate actors involved in online regulatory efforts. Related to this is a need for state and industry recognition and protection of digital rights. Chapter 7 offers two possible avenues: industry transparency reports and an Internet bill of rights modeled on Brazil's 2014 Marco Civil da Internet.

7

A Future for Digital Rights

The non-legally binding enforcement agreements traced in this book represent the first time that the largest, most powerful Internet firms agreed to coordinate their enforcement capabilities, not to serve the state, but to accommodate an elite group of multinational companies. By quietly establishing partnerships with U.S.-based macrointermediaries in the payment, search, advertising, marketplace, and domain name sectors, rights holders have accessed a regulatory capacity that was previously available only to powerful states. Before this, governments in the United States and United Kingdom had established similar partnerships to crack down on child pornography, illegal gambling, and online extremism.

The nonbinding agreements add the infringement of intellectual property rights to this list of serious social problems. More importantly, government officials in the United States and Europe forged the enforcement partnership between rights holders and macrointermediaries outside of traditional democratic, legislative processes. The result: prominent, mostly U.S. and European rights holders have the capacity and authority to crack down on the online trade in counterfeit goods and copyright-infringing content. Simply put, companies like Nike, Disney, and Apple have the explicit support of the U.S. government (and official support from the U.K. government and European Commission) to set and enforce rules globally on the Internet. Their rules, crafted in the

United States and Europe and exported globally, can potentially affect hundreds of millions of people who, every day, use the services of U.S. Internet companies and payment providers.

Rights holders have a long history of fighting for strengthened enforcement practices and ever-tougher rules in legislation and international agreements. Compliance-plus regulation, achieved through informal agreements with macrointermediaries, is only rights holders' latest enforcement project. The anticounterfeiting agreements build upon informal regulatory programs that the U.S. and U.K. governments created to devolve enforcement responsibility to intermediaries so they could block access to websites distributing child pornography and to the sites of those involved in extremism. In a classic example of mission creep, rights holders strategically extended intermediaries' responsibilities from fighting against the sexual abuse of children and national security threats to enhancing the regulation of intellectual property rights. Once enforcement programs were established to protect children and fight terrorists—subjects that rarely elicit moral objections—moral entrepreneurs were able expand these programs to other causes.

The nonbinding enforcement agreements are a key—if little known— element of the rapidly evolving regulation of intellectual property rights on the Internet. Throughout the book I have emphasized that this type of informal regulation presents serious procedural problems, such as weak oversight and wrongful takedowns, among others. The book also underlines equally serious problems in relation to fundamental principles of due process, rule of law, and privacy. These informal agreements, strategically crafted outside democratic and legislative processes, also raise critical questions about the appropriateness and limits of private regulation on the Internet, especially through non-legally binding agreements. What social problems, if any, should private actors address independently and voluntarily, outside the bounds of legislation and judicial orders? Because intermediaries have the technological capability to monitor their users and block flows of content, does that mean we should automatically extend this practice from child pornography to other issues, such as intellectual property? To what extent can (and should) we expect intermediaries to distinguish legality from illegality online, and to what degree are they capable of making such determinations? What kinds of penalties are appropriate for intermediaries to impose in informal regulatory programs, and should this include intermediaries' termination of services? What limitations are appropriate for intermediaries' work as regulators, particularly given the significant problems with intermediary-facilitated regulation examined throughout this book?

These are important questions that point to larger issues relating to the control over online flows of information and personal data, state-corporate surveillance partnerships, and the capacity and limitations of nonstate actors to shape the ways in which we can access information, goods, and services and even use certain technologies. This book began with reflections upon the Snowden files, especially revelations that the U.S. National Security Agency siphons information from major U.S.-based Internet firms—Google, Microsoft, Yahoo, and Facebook—to operate its surveillance programs.

It is no coincidence that these companies are central to both the U.S. government's national security programs and prominent rights holders' efforts to secure greater control over their intellectual property rights online. These macrointermediaries are structuring twenty-first-century society. With the capacity to amass and data-mine global flows of information, and as suppliers of critical Internet services essential to the daily lives of hundreds of millions of users worldwide, they command tremendous power. These Internet firms are important actors in the information-industrial complex (Powers and Jablonski 2015) that entrenches U.S. economic, political, and national security interests globally through the Internet. The anticounterfeiting regime, given its goal of extending (largely) U.S.-set rules globally and privileging Western legal and economic preferences, is an element of the information-industrial complex. As such, it is important to consider how the nonbinding agreements—and intermediary-facilitated regulation more generally—fit into broader systems of corporate and state surveillance and regulation on the Internet.

In addition to reflecting upon these broader issues, it is important to think about how the shortcomings of informal enforcement agreements can be addressed given the problems identified in this book. Corporate transparency is the most promising area in which to begin reform, because macrointermediaries can strengthen this aspect of their enforcement efforts without involvement from the state or rights holders, given sufficient pressure from their users. The second area involves strengthening and formalizing the protection of digital rights. Brazil's introduction of an Internet bill of rights in 2014, Marco Civil da Internet, provides both an instructive framework for identifying what is possible and a cautionary tale of challenges encountered.

EXTENDING STATES' REGULATORY CAPACITY

The Snowden files, first released in June 2013, provide important context to understanding the wider dynamics that are evolving between U.S.-based intermediaries and the U.S. government, of which the type examined in this book is only one example. While this online trademark-enforcement regime is an example of private actors leveraging state power to pursue their own objectives, the mass surveillance revealed by Snowden demonstrates how the state can and does coercively leverage access to these intermediaries for its own reasons. In this case, the U.S. government strategically extended its regulatory reach by working with (and through) intermediaries. The Snowden files reveal that the National Security Agency, in league with its U.K. counterpart, the Government Communications Headquarters, covertly hacked into and siphoned data from data centers operated by Google and Yahoo under the auspices of the Muscular program (see Greenwald 2014). In other words, the structure of the online world allows for both state and corporate surveillance. Understanding the one allows us to understand the other.

The surveillance programs described in the Snowden files underscore the utility of macrointermediaries to governments keen to further extend their control over flows of information and the online activities of hundreds of millions of people. Intermediaries' mass accumulation of data on their customers, done for their own commercial gain, presents a tempting target for government officials, as does intermediaries' capacity to block flows of information or remove content, as well as monitor their users' activities. Intermediaries' considerable latitude to amend and interpret their terms-of-service agreements is another feature valuable to states. Companies can easily institute new, or change existing, rules governing their services, and few users will bother to read—or will struggle to understand—the updated agreements. A brief consideration of the surveillance economy helps highlight some important overlapping interests between U.S. macrointermediaries and the U.S. government.

Surveillance Economy

The U.S. government has interests in common with companies that have surveillance-intensive business models that allow for the kinds of trademark enforcement described in this book (Schneier 2013). Also included in this group are social media networks, like Facebook and

Twitter. They share with the U.S. government an interest in shaping standards that discourage online anonymity and privacy in order to maximize the availability of personal information online. Because intermediaries' business models tend to rely heavily on advertising, they have a strong commercial interest in maintaining—and expanding—standards that enable them to gather, data-mine, and sell personal information.

Eric Schmidt, executive chairman of Alphabet, Google's parent company, candidly acknowledges his company's interest in accumulating information on its users: "With your permission you give us more information about you, about your friends, and we can improve the quality of our searches. We don't need you to type at all. We know where you are. We know where you've been. We can more or less know what you're thinking about" (Thompson 2010). Schmidt's comment, while admittedly an extreme example of corporate surveillance, demonstrates the importance that Internet firms place on amassing personal data that they can then mine for commercial purposes. Schmidt's new role as an advisor to the U.S. Department of Defense further illustrates the often-hidden relationships between Silicon Valley and the U.S. government's surveillance and defense sectors. U.S. secretary of defense Ash Carter announced in March 2016 that Schmidt would head the new Defense Innovation Advisory Board to advise the Pentagon on technological issues, including mobile apps and cloud technology (Alba 2016).

The National Security Agency, meanwhile, has an interest in amassing personal information from Internet users, including that which intermediaries gather from their users. By working through macrointermediaries, the U.S. government embeds its national security apparatus within Internet firms' platforms and services. These parties also have shared interests, although sometimes differing goals, in shaping policies and standards relating to Internet infrastructure and services. For example, on the issue of data retention and storage, their interests are relatively aligned in favoring broadly conceived standards in relation to the collection, retention, and use of personal data. Such standards facilitate both state and corporate surveillance.

In the case of encryption, however, there is a divergence of interests. The NSA, along with the Government Communications Headquarters, worked strategically for years to weaken encryption standards in order to facilitate their ability to siphon information from all corners of the Internet. In part, this effort involved NSA engineers shaping encryption protocols that would then be adopted by influential standard-setting bodies used by companies, governments, and civil-society agencies worldwide (Harris 2014, 89).[1] Unbeknownst to the standard-setting organizations, however, the NSA deliberately introduced hidden back-doors (Harris 2014, 89). The U.S. government's manipulation of encryption standard-setting processes provides a concrete illustration of the ways that the United States entrenches its legal, economic, and political preferences within the Internet's infrastructure and systems of applications.

Encryption backdoors are valuable to those who want to siphon information secretly. In contrast, firms that offer Internet services and infrastructure must protect their systems, users, and business partners from risks, including malware, that may result from using flawed, weakened code. Following publication of the Snowden files, Google, Yahoo, Twitter, and other firms announced plans to encrypt previously unprotected systems or upgrade their encryption systems (Greenwald 2014).

Territoriality and Geopolitical Borders

The anticounterfeiting regime's practice of using U.S.-based macrointermediaries to set and enforce rules globally highlights the intrinsic tension between political borders (territoriality) and the oft-expressed notion of a borderless Internet. Geopolitical borders did not disappear as the Internet developed. However, for many Internet users, especially cyber-utopians, the Internet's decentralized nature and global reach lessened or temporarily obscured the importance of national borders. States began reasserting their authority in the late 1990s to make rules that apply to the online environment (see Goldsmith and Wu 2006). In relation to the Internet, *territoriality* refers to the practice of state or corporate actors working to reinforce or diminish the effect of geopolitical borders (Powers and Jablonski 2015, 25). Since the late 1990s, the degree of state control over the structure and governance of the Internet and the role of nonstate actors has become a long-running battle. A central concern of many states and civil-society organizations worldwide is the considerable capacity of the U.S. government, working either directly or through industry, to shape rules, norms, and laws that favor its economic and security interests.

States' reassertion of national borders on the Internet disproportionately favors powerful states that can successfully export their preferred policies and norms. This explains how U.S. and European rights holders can set rules governing intellectual property that are exported globally through macrointermediaries and the reach of the U.S. government via the USTR. Given the scope and market share of major U.S.-based intermediaries, the U.S. government and rights holders have a significant advantage in exporting their rules and preferences, as well as in normalizing them as "universal" principles for the online realm. This is because the United States, as the birthplace of the Internet, has a historical advantage over other countries in shaping its development, especially given the commercial dominance of its Internet industry.

U.S.-based Internet firms aggregate U.S. power online because of the long-standing common interests between the U.S. government and its Internet industry (Carr 2015). "The fact that they're using international terms of service" as the basis for the nonbinding anticounterfeiting agreements allows for the "extraterritorial practical application in the United States law," observes Sherwin Siy, deputy legal director for the advocacy group Public Knowledge (interview, Siy 2012). Rights holders also strongly discourage national or company-specific regulatory measures that conflict with or are weaker than U.S. enforcement practices. As a result, rules drafted by U.S. intellectual property actors become de facto global standards that primarily benefit established corporate interests.

Prominent multinational rights holders are not the only ones who favor circumventing national legislative processes in pursuit of their interests. Globally operating Internet firms, too, are interested in ensuring that national laws do not impede or constrain the free flow of information across national borders. Google, for example, strongly lobbies against states' efforts to impose restrictions or regulations, including taxes, on the cross-border flow of data, because any such barriers would make it more difficult and costly for Google to index data and sell search-related advertising (Powers and Jablonski 2015, 85). Similarly, the NSA has an interest in fighting states' efforts to exert sovereign control over information flows within national borders (see Harris 2014).

Like the United States, other countries are attempting to reassert state control on the Internet, often through national laws that emphasize geopolitical boundaries. Concerns about disproportionate U.S. influence over the Internet became more pronounced after the Snowden files detailed the NSA's expansive Internet and telecommunications surveillance programs. Media outlets worldwide revealed how these programs surreptitiously collect data on hundreds of millions of people worldwide using popular email, video chat and messaging, file storage, and social networking applications (see Greenwald 2014). Other NSA surveillance programs targeted the private communications of world leaders, including those of German chancellor Angela Merkel and Brazilian president Dilma Rousseff.

One way to emphasize geopolitical boundaries on the Internet that received considerable attention in the wake of the Snowden files is "data localization" policies. Such policies generally involve confining the collection and processing of data to specific geographies or jurisdictions to enable national governments to exert greater control over how data is collected, stored, and processed, and by whom (Hill 2014). Several countries, including Brazil and Germany, considered introducing these policies following the Snowden revelations in relation to data gathered on their citizens. Depending on how these data localization rules are implemented, they could restrict the ways that globally operating intermediaries would be allowed to collect, use, and store personal data on people within the affected jurisdiction and transfer data outside that area. Such rules could, for example, restrict how marketplace intermediaries operating in the European Union transfer data on their European users outside that jurisdiction.

Proponents of data localization laws argue that these could provide a much-needed impetus to take power away from the U.S. government and big global Internet firms and shift it to elected officials within national legislatures and judicial systems in other nations. At the heart of many debates over territoriality, power, and law on the Internet are concerns over who sets and enforces certain rules on the Internet, whose interests are served, and how this may affect global flows of information. Related to these concerns are questions of jurisdiction: whose law applies and where? Regulating intellectual property and facilitating (albeit somewhat unwillingly) the NSA's surveillance programs are two ways that such Internet firms are reshaping ideas of state sovereignty in the online environment. Another case that has provoked heated debates over the role of macrointermediaries as global regulators and how (and where) state-based rules should be enforced online: Google and the right to be forgotten.

Google and the Right to Be Forgotten

The nonbinding agreements discussed in this book underline the degree to which macrointermediaries are global regulators. Speaking of the significant power of some Internet firms, retired U.S. general Keith Alexander commented that the "big Microsofts and Googles of the world" are "making decisions that have the impact of the kinds of decisions made in the halls of government" (Powers and Jablonski 2015, 195). Much as rights holders want to use macrointermediaries for their own ends, many states want to tap into this regulatory capacity to extend their preferred policies outside their traditional geographical jurisdictions. A case in point: in addition to regulating intellectual property on the Internet, alongside child pornography and extremism, Google has a new role in the European Union: enforcing E.U. data-protection rules in relation to personal data.

The case that led to Google's expanded regulatory responsibilities and generated a debate over state sovereignty and corporate power was Google Spain v. AEPD and Mario Costeja González. The European Court of Justice's May 2014 ruling is commonly known as the "right to be forgotten."

Based on the European Union's 1995 Data Protection Directive, the ruling stated that search intermediaries operating inside the European Union must abide by E.U. data protection rules. The court also ruled that individuals in the European Union have the right to request that search intermediaries remove search results containing personal information that is "inaccurate, inadequate, irrelevant or excessive" (paragraph 92). People seeking to remove personal information must submit an online request to a search intermediary. Under the court's ruling, the search intermediary is responsible for determining on a case-by-case basis whether the information should be removed or if the search results should remain untouched. Although search intermediaries remove specific search results, the information remains on web pages that the search engines indexed, such as those of media outlets. In other words, removed information will not be found using a search engine operating in the European Union but will still be available on the original source.

The ruling applies to all search intermediaries operating in the European Union. Since Google controls 90 percent of the European search market, it is the intermediary most affected by the decision. According to Google's Transparency Report, between the court ruling in May 2014 and May 29, 2016, Google received over 443,501 requests and evaluated just over 1.5 million URLs for removal from its search results. Google removed 43 percent of URLs relating to those requests. Of course, this is a mere fraction of the 558 million complaints Google received in 2015 in regard to copyright infringement. Its Transparency Report gives examples of some of the requests Google receives in relation to the right-to-be-forgotten ruling and those that it has denied. The search company reports that it has removed search results relating to decades-old criminal convictions, quashed convictions, and references to victims of crime. Google declined to remove search results relating to a decades-old criminal conviction of a high-ranking Hungarian government official, and a priest's conviction for possession of child sexual abuse imagery.

In September 2014, a French court, the Paris Tribunal de Grande Instance, ordered Google to implement the right-to-be-forgotten ruling in its global network, not simply its E.U. platforms. The European Union's body of privacy regulators, the Article 29 Working Party, has made the same demand. Isabelle Falque-Pierrotin, who heads the Article 29 group and leads France's Data Protection Authority (Commission nationale de l'informatique et des libertés), argues that the "location of the search user, not the search engine, is the most important" (Scott 2014). The right-to-be-forgotten ruling, Falque-Pierrotin contends, is a "rebalancing of the relationship between the data subjects and the industry representatives and the data controllers" (Halper 2015). As of this writing, Google is, unsurprisingly, resisting this demand. A Google spokesperson says that the company "respectfully disagree[s] with the idea that a national data protection authority can assert global authority to control the content that people can access around the world" (Hern 2015).

The European right-to-be-forgotten ruling and the anticounterfeiting regime raise important questions relating to the nature and territorial scope of intermediary-facilitated regulation on the Internet. In both cases, the state actors involved want to capitalize upon macrointermediaries' global scope in order to apply their preferred regulatory outcome worldwide. The European Union wants to export its conception of digital privacy globally, while the state actors in the anticounterfeiting regime, particularly the United States, are exporting their preferred standards for the protection of intellectual property rights. The practice of state and, increasingly, corporate actors working with major intermediaries to enforce certain laws or rules further problematizes the traditional distinction of territoriality of law and the nonterritoriality of the Internet (Floridi 2014).

The growing practice of intermediary-facilitated regulation also underscores the importance of debates on the authority of states and nonstate actors to make and enforce rules online, particularly at the transnational level, and on the legitimacy of these regulatory efforts. The anticounterfeiting regime and the European Court of Justice's ruling shift regulatory responsibility for interpreting and enforcing state-created rules to intermediaries. In the anticounterfeiting regime and right-to-be-forgotten case, states grant authority to macrointermediaries to act as arbiters to interpret certain rules and take appropriate action, whether it entails the removal of specific content or withdrawal of services from targeted sites. In these cases, powerful corporate actors, not governmental or judicial bodies, judge wrongdoing and sanction violations. However, state actors generally do not provide directives accompanying this responsibility that specify how intermediaries should interpret the nonbinding agreements or the right-to-be-forgotten ruling.

As a result, intermediaries' regulatory efforts on behalf of states—or, indeed, private actors—are often troublingly opaque. Intermediaries publicly provide few details regarding how they determine what content to remove and which services to withdraw, the scale of their enforcement efforts, and the processes they have for reviewing and auditing their regulatory practices. More seriously, there is little evidence that states require intermediaries to institute specific good governance practices in order to ensure effective oversight and accountability. These intermediaries effectively have the power of states or courts to enforce certain rules and standards but without any requirement to adhere to due-process and rule-of-law measures.

A CALL FOR TRANSPARENCY BY STATES

In short, the policy challenges posed by informal regulation and by macrointermediaries are not just arcane commercial issues. To the contrary, they go to the very heart of the political and economic order of a wired and interconnected twenty-first-century world. The questions and problems raised by these informal agreements mirror those we face when dealing with larger issues of ubiquitous state surveillance.

One way to push back against the problems inherent in the nonbinding agreements and, more broadly, in regulatory programs carried out by powerful macrointermediaries generally is to encourage the public to demand transparency. Transparency is often understood as a panacea that can right many wrongs: expose abuses by the powerful, render justice to the injured, and uncover the truth. Given the breadth of this conception, one must ask: transparency by whom, transparency for whom, and transparency for what purposes? The concept is commonly understood as integral to or broadly facilitative of democratic accountability. Traditionally, transparency has been viewed as a principle that can be used to shine a light on the actions of states. As a result, transparency can be understood as a principle that enables the general public to gain information about the operations, structure, and activities of a given entity, such as a government or company (Etzioni 2010, 1).

Although state and industry actors in the anticounterfeiting regime have repeatedly emphasized the importance of transparency, it is a principle sorely lacking in the negotiation and operation of the nonbinding agreements. This is particularly evident in relation to agreements that the U.S. and U.K. governments coordinated. While the European Commission negotiated its marketplace memorandum of understanding in secret, at least the commission published the text on its public website and periodically releases evaluations of enforcement activities carried out under the memorandum. Civil-society organizations have condemned the regime's lack of transparency. Corporate regulation on the Internet "should not be an excuse for invitation-only policy making," remarks Peter Bradwell from the U.K. Open Rights Group in relation to the roundtables that the Department for Culture, Media and Sport hosted (Bradwell 2011a).

David Sohn, of the Center for Democracy and Technology, argues that had consumer and civil-society organizations gotten a "seat at the table when discussing what these programs ought to look like," then there would be a better consideration of the possible consequences of the nonbinding agreements and necessary safeguards (interview, Sohn 2012). Calls for transparency are much less likely to be heard—and much less likely to result in meaningful change—after the rules are already in place.

Given the central role of state actors in facilitating the creation of informal anticounterfeiting agreements, they should bear some responsibility for ensuring that the agreements meet basic standards of good governance and that the public is aware of these private regulatory arrangements. The U.S. and U.K. governments should disclose the full texts of all nonbinding enforcement agreements that they have coordinated in this area. The government agencies involved should also clearly and publicly lay out guidelines to ensure that corporate signatories have appropriate due-process mechanisms.

At the very least, if each government agency publicly disclosed the text of the nonbinding agreements and drafted a set of clear guidelines explaining how measures should be implemented, the public would have a basic understanding of the nature, scope, and operation of these agreements. Individuals who wished to obtain more information on, complain about, or challenge the regulatory activities could contact the government agency responsible for coordinating the agreements. They could also file freedom-of-information requests to attempt to access or petition for further information.[2]

Industry Transparency Reports

With the rise of powerful transnational corporate actors, there is a shift to consider transparency in relation to corporate actors. As large Internet firms are increasingly acting as global regulators for states and other corporate actors, to what degree can, and more importantly, should, intermediaries be transparent in relation to their regulatory efforts on behalf of others?

Corporate transparency is often included as a feature of corporate social responsibility programs. Businesses, typically pressured by scandal or civil-society groups, seek to prove that they are good corporate citizens by addressing negative externalities of their commercial activities, such as environmental damage, or wrongdoing related to business processes, such as violations of labor standards or human rights (see Haufler 2010). As part of their corporate social responsibility programs, companies may disclose information about their commercial practices alongside efforts that show the companies' progress toward adherence to certain standards or compliance with certification measures to ensure deterrence of poor practices or wrongdoing.

Companies use information disclosure in this area to bolster their reputations and signify compliance with state laws, industry standards, or community norms. They also may use transparency reports to obtain a competitive advantage over rivals by claiming that their practices meet or even exceed standards intended to define good corporate practices in certain areas.

Tracking Efforts on Behalf of Governments and Rights Holders

Given the relative deficiency of state transparency in the anticounterfeiting regime, a push for industry transparency is a possible interim step to begin to raise public awareness of informal private regulation on the Internet and to stimulate a much-needed critical discussion of regulatory accountability and legitimacy in this area. Industry reports that disclose intermediaries' release of users' data to third parties or intermediaries' removal of data from the Internet are a relatively new development in the area of transparency reports. In contrast to mandated disclosure requirements, such as government-ordered listings of ingredients in food products, Internet firms voluntarily produce transparency reports relating to Internet data. Moreover, unlike social-responsibility reports that release information about a company's inner workings, Internet transparency reports typically divulge Internet firms' work on behalf of others.

Following revelations in the Snowden files that the National Security Agency targets U.S. Internet firms for their users' information, these companies faced anger from their customers and business partners. To reassure wary users and investors, these firms are increasingly publishing transparency reports that disclose how they facilitate surveillance and enforcement programs for government agencies, especially the NSA. Companies producing transparency reports include Microsoft, Yahoo, Twitter, Facebook, Dropbox, Apple, Tumblr, Reddit, and LinkedIn, as well as the telecommunications companies Verizon and AT&T.[3]

In addition to disclosing their dealings with governmental agencies in relation to users' data, Google and Twitter also track how they remove copyright-infringing content on behalf of copyright owners. Google, which was the first Internet firm to institute a transparency report, in 2010, discloses the greatest amount of information. The company said the goal for the report was to inform people about government requests for user data and content removal in the hope that "greater transparency will lead to less censorship" (Drummond 2010). Google reveals the numbers of requests it receives worldwide from governmental and law enforcement agencies for users' data and the removal of information in relation to court orders or subpoenas. To provide context to these numbers, Google also gives sanitized examples of those requests, as well as related outcomes.

In regard to complaints of copyright infringement, Google tracks the reporting organization (or individual) who submitted the request and the URL of the search result linking to the infringing web page. Google also tracks the number of URLs pertaining to each copyright-infringement complaint, and indicates the number of URLs requested for removal and those where no action was taken. Other companies that produce Internet transparency reports largely emulate Google's report, but they generally disclose less-detailed information than Google and focus on disclosing law enforcement requests for data, particularly relating to national security.

Working Toward Meaningful Transparency

Transparency reports are rapidly becoming an industry standard among major U.S. Internet and telecommunications firms. However, these companies must make significant changes in order for these reports to give a detailed, accurate picture of the firms' regulatory efforts on behalf of governments and corporations worldwide. At present, these reports provide only a limited account of the companies' regulatory activities. In some cases, Internet companies can be restricted in the type of information and amount of detail they are permitted to release publicly.

In contrast, there are few, if any, constraints on Internet firms' disclosure of their regulatory efforts on behalf of rights holders. All intermediaries that remove infringing content or withdraw their services from infringing sites can publicly publish records of their activities. Internet transparency reports are valuable to researchers and activists interested in examining corporate actors' online enforcement activities. Google's report, for example, enables researchers to track trends in the scale and nature of copyright-infringement takedown notices, as well as to identify problematic and abusive reporting practices (see Seng 2014). Civil-society groups, like the Electronic Frontier Foundation, have used Google's report to identify actors who deliberately submit requests to remove lawful content or seek to censor information.

Similar data collection efforts on corporate anticounterfeiting activities would be of significant value to researchers and consumer organizations. Regular disclosures could enable researchers and practitioners to track and suggest correctives in relation to errors, unfair or unduly harsh enforcement practices, and systematic problems in relation to weak due-process measures. If intermediaries also tracked the reasons that specific requests were denied, which Google currently does not do, this information would help researchers study patterns of wrongful or abusive complaints. Moreover, data on intermediaries' policing of copyright and trademark infringement would help develop a much-needed picture of the rapidly expanding brand-protection industry that undertakes monitoring and enforcement for rights holders.

To date, the anticounterfeiting regime has attracted little attention from scholars or the mainstream press, because the agreements are relatively new and there is little publicly available information on them. Sustained public pressure on companies that, like Facebook and Microsoft, publish transparency reports could persuade them to expand their transparency reports to track corporate requests for data. The creation of transparency reports in response to public anger over the NSA's surveillance programs demonstrates that Internet firms will respond to pressure from their customers and business clients if they perceive risks to their reputation or the loss of clients. This is particularly true where the firms have an interest in emphasizing their good management of users' data and, consequently, distancing themselves from controversial or unpopular regulatory efforts. Internet firms also have a pragmatic motive for publishing transparency reports: maintaining users' trust and loyalty. "People won't use technology they don't trust," says Microsoft's general counsel Brad Smith (Smith 2014).

Internet firms currently have few incentives to track enforcement efforts they undertake on behalf of private actors, in contrast to their strong financial and ideological motivations to disclose national security-related requests. This is because that there is no significant public pressure on companies to divulge the regulatory efforts they undertake for rights holders like Nike, Sony, or Disney that is equivalent to the pressure they received following revelations from the Snowden files. However, by pressuring macrointermediaries and the government agencies involved in this regime to disclose their policies and practices, along with enforcement results, we could begin cultivating public awareness of the existence of this global private regulatory regime. Industry disclosure could begin to provide information to establish a baseline of publicly available information.

To raise public awareness of intermediaries' regulatory programs, including anticounterfeiting efforts, it is not enough to produce a transparency report: the audience should be able to decide a course of action if they choose. Readers should be able to compare transparency reports among companies within an industry sector to determine, for example, which company has the most robust data-protection processes. It is a resource-intensive process for people to examine multiple transparency reports to determine firms' relative merits in their protection of users' data and detect changes in their policies or performance. However, even when consumers are aware of firms' policies there may be few opportunities for dissatisfied users to act upon that knowledge or choose viable market alternatives (Etzioni 2010). This is particularly the case regarding companies that dominate their respective markets, like Google, Apple, Twitter, and Facebook, along with the large payment providers Visa, MasterCard, and PayPal.

Focusing public attention on opaque corporate regulatory efforts can be a notable act of transparency in itself. Improved transparency alone, however, cannot address the considerable procedural and normative problems inherent in corporate online anticounterfeiting efforts. Transparency reports should be understood as part of a larger project to shine a much-needed light on state and corporate regulatory activities on the Internet. As discussed earlier, the states involved in this regime are not representing the interests of consumers or, more broadly, the general public.

Given these states' abdication of public interest in this area, greater political engagement by the public is needed. While it beyond the scope of this book to set out fully how this political engagement can best occur, it could involve enrolling competition watchdogs, privacy and human rights commissioners, and agencies responsible for promoting net neutrality, good governance, and openness on the Internet. *Net neutrality* refers to the principle of treating the flow of all data on the Internet equally, rather than privileging or imposing costs on certain types of content or platforms. This project includes fostering and engaging in debates over the right to privacy and the shifting nature of privacy in an era of mass surveillance by both states and corporations. Alongside these efforts, there must be an accompanying push to protect digital rights.

A FUTURE WITH DIGITAL RIGHTS

Brazil's introduction of an Internet bill of rights demonstrates that it is possible to challenge, albeit incrementally, entrenched state-corporate interests on the Internet. Former Brazilian president Dilma Rousseff passed the Marco Civil da Internet into law on April 23, 2014, an "Internet constitution" that is the first of its kind in the world. Rousseff's announcement of the bill strategically coincided with a prestigious conference on Internet issues held in in Sao Paulo, Brazil, by NETmundial, a global, multistakeholder initiative on Internet governance. A key element of Marco Civil was an open consultation process that offers a useful roadmap for other countries to foster awareness of digital-rights issues and incorporate people's concerns. The Brazilian government posted a first draft of the bill on an open-access online platform for an eighteen-month public review. The government then invited interested parties, including businesses, individuals, and nongovernmental organizations, to comment on and suggest amendments to the bill. Nearly two thousand people provided comments on the bill, and the government incorporated some of their suggestions into the next version of the bill.

A member of Access Now, a transnational digital-rights group that campaigned for Marco Civil, describes the consultative process: "It was truly a hybrid and transparent forum: users, civil society organizations, telcos, governmental agencies, all provided comments side-by-side. Each contributor could see the others' contributions, and all cards on the table had to be considered" (Lemos 2014).

Marco Civil covers a wide range of issues, from intermediary liability and net neutrality to privacy and freedom of expression. Article 9 of the law safeguards the principle of net neutrality by obliging intermediaries to treat the flow of data without discrimination, except under certain conditions. In article 3, it also establishes a set of rights and principles that, among other provisions, includes the protection of privacy and personal data. According to activists from the Brazilian civil-society group Institute for Technology and Society, some of whom helped draft the bill, Marco Civil has significantly transformed regulation on the Internet in Brazil. The law has strengthened adherence to due-process mechanisms on the part of the Brazilian judiciary, which formerly had a history of arbitrary, conflicting rulings, and it has standardized the requirement for police to acquire warrants before examining users' data in criminal investigations (Lemos 2015). Importantly, Marco Civil has been useful in limiting the Brazilian government's undue influence over Internet content by clarifying Internet intermediaries' liability for hosting third-party content, which is similar to laws in other countries (Lemos 2015).

Given the breadth and complexity of the issues addressed in Marco Civil, the law's path was neither straightforward nor rapid. Approximately seven years passed from the conception and drafting of the bill and lengthy public consultation before the Brazilian Congress granted approval (Lemos 2015). Following its introduction in 2011, Brazil's Congressional House postponed voting on the bill several times. Marco Civil was, for example, delayed for over two years in the Brazilian Chamber of Deputies as Internet firms lobbied to water down provisions in relation to privacy, among other issues (Moncau and Mizukami 2014). The bill gained political importance when the Snowden files revealed that the NSA monitored the communications of President Rousseff and some of her key aides, which spurred Rousseff to push forward the bill. As with other state efforts to establish laws governing the Internet, the Brazilian government attempted to balance its security interests with advocates' demands for privacy and limited state and corporate surveillance. For digital-rights organizations, a key drawback to

Marco Civil is its mandatory data-retention provision in article 10, which forces Internet service providers to keep logs of users' traffic for particular time frames. In addition, under article 8, the law permits intermediaries to collect users' personal data if the collection can be justified, is not forbidden, and is specified in Internet firms' terms-of-use agreements.

The issue of data localization sparked one of the most heated debates over the bill. Following the revelation that the NSA was monitoring the communications of Brazilian government officials, Rousseff proposed that all Internet firms' data on Brazilians should be held on servers within the country. For the Brazilian government, this data-localization policy would give it greater control over the way in which data on Brazilians could be acquired, stored, and used. However, the proposal sparked an outcry from technologists, civil-advocacy groups, and Internet firms, who stated that such measures would fragment the globally interconnected infra-structure that enables the free flow of information. Such a measure would impose additional costs and requirements on intermediaries that operate internationally, such as Google and Microsoft, and routinely transfer data among data centers located in different political jurisdictions. Civil-society advocates also argued against the proposal, claiming it would not effec-tively protect users' rights and would negatively affect the effective and secure global functioning of the Internet. In the face of this backlash, the Brazilian government dropped the data-localization requirement.

Civil-society groups in Brazil and internationally readily admit that Marco Civil is not perfect. What's important, however, is that it codified protection for digital rights and protection of personal data into law, even in the face of strong opposition, and set the stage for similar laws elsewhere.

CONCLUSION

The state-backed anticounterfeiting regime, based on a series of back-room handshake deals, raises fundamental questions about how intel-lectual property should be policed online and by whom, and about the role of the state. More broadly, the regime and intermediary-facilitated regulation generally elicit debates about who owns our data, opaque state-corporate regulatory partnerships, and what rights we have to control how states and corporations use our digital footprints.

As daunting as the challenges are to reform this anticounterfeiting regulatory regime—and they are considerable—there is hope. The big lesson that Marco Civil provides is that it is possible to implement a law that protects digital rights, including privacy, freedom of expression, data protection, and net neutrality. The Brazilian government and civil-society groups effectively cultivated public awareness of and political engagement with digital rights. The campaign for Marco Civil, along with the groundbreaking protests against the Stop Online Piracy Act and Protect Intellectual Property Act, demonstrate that there is considerable public interest in the topic of regulation on (and of) the Internet. The events also show that even with relatively technical issues like intellectual property, intermediary liability, net neutrality, and digital privacy, it is possible to raise public awareness and encourage meaningful political engagement. Similarly, ongoing protests against the NSA in relation to the secretive surveillance programs demonstrate significant public interest in issues of digital privacy and concern over corporate-state surveillance partnerships. As part of a campaign called "The Day We Fight Back," for example, tens of thousands of people from fifteen countries protested against NSA surveillance on the Internet on February 11, 2014.

The codification of an Internet bill of rights in law shows that the state can be brought back in to regulate on behalf of the public interest. Tim Berners-Lee, who created the World Wide Web, characterized Marco Civil as "a very good example of how governments can play a positive role in advancing web rights and keeping the web open" (Lemos 2015). The challenge, however, is to bring back the state when it and powerful corporations have a shared interest in working informally, secretively, and undemocratically.

Notes

1. SECRET HANDSHAKE DEALS

1. The European Commission, the European Union's executive body, is not quite a state; but because it has legislative and regulatory powers, for the purposes of this book it is considered a state actor.

2. The term *macrointermediaries* is based on the concept of "macrogate-keepers" used to describe companies that facilitate the flow of information on the Internet (see Barzilai-Nahon 2009).

3. This is demonstrated in studies that examine the concentration of owner-ship of these rights (see Office for Harmonization in the Internal Market 2013; U.S. Department of Commerce 2012).

4. All figures are in U.S. dollars unless otherwise noted.

5. *Parallel trade* refers to the distribution of legitimate, noncounterfeited goods from one country or region to another without the authorization of the intellectual-property rights owner. Rights holders generally object to this prac-tice because they may use differential pricing in which an identical product is assigned higher prices in certain countries or regions in order to maximize profits.

6. The term *generic pharmaceuticals* refers to genuine drugs that are no longer covered by a patent and that are identical to—in terms of active medici-nal ingredients—but typically cheaper than, brand-name versions of the same drug. *Counterfeit pharmaceuticals* refers to medication that is deliberately and fraudulently mislabeled and which may have the wrong, or incorrect quantities of, active ingredients. *Substandard medication* refers to flawed medication, which can be genuine or counterfeit medication.

7. Lessig (1999) terms this idea *code is law,* and his ideas have been cri-tiqued, often harshly. For example, Mayer-Schönberger (2008) contends that Lessig misunderstands the dynamism of the relationship of technology and

society, as emphasized by science and technology studies, and that Lessig instead adopts a one-dimensional relationship.

2. INTERNET FIRMS BECOME GLOBAL REGULATORS

1. The U.S. government and critics of WikiLeaks, including some in the mainstream U.S. press like Fox News, treated WikiLeaks differently from "traditional" media outlets. This raises broader questions about who constitutes a "journalist" and the degree to which so-called nontraditional media organizations like WikiLeaks should be protected under the First Amendment in the United States. For a critical examination of these issues, see Benkler (2011).

2. The ACTN was later renamed as the Advisory Committee for Trade Policy and Negotiations.

3. For detailed analyses of GATT negotiations, including intellectual property rights, see Drahos and Braithwaite (2002), Matthews (2002), and Sell (2003).

4. For a detailed history of the development of the Internet from the early 1960s and the roles played by U.S. and European researchers, see Ziewitz and Brown (2013).

5. See chapter 2 of Powers and Jablonski (2015) for a detailed discussion of the emergence of the information-industrial complex and the ways that it intersects with the military-industrial complex.

6. One result of these roundtable meetings was a non-legally binding agreement called the Voluntary Copyright Alert Program, which replaced the controversial three-strikes program prescribed in the Digital Economy Act. The Voluntary Copyright Alert Program, announced in July 2014, largely focuses on warning subscribers involved in unauthorized downloading instead of threatening to withdraw their Internet access.

7. Espinel continues to shape U.S. policy making in relation to intellectual property in her role as president and chief executive officer of the BSA. In October 2014, President Obama appointed Espinel to the Advisory Committee for Trade Policy and Negotiations, discussed earlier in the chapter, which is the main advisory group for the U.S. government on trade issues. Espinel's shift to lobbying illustrates the revolving door between government and the private sector in relation to intellectual-property policy making.

3. REVENUE CHOKEPOINTS

1. The IWF's legal status is complex, and an in-depth discussion of its operation is beyond the scope of this book. For such a discussion, see Laidlaw (2012), who concludes that the IWF describes itself as a nongovernmental self-regulatory body but acts like a public authority.

2. In 2003, following the 9/11 terrorist attacks in the United States, the organization was renamed the Bureau of Alcohol, Tobacco, Firearms, and Explosives and shifted from the Department of the Treasury to the Department of Justice, but it retained the acronym ATF.

3. These documents are not publicly available but are on file with the author.

4. Under many laws protecting copyright, including the U.S. DMCA, breaking a digital lock is prohibited even when the law permits people to exercise their legal rights to access the information (see Haggart 2014). In other words, even if the law permits certain actions, the digital lock, set by copyright owners, supersedes the law.

4. ACCESS CHOKEPOINTS

1. While the terms *Internet* and *World Wide Web* (or *web*) are often used interchangeably, they refer to different entities. The Internet is a series of interconnected computers, and the web, which is a system of hypertext-linked web pages, is one of the services that operates on the Internet.

2. Google makes this statement on its web page describing how content can be removed; see https://support.google.com/legal/troubleshooter/1114905?rd 2#ts=1115655,1282899.

3. In October 2015, Google executives announced that they had created a new company—Alphabet, Inc.—to separate Google (search and advertising businesses, YouTube, mapping, applications, and the Android system) from the company's other business lines, including the Nest smart-home products and more experimental ventures, including robotics and autonomous vehicle ventures (known as Google X).

4. Google's Transparency Report is available at www.google.com /transparencyreport/?hl=en.

5. Other intermediaries produce similar transparency reports based on Google's efforts, but as is discussed in chapter 6, these reports are not as detailed as Google's disclosures and largely do not cover removal of content related to the infringement of intellectual property rights.

6. As of October 2015, Eric Schmidt transitioned from serving as Google's CEO to functioning as the executive chair of Alphabet, Inc., Google's new parent company.

7. The Open Rights Group obtained a copy of the rights holders' proposal through a Freedom of Information Act request and published a link to the document in its analysis of the roundtable discussions (see Bradwell 2012).

8. The Open Rights Group obtained a copy of this nonbinding code of conduct through a Freedom of Information Act request. A link to the document is available in its analysis of the roundtable discussions (see Bradwell 2012).

9. Google also fails to define the threshold for "high" in its 2014 *How Google Fights Piracy,* which explains its policies and enforcement programs (see Google 2014).

10. Jones left GoDaddy in 2012 and made an unsuccessful bid for the Republican nomination in the 2014 gubernatorial election in Arizona.

11. eNom is one of the companies operated by Rightside, a U.S.-based company that operates domain registrars and registries and is listed as a CSIP member.

12. I completed this report while working as a strategic criminal intelligence analyst with Criminal Intelligence Service Canada, a law enforcement organization in Canada focusing on organized crime.

13. LegitScript's certification program is the only one that the National Association of Boards of Pharmacy recognizes outside its VIPPS program (Verified Internet Pharmacy Practice Site), which designates pharmacies operating in compliance with U.S. federal and state laws.

14. That is, unless, as discussed earlier, the domain registrar also provides web-hosting services to the targeted site and can thus seize the site's content.

5. MARKETPLACE CHOKEPOINTS

1. For eBay's fees and services, see http://pages.ebay.com/help/sell/fees.html #if_auction.

2. Yahoo's board of directors considered selling its stake in Alibaba several times, because Yahoo has struggled with serious economic problems for several years. But as of May 2016, Yahoo retains its Alibaba stake.

3. For eBay's "Notice of Claimed Infringement" form, which rights holders use to report infringement to the marketplace, see http://pics.ebay.com/aw/pics /pdf/us/help/community/NOCI1.pdf.

4. For a detailed and highly readable analysis of eBay's legal battles with rights holders in the United States and Europe over complaints of counterfeit goods, see Rimmer (2011).

5. Tiffany appealed the decision to the U.S. Supreme Court, arguing that the case posed important questions about the division of enforcement responsibilities between rights holders and intermediaries. The Supreme Court rejected Tiffany's appeal without comment.

6. The European Economic Area includes the European Union and member states of the European Free Trade Area, Iceland, Liechtenstein, and Norway.

7. For a full list of signatories, see European Commission (2013).

8. For information in English on how to submit a complaint to Taobao, see http://qinquan.taobao.com/?_localeChangeRedirectToken=1.

9. For a list of the IACC's rights holder members, see www.iacc.org/member-companies.html.

6. CHANGING THE ENFORCEMENT PARADIGM

1. For example, the American Assembly, a nonpartisan public affairs forum based at Columbia University, surveyed unauthorized downloading sites and found they were low-cost operations that in some cases relied upon donations (Karaganis 2012).

2. Testimony before Congress on PIPA and SOPA was largely limited to pro-enforcement actors, such as the Motion Picture Association of America and Pfizer, as well as intermediaries that supported aspects of the bills, such as MasterCard and GoDaddy. Google was the only witness invited that largely opposed the bills.

3. E-Commerce Directive article 47 prevents member states from imposing a general obligation on service providers to monitor their platforms, but it allows monitoring in a specific case.

4. For example, an ex-Coach employee filed a class-action lawsuit against the U.S.-based luxury goods firm in 2011, alleging that the company tried to use trademark law to block the legal sale of secondhand Coach products on eBay (see Gina Kim v. Coach, Inc., and Coach Services, Inc., 2011).

5. As discussed in chapter 4, the Open Rights Group obtained the informal agreement drafted by rights holders for search intermediaries and the responses from search intermediaries (see Bradwell 2012). DCMS officials reversed their earlier stance against disclosing the minutes relating to the DCMS roundtable discussions, and they posted minutes from the May 2013 meeting on the departmental website.

6. I received copies of the two informal agreements relating to the payment providers from a colleague, who in turn received them from a trade association.

7. A FUTURE FOR DIGITAL RIGHTS

1. One of these standard-setting bodies was the National Institute of Standards and Technology, a U.S. government agency that sets standards in relation to industrial equipment and scientific instruments. Security expert Bruce Schneier raised an alarm about the NSA's practices in 2007, when he found weaknesses in an algorithm championed by the NSA (see Harris 2014, chap. 4).

2. This strategy would likely have mixed success. Freedom-of-information requests granted by the Department for Culture, Media and Sport yielded minutes of the roundtable meetings and the search intermediaries' code of conduct (as well as rights holders' proposal for search intermediaries). In contrast, such requests were unsuccessful in the United States, where the government claimed that the information would disclose trade or commercial secrets (see Masnick 2014).

3. Links to U.S. firms' transparency reports are available on Google's Transparency Report site, www.google.com/transparencyreport/.

References

AGREEMENTS, BILLS, LEGAL CASES, AND LEGISLATION

Agreement on Trade-Related Aspects of Intellectual Property (TRIPS), opened for signature April 15, 1994 (entered into force January 1, 1995). Agreement Establishing the World Trade Organization, Annex 1C, Legal Instruments—Results of the Uruguay Round. www.wto.org/english/docs_e/legal_e/27-trips .pdf.

Combating Online Infringement and Counterfeits Act (S. 3804, September 20, 2010) 111th Congress, 2009–2010, not enacted. www.govtrack.us/congress /bills/111/s3804.

Digital Economy Act (Pub. L. c. 24, April 8, 2010), Parliament of the United Kingdom. www.legislation.gov.uk/ukpga/2010/24/contents.

Digital Millennium Copyright Act (Pub. L. 105–304, October 28, 1998), 105th Congress, 1997–1998. www.govtrack.us/congress/bills/105/hr2281.

E-Land International Fashion (Shanghai Huangpu District People's Court) Co. v. Zhejiang Taobao Internet Co. (2010). In Chinese only; English summary available at www.sipa.gov.cn/gb/zscq/zscqjel/node160/node202 /userobject1ai9322.html.

Electronic Commerce (EC Directive) Regulation 2002 (Pub. L. No. 2013, August 21, 2002, implemented the European Commission E-Commerce Directive). www.legislation.gov.uk/uksi/2002/2013/pdfs/uksi_20022013_en.pdf.

European Union 1995 Data Protection Directive. Directive 95/46/EC of the European Parliament and of the Council of 24 October 1995 on the Protection of Individuals with Regard to the Processing of Personal Data and on the Free Movement of Such Data. November 23, 1995. http://eur-lex.europa .eu/LexUriServ/LexUriServ.do?uri=CELEX:31995L0046:en:HTML.

European Union Directive on Electronic Commerce on Certain Legal Aspects of Information Society Services, in Particular Electronic Commerce, in the

Internal Market (2000/31/EC, June 8, 2000), European Parliament. http://ec.europa.eu/internal_market/e-commerce/directive/index_en.htm.

Gina Kim v. Coach, Inc., and Coach Services, Inc., Complaint for Damages, U.S. District Court, Western District of Washington (February 8, 2011). www.scribd.com/doc/48651879/Kim-v-Coach-Complaint.

Google Spain, SL, Google, Inc., v. Agencia Española de Protección de Datos (AEPD), Mario Costeja González, Case no. C-131/12, European Court of Justice (May 13, 2014). http://eur-lex.europa.eu/legal-content/EN/TXT/?uri=CELEX:62012CJ0131.

High Performance Computing and Communication Act of 1991 (Pub. L. 102–194, January 3, 1991), 102nd Congress, 1992–1993. www.nitrd.gov/congressional/laws/pl_102–194.aspx.

L'Oréal, SA, v. eBay France, SA (Case RG 07/11365), 2009. Tribunal de Grande Instance, Paris, May 13, 2009.

L'Oréal, SA, and Others v. eBay International, AG, and Others (C-324/09), 2011, EUECJ (July 12, 2011).

Marco Civil de Internet (Brazilian Civil Rights Framework for the Internet) (Pub. L. 12.965, April 22, 2014), Brazilian Senate. English version available at http://infojustice.org/wp-content/uploads/2013/11/Marco-Civil-English-Translation-November-2013.pdf.

Omnibus Trade and Competitiveness Act (Pub. L. 100–418, August 23, 1988), 100th Congress, 1987–1988. www.govtrack.us/congress/bills/100/hr4848/text.

Online Protection and Enforcement of Digital Trade Act (S. 2029, January 17, 2011) 111th Congress, 2009–2010, not enacted; Online Protection and Enforcement of Digital Trade Act (H.R. 3728, January 18, 2012) 112th Congress, 2011–2013, not enacted. www.keepthewebopen.com/assets/pdfs/OPEN.pdf.

Paris Convention for the Protection of Industrial Property, first enacted March 20, 1883, and last amended on September 28, 1979. www.wipo.int/treaties/en/text.jsp?file_id=288514.

Preventing Real Online Threats to Economic Creativity and Theft of Intellectual Property Act (S. 968, May 12, 2011) 112th Congress, 2011–2013, not enacted. www.govtrack.us/congress/bills/112/s968.

Prioritizing Resources and Organization for Intellectual Property Act of 2008 (Pub. L. 110–403, October 13, 2008), 110th Congress, 2007–2009. www.gpo.gov/fdsys/pkg/PLAW-110publ403/pdf/PLAW-110publ403.pdf.

SA Louis Vuitton Malletier v. eBay, Inc., Tribunal de Commerce de Paris, Premiere Chambre B (Paris Commercial Court), Case No 200677799 (June 30, 2008).

Stop Online Piracy Act (H.R. 3261, October 26, 2011), 112th Congress, 2011–2013, not enacted. www.govtrack.us/congress/bills/112/hr3261.

Tiffany, Inc. v. eBay, Inc., 576 F. Supp. 2d 463 (U.S. District Court, Southern District, New York, 2008). www.eff.org/cases/tiffany-v-ebay.

Tiffany, Inc., v. eBay, Inc., 600 F 3d 93 (2d Cir New York, 2010), www.eff.org/cases/tiffany-v-ebay.

Tort Law of the People's Republic of China (PRC Presidential Order No. 21, July 1, 2010). www.wipo.int/wipolex/en/details.jsp?id=6596.

Trans-Pacific Partnership Agreement (negotiations opened November 11, 2011, negotiations concluded February 2016; not in force), Intellectual Property Rights Chapter Consolidated Text, Advanced Intellectual Property Chapter for All 12 Nations with Negotiating Positions. 19th Round of Negotiations at Bandar Seri Begawan, Brunei, August 30, 2013, WikiLeaks release November 13, 2013. https://wikileaks.org/tpp/static/pdf/Wikileaks-secret-TPP-treaty-IP-chapter.pdf.

INTERVIEWS (ALL INTERVIEWS BY AUTHOR)
United States
Bainbridge, Julie, senior brand protection manager, PayPal, telephone interview, July 1, 2012.
Barchiesi, Bob, president, International Anti-Counterfeiting Coalition, in-person interview, digital recording, April 24, 2012, Washington, DC.
Brenner, Brett, Electrical Safety Foundation International (trade association), in-person interview, April 24, 2012, Arlington, VA.
Elings, Roxanne, cochair, Global Trademarks/Brand Management Practice, Greenberg Traurig, in-person interview, digital recording, March 20, 2012, New York City.
Garner, Tracy, program manager, Schneider Electric (rights holder), interview by Skype, May 9, 2012.
Government official, senior policy advisor, Office of the U.S. Intellectual Property Enforcement Coordinator, in-person interview, May 18, 2012, Washington, DC.
Kubic, Tom, CEO, Pharmaceutical Security Institute (trade association), in-person interview by author, May 10, 2012, Arlington, VA.
Lawyer, Hong Kong law firm, in-person interview, May 7, 2012, Washington, DC.
NIPRC Center official, National Intellectual Property Rights Coordination Center, in-person interview, May 16, 2012, Arlington, VA.
Siy, Sherwin, deputy legal director, Public Knowledge, in-person interview, digital recording, May 11, 2012, Washington, DC.
Sohn, David, general counsel, Center for Democracy and Technology, in-person interview, digital recording, May 15, 2012, Washington, DC.
Volpi, Vincent, CEO, PICA Corporation (investigative firm), interview by Skype, June 25, 2012.

United Kingdom
Croker, Damian, CEO, BrandStrike Limited, in-person interview, digital recording, September 25, 2012, London.
Croxon, Siân, partner, DLA Piper, in-person interview, digital recording, September 14, 2012, London.
Director, private security firm, in-person interview, digital recording, September 12, 2012, London.
Gray, Alastair, head of the London branch of Cerberus Investigations, in-person interview, September 4, 2012, London.

Guthrie, Robert, associate, S. J. Berwin, in-person interview, digital recording, October 5, 2012, London.

Hyde-Blake, Gavin, director of research and investigation, Eccora, in-person interview, digital recording, September 19, 2012, London.

Kotecha, Amit, senior mobile and networks manager, Internet Advertising Bureau, in-person interview, digital recording, October 8, 2012, London.

Mee, Duncan, co-owner, Cerberus Investigations, in-person interview, digital recording, September 4, 2012, London.

Newman, Jeremy, partner, Rouse Legal, in-person interview, digital recording, September 10, 2012, London.

Orchard, Ruth, director, Anti-Counterfeiting Group, High Wycombe, England, Skype interview, digital recording, September 17, 2012.

Ramm, James, director, Commercial Security International, in-person interview, digital recording, October 10, 2012, London.

Sharp, Kieron, director general, Federation Against Copyright Theft, Middlesex, England, Skype interview, digital recording, October 9, 2012.

Waring, Tim, director, Intelligence Technologies, Suffolk, England, Skype interview, digital recording, October 3, 2012,.

Watson, Allan, director, global operations, Gamble Investigations International, in-person interview, digital recording, September 12, 2012, London.

Winter, Susie, director general, Alliance for Intellectual Property, in-person interview, digital recording, September 12, 2012, London.

Wishart, Bob, head of national operational delivery, Regional Fraud Project, City of London Police, in-person interview, digital recording, September 6, 2012, London.

Wood, David, director of antipiracy, British Recorded Music Industry (BPI), in-person interview, digital recording, September 12, 2012, London.

Canada

Lipkus, David, associate, Kestenberg, Siegal, Lipkus, Toronto, in-person interview, August 10, 2012, Toronto.

WORKS CITED

Ad Networks. 2013. "Best Practices Guidelines for Ad Networks to Address Piracy and Counterfeiting." www.2013ippractices.com/bestpracticesguidelines foradnetworkstoaddresspiracyandcounterfeiting.html.

Alba, Davey. 2016. "Pentagon Taps Eric Schmidt to Make Itself More Google-ish." *Wired,* March 2. www.wired.com/2016/03/ex-google-ceo-eric-schmidt-head-pentagon-innovation-board/.

Alibaba Group. 2014. "Form F-1 Registration Statement for Alibaba Group Holding Limited." Filed with Securities and Exchange Commission on May 6, 2014, Washington, DC. www.sec.gov/Archives/edgar/data/1577552/000119312514184994/d709111df1.htm.

———. 2015. *Alibaba Group 2015 Annual Report.* http://ar.alibabagroup .com/2015/index.html#YearInReview.

———. 2015a. "The Facts about Alibaba Group and IPR." *Alizila,* January 30. www.alizila.com/facts-about-alibaba-group-and-ipr.

Allen, Larry. 2012. "Rooting Out Rogue Merchants I: Online Advertising's Response to Counterfeiting." Presentation by the senior vice president, business development and global platform sales, 24/7 Media, at the International Anti-Counterfeiting Coalition Spring Conference, Grand Hyatt Hotel, Washington, DC, May 2–4.

Alliance for Safe Online Pharmacies. N.d. "What We Do." Accessed January 3, 2016. http://safeonlinerx.com/about-us/what-we-do/. .

———. N.d.a "Our Principles." Accessed May 13, 2016. http://safeonlinerx .com/about-us/our-principles/.

Alphabet. 2016. *Google Annual Report 2015.* www.sec.gov/Archives/edgar /data/1288776/000165204416000012/goog10-k2015.htm.

American Express. 2013. "American Express Merchant Reference Guide U.S." www209.americanexpress.com/merchant/singlevoice/singlevoiceflash/ USEng/pdffiles/MerchantPolicyPDFs/US_%20RefGuide.pdf.

———. 2015. *American Express Company 2015 Annual Report 2015.* https: //materials.proxyvote.com/Approved/025816/20160304/AR_276402 /HTML1/tiles.htm.

Anderson, Nate. 2010. "Senator: Web Censorship Bill a 'Bunker-Busting Cluster Bomb.'" *Wired,* November 20. www.wired.com/2010/11/senator-web-censorship-bill-a-bunker-busting-cluster-bomb/.

Andreas, Peter. 2010. "The Politics of Measuring Illicit Flows and Policy Effectiveness." In *Sex, Drugs, and Body Counts: The Politics of Numbers in Global Crime and Conflict,* edited by Peter Andreas and Kelly M. Greenhill, pp. 23–44. Ithaca, NY: Cornell University Press.

Association of National Advertisers. 2012. "Statement of Best Practices Addressing Online Counterfeiting and Piracy." May 3, 2012. www.ana.net /content/show/id/23417.

Avant, Deborah D., Martha Finnemore, and Susan K. Sell, eds. 2010. *Who Governs the Globe?* Cambridge: Cambridge University Press.

BAE Systems Detica. 2012. "The Six Business Models for Copyright Infringement." June 27. www.prsformusic.com/aboutus/policyandresearch /researchandeconomics/Pages/default.aspx.

Bagchi, Moinak, Murdoch, Sonja, and Jay Scanlan. 2015. "The state of global media spending." McKinsey & Company, www.mckinsey.com/industries /media-and-entertainment/our-insights/the-state-of-global-media-spending

Baney, Libby. 2015. "Cheers! Registries and Registrars Doing the Right Thing by Patients." *CircleID,* December 18. www.circleid.com/posts/20151218 _cheers_registries_and_registrars_doing_the_right_thing_by_patients/.

Barchiesi, Bob. 2011. "Message from the President IACC Portal Program: Letter from Bob." *Get Real,* August 18.

———. 2012. "IACC Payment Processor Portal Training Workshop." Presentation by the president of the IACC at the International Anti-Counterfeiting Coalition Spring Conference, Washington, DC, May 2–4.

Barea, Adam. 2013. "Combating Rogue Online Pharmacies." *Google Public Policy Blog,* June 18. http://googlepublicpolicy.blogspot.ca/2013/06/combating-rogue-online-pharmacies.html.

Barone, Joe. 2012. "Rooting Out Rogue Merchants I: Online Advertising's Response to Counterfeiting." Presentation by the managing director, digital advertising operations, GroupM, at the International Anti-Counterfeiting Coalition Spring Conference, Grand Hyatt Hotel, Washington, DC, May 2–4.

Barzilai-Nahon, Karine. 2009. "Toward a Theory of Network Gatekeeping: A Framework for Exploring Information Control." *Journal of the American Society for Information Science and Technology* 59 (9): 1493–1512.

Bason, Tamlin H. 2012. "IP Czar: Voluntary Industry Agreements Could Be Key to Combatting IP Infringement." *Bloomberg BNA,* May 17. www.bna.com/ip-czar-voluntary-industry/.

Bendrath, Ralf, and Milton Mueller. 2011. "The End of the Net as We Know It? Deep Packet Inspection and Internet Governance." *New Media Society* 13 (7): 1142–1160.

Benkler, Yochai. 2011. "A Free Irresponsible Press: WikiLeaks and the Battle over the Soul of the Networked Fourth Estate." *Harvard Civil Rights–Civil Liberties Law Review* 46:311–397.

———. 2011a. "WikiLeaks and the Protect-IP Act: A New Public-Private Threat to the Internet Commons." *Daedalus* 140 (4): 154–164.

Berkens, Michael. 2011. "Here Is GoDaddy's Statement in Support of the Stop Online Piracy Act House Hearing Tomorrow." *The Domains,* November 15. www.thedomains.com/2011/11/15/here-is-godaddys-statement-in-support-of-the-stop-online-privacy-act-house-hearing-tomorrow/.

Blakeney, Michael. 1995. "Intellectual Property in World Trade." *International Trade Law and Regulation* 1:76–81.

boyd, danah, and Kate Crawford. 2012. "Critical Questions for Big Data: Provocations for a Cultural, Technological and Scholarly Phenomenon." *Information, Communication and Society* 15 (5): 662–679.

Bracha, Oren, and Frank Pasquale. 2008. "Federal Search Commission? Access, Fairness, and Accountability in the Law of Search." *Cornell Law Review* 93:1149–1210.

Bradwell, Peter. 2011. "Government and Private Policing." *Open Rights Group* (blog), December 14. www.openrightsgroup.org/blog/2011/private-copyright-policing-update.

———. 2011a. "Website Blocking Part 1: Two-Tier Policy Making." *Open Rights Group* (blog), November 9. www.openrightsgroup.org/blog/2011/website-blocking-part-1:-two-tier-policy-making.

———. 2012. "The Spirit of 'Transparency' Haunts Copyright Roundtables." *Open Rights Group* (blog), May 3. www.openrightsgroup.org/blog/2012/the-spirit-of-transparency-and-the-copyright-roundtables.

Braithwaite, John. 2005. *Neoliberalism or Regulatory Capitalism.* Regulatory Institutions Network. Occasional Paper 5. Canberra: Australian National University. www.anu.edu.au/fellows/jbraithwaite/pubsbyyear/index.php?p=1.

Braithwaite, John, and Peter Drahos. 2000. *Global Business Regulation.* Cambridge: Cambridge University Press.

Brewer-Hay, Richard. 2008. "UPDATED: eBay Wins Tiffany Court Case." eBay blog, 14 July. http://blog.ebay.com/ebay-wins-tiffany-court-case/.

———. 2008a. "eBay Vows to Fight Following Overreach by LVMH." eBay blog, 30 June. http://blog.ebay.com/ebay-vows-to-fight-following-overreach-by-lvmh/.

———. 2010. "[UPDATED 11/29] Breaking: eBay Victorious in Tiffany Case #ebaynews." eBay blog, 1 April. http://blog.ebay.com/breaking-ebay-victorious-in-tiffany-case-ebaynews/.

Brey, Philip. 2005. "Artifacts as Social Agents." In *Inside the Politics of Technology: Agency and Normativity in the Co-Production of Technology and Society,* edited by H. Harbers, pp. 61–84. Amsterdam: Amsterdam University Press.

Bridy, Annemarie. 2015. "Internet Payment Blockades." *Florida Law Review* 67 (5): 1523–1568.

———. 2015a. "Copyright's Digital Deputies: DMCA-Plus Enforcement by Internet Intermediaries." In *Research Handbook on Electronic Commerce Law,* edited by John A. Rothchild. Cheltenham, U.K.: Edward Elgar, forthcoming. http://ssrn.com/abstract=2628827.

Brodeur, Jean-Paul. 2007. *The Policing Web.* Oxford: Oxford University Press.

Brown, Ian, and Christopher T. Marsden. 2013. *Regulating Code: Good Governance and Better Regulation in the Information Age.* Cambridge, MA: MIT Press.

Brownsword, Roger. 2004. "What the World Needs Now: Techno-Regulation, Human Rights and Human Dignity." In *Global Governance and the Quest for Justice.* Vol. 4: *Human Rights,* edited by Roger Brownsword, 203–234. Oxford: Hart Publishing.

———. 2011. "Lost in Translation: Legality, Regulatory Margins, and Technological Management." *Berkeley Technology Law Journal* 26:1321–1366.

Business Action to Stop Counterfeiting and Piracy. 2009. *Research Report on Consumer Attitudes and Perceptions on Counterfeiting and Piracy.* International Chamber of Commerce. www.iccwbo.org/advocacy-codes-and-rules/bascap/consumer-awareness/consumer-perceptions/.

Büthe, Tim. 2010. "Private Regulation in the Global Economy: A P(Review)." *Business and Politics* 12:1–38.

Cannon, Mike. 2014. "Google Domain Registration Service Will Kill GoDaddy's Business." *TechTimes,* June 25. www.techtimes.com/articles/9146/20140625/google-domain-registration-service-will-kill-godaddys-business.htm.

Cardozo, Nate. 2014. "What Were They Thinking? Microsoft Seizes, Returns Majority of No-IP.com's Business." Electronic Frontier Foundation, July 15. www.eff.org/deeplinks/2014/07/microsoft-and-noip-what-were-they-thinking.

Carr, Madeline. 2012. "The Political History of the Internet: A Theoretical Approach to the Implications for U.S. Power." In *Cyberspaces and Global Affairs,* edited by S. S. Costigan and J. Perry, 173–188. Surrey, U.K.: Ashgate.

———. 2015. "Power Plays in Global Internet Governance." *Millennium: Journal of International Studies* 43 (2): 640–659.

Castle, Stephen, and Douglas Dalby. 2013. "Horse Meat in Food Stirs a Furor in the British Isles." *New York Times,* February 8. www.nytimes

.com/2013/02/09/world/europe/horse-meat-in-food-stirs-furor-in-british-isles.html.

Center for Safe Internet Pharmacies. 2014. "Principles of Participation for Members." www.safemedsonline.org/who-we-are/principles-participation/.

Charman-Anderson, Suw. 2012. "PayPal Forced into Erotica U-Turn." *Forbes,* March 14. www.forbes.com/sites/suwcharmananderson/2012/03/14/paypal-forced-into-erotica-u-turn/.

China, Incitez. 2015. "China Search Engine Market Overview in 2014." China Internet Watch, March 16. www.chinainternetwatch.com/12678/search-engine-market-overview-2014/.

Citron, Danielle. 2008. "Technological Due Process." *Washington University Law Review* 85 (6): 1249–1313.

City of London Police. 2015. "Operation Creative and the Infringing Website List (IWL)." April 20. www.cityoflondon.police.uk/advice-and-support/fraud-and-economic-crime/pipcu/Pages/Operation-creative.aspx.

Clarke, Ronald V. 1997. *Situational Crime Prevention: Successful Case Studies.* Guilderland, NY: Harrow and Heston.

Clifton, Marjorie. 2012. "The Fight to Combat Illegal Online Pharmacies." BiotechNow, August 1. www.biotech-now.org/health/2012/08/the-fight-to-combat-illegal-online-pharmacies.

CNBC. 2014. "Alibaba's Counterfeit Troubles." Interview with Bob Barchiesi, president of the International Anti-Counterfeiting Coalition. August 11. http://video.cnbc.com/gallery/?video=3000301246.

CNN Money. 2015. "GoDaddy Races onto Wall Street: Stock Soars 30% after IPO." April 1. http://money.cnn.com/2015/04/01/investing/godaddy-ipo-tech-danica-patrick/.

Costa, Dioga. 2015. "Hosting Market: GoDaddy Crushes the Competition." Tech.Co, July 22. http://tech.co/hosting-market-godaddy-2015-07.

Cutler, A. Claire, Virginia Haufler, and Tony Porter. 1999. *Private Authority and International Affairs.* Albany: State University of New York Press.

Datta, Amit, Michael Carl Tschantz, and Anupam Datta. 2015. "Automated Experiments on Ad Privacy Settings: A Tale of Opacity, Choice, and Discrimination." *Proceedings on Privacy Enhancing Technologies* 1:92–112.

de Chernatony, Leslie, and Francesca Dall'Olmo Riley. 1998. "Defining a "Brand": Beyond the Literature with Experts' Interpretations." *Journal of Marketing Management* 14:417–443.

de Chernatony, Malcolm McDonald Leslie, and Elaine Wallace. 2011. *Creating Powerful Brands.* Oxford: Butterworth-Beinemann.

Dedrick, Jason, Kenneth L. Kraemer, and Greg Linden. 2009. "Who Profits from Innovation in Global Value Chains?: A Study of the iPod and Notebook PCs." *Industrial and Corporate Change* 19:81–116.

Deibert, Ronald J., John G. Palfrey, Rafal Rohozinski, and Jonathan Zittrain. 2011. *Accessed Contested: Security, Identity, and Resistance in Asian Cyberspace.* Cambridge, MA: Open Net Initiative and MIT Press.

DeNardis, Laura. 2014. *The Global War for Internet Governance.* New Haven, CT: Yale University Press.

Department for Culture, Media and Sport. 2013. "Minutes of the Online Infringement of Copyright Roundtable, 15 May 2013." June 4. www.gov .uk/government/publications/online-infringement-of-copyright-roundtable-minutes-15-may-2013.

Department of Justice. 2011. "Google Forfeits $500 Million Generated by Online Ads and Prescription Drug Sales by Canadian Online Pharmacies." U.S. Department of Justice Press Release, August 24. www.justice.gov/opa /pr/google-forfeits-500-million-generated-online-ads-prescription-drug-sales-canadian-online.

Digital Strategy Consulting. 2013. "Third of UK Brands 'Have No Idea Where Display Ads Appear Online.'" November 22. www.digitalstrategyconsulting .com/intelligence/2013/11/third_of_uk_brands_have_no_idea_where_display _ads_appear_online.php.

Dou, Eva. 2016."Jack Ma Says Fakes 'Better Quality and Better Price Than the Real Names.'" *Washington Post,* June 15, http://blogs.wsj.com/chinarealtime /2016/06/15/jack-ma-says-fakes-better-quality-and-better-price-than-the-real-names/.

Dougherty, Dan. 2011. "Combating Counterfeits: eBay's Global Approach." *Landslide* 4 (2): 1–3.

Drahos, Peter. 1995. "Global Property Rights in Information: The Story of TRIPS at the GATT." *Prometheus* 13:6–19.

———. 2007. "Four Lessons for Developing Countries from the Trade Negotiations over Access to Medicines." *Liverpool Law Review* 28 (1): 11–39.

Drahos, Peter, and John Braithwaite. 2002. *Information Feudalism: Who Owns the Knowledge Economy?* Oxford: Oxford University Press.

Drummond, David. 2010. "Greater Transparency around Government Requests." *Google Official Blog,* April 20. http://googleblog.blogspot.com. au/2010/04/greater-transparency-around-government.html.

eBay. 2013. *eBay Inc., Form 10-K, for the Fiscal Year Ended December 31, 2012* (annual report). https://investors.ebayinc.com/secfiling.cfm?filingID =1065088–13–4&CIK=.

———. 2014. "eBay User Agreement." Last modified August 14. http://pages .ebay.com/help/policies/user-agreement.html.

———. 2015. *2015 Annual Report.* https://investors.ebayinc.com/annuals.cfm.

———. N.d. "Prohibited and Restricted Items—Overview." Accessed July 15, 2015. http://pages.ebay.co.uk/help/policies/items-ov.html.

Eberlein, Burkhard, and Edgar Grande. 2005. "Beyond Deregulation: Transnational Regulatory Regimes and the EU Regulatory State." *Journal of European Public Policy* 12 (1): 89–112.

The Economist. 2010. "Alibaba: China's King of e-Commerce." December 29. www.economist.com/node/17800299/.

Electronic Frontier Foundation. 2015. "Comments of EFF to the USTR 2015 Special 301 Review." Docket number USTR-2014–0025. www.eff.org /document/comments-eff-ustr-2015-special-301-review.

Elkin-Koren, Niva. 2001. "Let the Crawlers Crawl: On Virtual Gatekeepers and the Right to Exclude Indexing." *University of Dayton Law Review* 26:180–209.

Elliott, Martin. 2012. "Rooting Out Rogue Merchants." Presentation by the director of corporate risk management, Visa International, at the International Anti-Counterfeiting Coalition Spring Conference, Grand Hyatt Hotel, Washington, DC, May 2–4.

Ellison, David. 2012. "UK Advertisers Grasping Nettle of Online Brand Protection." News ISBA: The Voice of British Advertisers, August 9. www.isba .org.uk/news/2013/08/09/uk-advertisers-grasping-nettle-of-online-brand-protection.

eMarketer. 2016. "Worldwide Ad Spending Growth Revised Downward." April 21. www.emarketer.com/Article/Worldwide-Ad-Spending-Growth-Revised-Downward/1013858.

Enigmax. 2013. "PayPal Demands Invites to Private BitTorrent Trackers." *TorrentFreak*, January 8. https://torrentfreak.com/paypal-demands-invites-to-private-bittorrent-trackers-130108/.

Erickson, Jim. 2011. "Alibaba.com Unveils New Anti-fraud Plan." Alizila, May 12. www2.alizila.com/alibabacom-unveils-new-anti-fraud-plan.

———. 2012. "U.S. Removes Taobao from 'Notorious' List of Pirate Markets." Alizila, December 14. www2.alizila.com/us-removes-taobao-notorious-list-pirate-markets.

———. 2012a. "Taobao Marketplace to Name and Shame Shady Online Merchants." Alizila, March 8. www.alizila.com/taobao-marketplace-name-and-shame-shady-online-merchants.

Ernesto. 2011. "BitTorrent.com and Archive.org Blacklisted as Pirate Sites by Major Advertiser." *TorrentFreak*, June 10. https://torrentfreak.com/bittorrent-com-and-archive-org-blacklisted-as-pirate-sites-110610/.

———. 2012. "PayPal Bans BitTorrent Friendly VPN Provider." *TorrentFreak*, June 22. https://torrentfreak.com/paypal-bans-bittorrent-friendly-vpn-provider-120622/.

———. 2015. "Google Asked to Remove 558 'Pirate' Links in 2015." *TorrentFreak*, December 30. https://torrentfreak.com/google-asked-remove-558-million-pirate-links-2015/.

———. 2015a. "Google Asked to Remove One Billion 'Pirate' Search Results." *TorrentFreak*, October 29. https://torrentfreak.com/google-asked-to-remove-one-billion-pirate-search-results-151029/.

———. 2016. "PayPal Starts Banning VPN and SmartDNS Services." *TorrentFreak*, February 5. https://torrentfreak.com/paypal-starts-banning-vpn-and-smartdns-services-160205/.

———. 2016a. "Google Asked to Remove 100,000 'Pirate Links' Every Hour." *TorrentFreak*, March 6. https://torrentfreak.com/google-asked-to-remove-100000-pirate-links-every-hour-160306/.

Espinel, Victoria. 2011. "Remarks of Victoria Espinel, White House Intellectual Property Enforcement Coordinator." Marielle Gallo "IP Forum" IPR Enforcement in the Digital Era, Brussels, Belgium, November 22.

———. 2011a. "Testimony of Victoria A. Espinel, Intellectual Property Enforcement Coordinator, Office of Management and Budget." Hearing before the Subcommittee on Intellectual Property, Competition, and the Internet,

Committee on the Judiciary, U.S. House of Representatives, 112th Congress, March 1, 2012. Washington, DC.

———. 2012. "Testimony of Victoria A. Espinel, U.S. Intellectual Property Enforcement Coordinator, Office of Management and Budget." Hearing before the U.S. House of Representatives, Committee on the Judiciary, Subcommittee on Intellectual Property, Competition, and the Internet, September 20, 2012, Washington, DC.

———. 2013. "Coming Together to Combat Online Piracy and Counterfeiting." White House blog, July 15. www.whitehouse.gov/blog/2013/07/15/coming-together-combat-online-piracy-and-counterfeiting.

Etzioni, Amitai. 2010. "Is Transparency the Best Disinfectant?" *Journal of Political Philosophy* 18 (4): 389–404.

European Commission. 2004. "Directive 2004/48/EC of the European Parliament and of the Council on the Enforcement of Intellectual Property Rights—April 29, 2004." *Official Journal of the European Union.* http://eur-lex.europa.eu/legal-content/EN/TXT/?uri=CELEX:32004L0048R%2801%29.

———. 2009. "Communication from the Commission to the Council, the European Parliament and the European Economic and Social Committee: Enhancing the Enforcement of Intellectual Property Rights in the Internal Market." http://eur-lex.europa.eu/legal-content/EN/TXT/?uri=celex:52009DC0467.

———. 2011. "Memorandum of Understanding." http://ec.europa.eu/growth/industry/intellectual-property/enforcement/index_en.htm#Sale.

———. 2012. *A European Consumer Agenda—Boosting Confidence and Growth. Communication from the Commission to the European Parliament, the Council, the Economic and Social Committee and the Regions.* Brussels. http://eur-lex.europa.eu/procedure/EN/201588.

———. 2012a. "Memorandum of Understanding on the Sale of Counterfeit Goods via the Internet—2nd Quarterly Meeting—26 January 2012—Summary." Directorate General Internal Market and Services.

———. 2013. *Report from the Commission to the European Parliament and the Council on the Functioning of the Memorandum of Understanding on the Sale of Counterfeit Goods via the Internet.* Brussels. http://eur-lex.europa.eu/LexUriServ/LexUriServ.do?uri=COM:2013:0209:FIN:EN:PDF.

Ferrante, Michele. 2014. "Online Counterfeit in China: Court Practice and Remedies against Infringing Websites." American Bar Association, Section of Intellectual Property Law, 29th Annual Intellectual Property Law Conference, Arlington, VA, April 2–4, 2014.

Firth, James. 2011. "Live Tweets from Ed Vaizey Round Table on Content Protection and Web Blocking." SRoC: Slightly Right of Centre, December 7. www.sroc.eu/2011/12/live-tweets-from-ed-vaizey-round-table.html.

Fisher, Daniel. 2015. "Visa Moves at the Speed of Money." *Forbes,* June 5. www.forbes.com/sites/danielfisher/2015/05/06/visa-moves-at-the-speed-of-money/.

Floridi, Luciano. 2014. "Right to Be Forgotten Poses More Questions Than Answers." *The Guardian,* November 11. www.theguardian.com/technology/2014/nov/11/right-to-be-forgotten-more-questions-than-answers-google.

Flynn, Sean M. 2010. "Special 301 and Access to Medicine in the Obama Administration." *Intellectual Property Brief* 2 (2): 5–13.

Flynn, Sean M, Baker Brook, Margot Kaminski, and Jimmy Koo. 2012. "The U.S. Proposal for an Intellectual Property Chapter in the Trans-Pacific Partnership Agreement." *American University International Law Review* 28 (1): 105–202.

Franklin, Sarah. 1995. "Science as Culture, Cultures of Science." *Annual Review of Anthropology* 24:163–184.

Franzen, Carl. 2012. "How the Web Killed SOPA and PIPA." *Talking Points Memo,* January 20. http://talkingpointsmemo.com/idealab/how-the-web-killed-sopa-and-pipa.

Gasser, Urs, and Wolfgang Schulz. 2015. *Governance of Online Intermediaries: Observations from a Series of National Case Studies.* Berkman Center for Internet and Society Research Publication Series, Research Publication No. 2015–5. Cambridge, MA: Harvard University. https://cyber.law.harvard.edu/publications/2015/online_intermediaries.

Gentry, J.W. 2001. "How Now Ralph Lauren? The Separation of Brand and Product in a Counterfeit Culture." *Advances in Consumer Research* 28:258–265.

Gesenhues, Amy. 2014. "Yandex Reports 62% Share of Russian Search Market with Q1 2014 Revenue Up 36%." Search Engine Land, April 24. http://searchengineland.com/yandex-reports-36-growth-q1–2014-now-owns-62-share-russian-search-market-189860.

Gillan, Audrey. 2008. "Chinese Tainted Milk Powder Leaves 6,200 Children Ill." *The Guardian,* September 17. www.theguardian.com/world/2008/sep/17/china.

Gioconda Law Group and RogueFinder. 2012. "Study of 'Rogue Websites' Selling Counterfeit Goods." May 15. http://docslide.us/documents/rogue-finder-study.html.

GoDaddy. 2016. "GoDaddy Universal Terms of Service Agreement." Last updated March 28. https://au.godaddy.com/legal-agreements.aspx.

Goldman, Eric. 2012. "Celebrating (?) the Six-Month Anniversary of SOPA's Demise." *Forbes,* July 18. www.forbes.com/sites/ericgoldman/2012/07/18/celebrating-the-six-month-anniversary-of-sopas-demise/.

Goldsmith, Jack, and Tim Wu. 2006. *Who Controls the Internet? Illusions of a Borderless World.* Oxford: Oxford University Press.

Google. 2013. "How Google Fights Piracy." September 10. https://docs.google.com/file/d/0BwxyRPFduTN2dVFqYml5UENUeUE/edit.

———. 2014. "How Google Fights Piracy." October 17. https://drive.google.com/file/d/0BwxyRPFduTN2NmdYdGdJQnFTeTA/view.

———. 2016. "Transparency Report." Last updated March 30. Accessed February 16, 2016. www.google.com/transparencyreport/removals/copyright/search/?q=Tory+Burch.

———. N.d. "Advertising Policies Help." Accessed June 14, 2015. https://support.google.com/adwordspolicy/answer/6015406.

———. N.d.a. "Removal Policies." Accessed June 14, 2015. https://support.google.com/websearch/answer/2744324.

———. N.d.b. "Help for Trademark Owners." Accessed June 14, 2015. https://support.google.com/adwordspolicy/answer/2562124?hl=en-AU.

———. N.d.c. "Removing Content from Google." Accessed June 14, 2015. https://support.google.com/legal/troubleshooter/1114905?hl=en#ts=111565 5%2C1282899.

Government Accountability Office. 2013. *Internet Pharmacies: Federal Agencies and States Face Challenges Combating Rogue Sites, Particularly Those Abroad.* Washington, DC. www.gao.gov/products/GAO-13-560.

Graz, Jean-Christophe, and Andreas Nölke. 2008. "Introduction: Beyond the Fragmented Debate on Transnational Private Governance." In *Transnational Private Governance and Its Limits,* edited by J. C. Graz and A. Nölke, 2–26. New York: Routledge.

Green Sheet. 2005. "Card Companies Agree to Ban Transactions from Online Cigarette Sales." www.greensheet.com/gs_archive.php?issue_number=050401 &story=4.

Greenwald, Glenn. 2014. *No Place to Hide: Edward Snowden, the NSA and the U.S. Surveillance State.* New York: Metropolitan Books.

Guadamuz, Andrés. 2011. *Networks, Complexity and Internet Regulation: Scale-Free Law.* Cheltenham, U.K.: Edward Elgar.

Gupta, Vikaram. 2015. "Fighting Bad Advertising Practices on the Web—2014 Year in Review." Google Inside Adwords, February 3. http://adwords.blogspot.com/2015/02/fighting-bad-advertising-practices-on.html.

Haggart, Blayne. 2014. *Copyfight: The Global Politics of Digital Copyright Reform.* Toronto: University of Toronto Press.

Halbert, Debora. 1997. "Intellectual Property Piracy: The Narrative Construction of Deviance." *International Journal for the Semiotics of Law* 10:55–78.

Halimi, Natalie. 2015. "Pirate Bay Rises from the Ashes (Again): A Stats'-Eye View." *Venture Beat,* February 5. http://venturebeat.com/2015/02/05/pirate-bay-rises-from-the-ashes-again-a-stats-eye-view/.

Hall, Peter A. 1993. "Policy Paradigms, Social Learning, and the State: The Case of Economic Policymaking in Britain." *Comparative Politics* 25 (3): 275–296.

Halper, Mark. 2015. "Isabelle Falque-Pierrotin: Privacy Needs to Be the Default, Not an Option." *Wired,* June 25. www.wired.com/2015/06/isabelle-falque-pierrotin-privacy-needs-default-not-option/.

Harris, Shane. 2014. *@War: The Rise of the Military-Internet Complex.* New York: Houghton Mifflin Harcourt.

Haufler, Virginia. 2010. "Disclosure as Governance: The Extractive Industries Transparency Initiative and Resource Management in the Developing World." *Global Environmental Politics* 10 (3): 53–73.

Healey, Jon. 2013. "A Non-SOPA Broadside Aimed at Online Piracy Hotbeds." *Los Angeles Times,* July 15. http://articles.latimes.com/2013/jul/15/news/la-ol-online-advertising-movie-music-piracy-20130715/2.

Hern, Alex. 2015. "Google Says Non to French Demand to Expand Right to Be Forgotten Worldwide." *The Guardian,* July 30. www.theguardian.com/technology/2015/jul/30/google-rejects-france-expand-right-to-be-forgotten-worldwide.

Hill, Jonah Force. 2014. "The Growth of Data Localization Post-Snowden: Analysis and Recommendations for U.S. Policymakers and Industry Leaders." Presentation to The Hague Institute for Global Justice, Conference on the Future of Cyber Governance, 2014. http://ssrn.com/abstract=2430275.

Holpuch, Andrea. 2015. "Facebook Users Plan Protest against Site's 'Real Name' Policy at Headquarters." *The Guardian,* May 30. www.theguardian.com/technology/2015/may/30/facebook-real-name-policy-protest.

Horten, Monica. 2011. "European Commission Brokers eBay Counterfeit Takedown Agreement." IPtegrity, May 5. www.iptegrity.com/index.php/ipred/640-european-commission-brokers-ebay-counterfeit-takedown-agreement.

Horton, John C. 2015. "Executive Summary of Testimony by John C. Horton, LegitScript President," Stakeholder Perspectives on ICANN: The .Sucks Domain and Essential Steps to Guarantee Trust and Accountability in the Internet's Operation." Hearing before the Subcommittee on Courts, Intellectual Property, and the Internet, Committee on the Judiciary, House of Representatives, 114th Congress, May 13. http://judiciary.house.gov/index.cfm/hearings?Id=7E5AF16E-B1F8-45B8-803B-9E389A9B745E&Statement_id=4CA88248-9DD9-4C6F-A7EC-EB17098C9AFC.

Humphries, Fred. 2013. "Microsoft Applauds Release of Best Practice Guidelines for Ad Networks to Address Piracy and Counterfeiting." *Microsoft on the Issues: The Official Microsoft Blog,* July 13. http://blogs.technet.com/b/microsoft_on_the_issues/archive/2013/07/15/microsoft-applauds-release-of-best-practice-guidelines-for-ad-networks-to-address-piracy-and-counterfeiting.aspx.

Hunt, Jeremy. 2011. "Boldness Be My Friend." Speech to the Royal Television Society Cambridge Convention, Department for Culture, Media and Sport, September 14. www.gov.uk/government/speeches/royal-television-society--2.

Hutchinson, Lee. 2013. "PayPal Freezes $45,000 of Mailpile's Crowdfunded Dollars (Updated)." *Ars Technica,* September 5. http://arstechnica.com/business/2013/09/paypal-freezes-45000-of-mailpiles-crowdfunded-dollars/.

Immigration and Customs Enforcement. 2014. "Operation in Our Sites." May 22. www.ice.gov/doclib/news/library/factsheets/pdf/operation-in-our-sites.pdf.

Intellectual Property Enforcement Coordinator. 2010. *Joint Strategic Plan on Intellectual Property Enforcement.* June. www.whitehouse.gov/omb/intellectualproperty/sir.

———. 2012. *2011 U.S. Intellectual Property Enforcement Coordinator Annual Report on Intellectual Property Enforcement.* Washington, DC. March 20. www.whitehouse.gov/omb/intellectualproperty.

Intellectual Property Office. 2011. *Prevention and Cure: The UK IP Crime Strategy 2011.* www.ipo.gov.uk/ipcrimestrategy2011.pdf.

Interactive Advertising Bureau. 2013. "Quality Assurance Guideline, Version 2.0." July 25. www.iab.net/about_the_iab/recent_press_releases/press_release_archive/press_release/pr-072513.

Interbrand. 2015. "Interbrand Best Global Brands 2015." http://interbrand.com/best-brands/best-global-brands/2015/ranking/.

International Anti-Counterfeiting Coalition. 2011. "The International Anti-Counterfeiting Coalition Developing New Online Tools to Choke Off Money to Rogue Websites." IACC Press Release, September 27. www.iacc.org /announcements/iacc-has-new-tools-to-cut-off-money-to-bad-sites.

———. 2011a. *IACC Special 301 Report Submission*. Report submitted to Office of the United States Trade Representative in relation to 2011 Special 301 Review: Identification of Countries under Section 182 of the Trade Act of 1974: Request for Public Comment. 75 Fed. Reg. 82424–26 (December 30, 2010). February 15. www.iacc.org/advocacy/key-issues.

———. 2012. *Executive Summary, IACC Payment Processor Portal Program: First Year Statistical Review*. Prepared by Kristina Montanaro, IACC associate counsel and director of special programs, for presentation to the U.S. Intellectual Property Enforcement Coordinator. http://docplayer.net /2433238-International-anticounterfeiting-coalition-iacc-payment-processor-portal-program-first-year-statistical-review.html.

———. 2012a. *IACC Special 301 Report Submission*. Report submitted to Office of the United States Trade Representative in relation to 2012 Special 301 Review: Identification of Countries under Section 182 of the Trade Act of 1974: Request for Public Comment. 76 Fed. Reg. 81555–56 (December 28, 2011). February 10. www.iacc.org/advocacy/key-issues.

———. 2012b. "IACC Announces Collaborations with Taobao and DHGate to Fight Counterfeiting." *PR Newswire*, www.prnewswire.com/news-releases /international-anticounterfeiting-coalition-announces-collaborations-with-taobao-dhgate-to-fight-counterfeiting-online-170518046.html.

———. 2013. "IACC and Taobao Marketplace Sign Agreement to Combat Counterfeiting Online." August 15. www.iacc.org/announcements/international-anticounterfeiting-coalition-and-taobao-marketplace-sign-agreement-to-combat-counterfe.

———. N.d. "RogueBlock." Accessed February 16, 2016. www.iacc.org/online-initiatives/rogueblock.

International Federation of the Phonographic Industry. 2011. "PayPal Works with Police and Industry to Tackle Copyright Infringing Websites." IFPI press release, July 21. www.ifpi.org/content/section_news/20110721.html.

International Trademark Association. 2009. "Addressing the Sale of Counterfeits on the Internet." www.inta.org/TrademarkBasics/FactSheets/Pages /Counterfeiting.aspx

Internet Corporation for Assigned Names and Numbers. 2012. ".com Registry-Registrar Agreement." December 1. www.icann.org/resources/pages/appendix-08–2012–12–07-en.

———. 2013. "New gTLD Registry Agreement. Specification 11: Public Interest Commitments." July 2. newgtlds.icann.org/en/applicants/agb/agreement-approved-02jul13-en.pdf.

Interpol. 2013. "International Operation Targets Online Sale of Illicit Medicines." Interpol Media release, June 27. www.europol.europa.eu/latest_news /international-operation-targets-online-sale-illicit-medicines-europol-supported-campaign.

———. 2015. "Interpol-Coordinated Operation Strikes at Organized Crime with Seizure of 20 Million Illicit Medicines." Interpol Media release, June 18. www.interpol.int/News-and-media/News/2015/N2015–082.

Introna, Lucas D., and Helen Nissenbaum. 2000. "Shaping the Web: Why the Politics of Search Engines Matters." *Information Society* 16:69–185.

Jackson, Mark. 2014. "Update: UK ISPs Agree Voluntary Internet Piracy Warning Letters Scheme." *ISPreview,* June 19. www.ispreview.co.uk/index.php/2014/07 /big-uk-isps-agree-voluntary-internet-piracy-warning-letters-scheme.html.

Jaffe, Daniel L. 2012. "Rooting Out Rogue Merchants I: Online Advertising's Response to Counterfeiting." Presentation by the executive vice president, Association of National Advertisers, at the International Anti-Counterfeiting Coalition Spring Conference, Grand Hyatt Hotel, Washington, DC, May 2–4.

Johnson, Travis. 2013. "Request of the United States Patent and Trademark Office for Public Comments: Voluntary Best Practices Study, 78 Fed. Reg. 37210 (June 20, 2013)." Comments Regarding USPTO's Joint Strategic Plan for Intellectual Property Enforcement Voluntary Best Practices Study. International Anti-Counterfeiting Coalition, Washington, DC. www.uspto.gov /ip/officechiefecon/comments_joint_strategic_plan.jsp.

Joint Industry Committee for Web Standards. 2015. "DTSG UK Good Practice Principles." www.jicwebs.org/digital-trading-standards-group-good-practice-principles/good-practice-principles.

Jones, Christine N. 2011. "Statement of Christine N. Jones, Executive Vice-President, General Counsel and Corporate Secretary, the GoDaddy Group, Inc." Hearing on "Promoting Investment and Protecting Commerce Online: Legitimate Sites v. Parasites, Part II." Before the House of Representatives Committee on the Judiciary, Subcommittee on Intellectual Property, Competition and the Internet, April 6, 2011. Washington, DC.

Jordana, Jacint, and David Levi-Faur. 2004. *The Politics of Regulation: Institutions and Regulatory Reforms for the Age of Governance.* Cheltenham, U.K.: Edward Elgar Publishing.

Karaganis, Joe. 2012. "Meganomics: The Future of "Follow-the-Money" Copyright Enforcement." *TorrentFreak,* January 24. https://torrentfreak.com /meganomics-the-future-of-follow-the-money-copyright-enforcement-120124/.

Kidman, Alex. 2011. "Angry Birds CEO Not Angry with Counterfeiters." Gizmodo, November 3. www.gizmodo.com.au/2011/11/angry-birds-ceo-not-angry-with-counterfeiters/.

Kirkpatrick, Linda. 2011. "Testimony of Linda Kirkpatrick, Group Head, Franchise Development/Customer Performance Integrity, MasterCard Worldwide, Hearing on H.R. 3261, the Stop Online Piracy Act." Before the Committee of the Judiciary, U.S. House of Representatives, 112th Congress, November 16, 2011. Washington, DC.

———. 2012. "Rooting Out Rogue Merchants: The IACC Payment Processor Portal Mid-Year Review and Vision for the Future." Presentation by the group head, franchise development and customer compliance, MasterCard, at the International Anti-Counterfeiting Coalition Spring Conference, Grand Hyatt Hotel, Washington, DC, May 2–4.

Kohl, Uta. 2013. "Google: The Rise and Rise of Online Intermediaries in the Governance of the Internet and Beyond (Part 2)." *International Journal of Law and Information Technology* 21 (2): 187–234.

Kolsun, Barbara, Heather McDonald, and Darren Pogoda. 2004. "Panel III: The New Campaign against Counterfeiting and Piracy." *Fordham Intellectual Property, Media and Entertainment Law Journal* 14:955–1003.

Kraemer, Kenneth L., Greg Linden, and Jason Dedrick. 2011. "Who Captures Value in the Apple iPad and iPhone?" Personal Computing Industry Centre. http://pcic.merage.uci.edu/papers.htm

Krasner, Stephen D. 1982. "Structural Causes and Regime Consequences: Regimes as Intervening Variables." *International Organization* 36:185–205.

Kravets, David. 2009. "Bongs, Virginity and Other Stuff You Can't Sell on eBay." *Wired*, February 11. www.wired.com/2009/02/bongs-virginity/.

Laidlaw, Emily. 2012. "The Responsibilities of Free Speech Regulators: An Analysis of the Internet Watch Foundation." *International Journal of Law and Information Technology* 20:312–345.

———. 2015. *Regulating Speech in Cyberspace: Gatekeepers, Human Rights and Corporate Responsibility*. Cambridge: Cambridge University Press.

Lasar, Matthew. 2011. "New Music Industry Plan: Halt Flow of Money to Pirate Music Sites." *Ars Technica*, March 4. http://arstechnica.com/business/2011/03/new-music-industry-plan-halt-flow-of-money-to-pirate-music-sites/.

Latour, Bruno. 2005. *Reassembling the Social: An Introduction to Actor-Network Theory*. Oxford: Oxford University Press.

Leenes, Ronald. 2011. "Framing Techno-Regulation: An Exploration of State and Non-State Regulation by Technology." *Legisprudence* 5:143–169.

LegitScript. 2016. *The Internet Pharmacy Market in 2016: Trends, Challenges, and Opportunities*. Prepared by LegitScript.com for the Center for Safe Internet Pharmacies. https://blog.legitscript.com/2016/01/internet-rx-market-csip-report/.

———. N.d. "Threat Assessment and Enforcement." Accessed May 2, 2015. www.legitscript.com/services/enforcement/.

Lemos, Ronaldo. 2014. "A Bill of Internet Rights for Brazil." Accessed March 16. www.accessnow.org/blog/2014/03/26/a-bill-of-internet-rights-for-brazil.

———. 2015. "Brazil's Internet Law, the Marco Civil, One Year Later." *Net Politics*, June 1. http://blogs.cfr.org/cyber/2015/06/01/brazils-internet-law-the-marco-civil-one-year-later/.

Lessig, Lawrence. 1999. *Code and Other Laws of Cyberspace*. New York: Basic Books.

Levi, Michael. 2010. "Combating the Financing of Terrorism: A History and Assessment of the Control of 'Threat Finance.'" *British Journal of Criminology* 50 (4): 650–669.

Levi-Faur, David. 2013. "The Odyssey of the Regulatory State: From a 'Thin' Monomorphic Concept to a 'Thick' and Polymorphic Concept." *Law and Policy* 35:29–50.

Levine, Yasha. 2014. "Al Gore Says Silicon Valley Is a "Stalker Economy." *Pando*, June 11. https://pando.com/2014/06/11/al-gore-says-silicon-valley-is-a-stalker-economy/.

Liang, Ni. 2014. "Intellectual Property Protection Practices of Alibaba Group under the Internet Platform-Based Business Model." Prepared by Ni Liang, senior director, security department, Alibaba Group, China. World Intellectual Property Organization, Advisory Committee on Enforcement, Ninth Session, February 12. Geneva. www.wipo.int/meetings/en/doc_details.jsp?doc_id=267716.

Lindenbaum, Jeffrey A., and David Ewen. 2012. "Catch Me If You Can: An Analysis of New Enforcement Measures and Proposed Legislation to Combat the Sale of Counterfeit Products on the Internet." *Pace Law Review* 32:567–640.

Liu, He (Lonnie), Kirill Levchenko, Márk Félegyházi, Christian Kreibich, Gregor Maier, Geoffrey M. Voelker, and Stefan Savage. 2011. "On the Effects of Registrar-Level Intervention." In *LEET '11 Proceedings of the 4th USENIX Conference on Large-Scale Exploits and Emergent Threats*. Berkeley, CA: USENIX Association. http://dl.acm.org/citation.cfm?id=1972441.1972448.

Lyon, David. 2014. "Surveillance, Snowden, and Big Data: Capacities, Consequences, Critique." *Big Data and Society,* July:1–13.

MacAskill, Ewan. 2010. "Julian Assange like a High-Tech Terrorist Says Joe Biden." *The Guardian,* December 20. www.theguardian.com/media/2010/dec/19/assange-high-tech-terrorist-biden.

MacCarthy, Mark. 2010. "What Payment Intermediaries Are Doing about Online Liability and Why It Matters." *Berkeley Technology Law Journal* 25:1038–1120.

Mackenzie, Simon. 2010. "Counterfeiting as Corporate Externality: Intellectual Property Crime and Global Insecurity." *Crime Law and Social Change* 54:21–38.

MacKinnon, Rebecca. 2012. *Consent of the Networked: The Worldwide Struggle for Internet Freedom.* New York: Basic Books.

Mac Síthigh, Daíthí. 2013. "The Fragmentation of Intermediary Liability in the UK." *Journal of Intellectual Property Law and Practice* 8:521–531.

Mann, Ronald J., and Seth R. Belzley. 2005. "The Promise of Internet Intermediary Liability." *William and Mary Law Review* 47:239–307.

Manning, Chelsea. 2013. "Bradley Manning's Personal Statement to Court Martial: Full Text." *The Guardian,* March 1. www.theguardian.com/world/2013/mar/01/bradley-manning-wikileaks-statement-full-text.

———. 2014. "The Fog Machine of War." *New York Times,* June 14 www.nytimes.com/2014/06/15/opinion/sunday/chelsea-manning-the-us-militarys-campaign-against-media-freedom.html?_r=2.

Masnick, Mike. 2011. "Class Action Lawsuit Filed against Coach over Bogus Takedowns, Trademark Bullying." *Techdirt* (blog), February 14. www.techdirt.com/articles/20110211/21555413069/class-action-lawsuit-filed-against-coach-over-bogus-takedowns-trademark-bullying.shtml.

———. 2014. "White House Withholds Details of Its Role in 'Voluntary' Agreement between Payment Processors and Copyright Industries." *Techdirt* (blog), February 21. www.techdirt.com/articles/20140220/16152426303

/white-house-withholds-details-its-role-voluntary-agreement-between-payment-processors-copyright-industries.shtml.

MasterCard. 2014. *MasterCard Annual Report 2014.* http://investor.mastercard
.com/investor-relations/financials-and-sec-filings/annual-reports/default
.aspx.

———. N.d. "MasterCard Anti-Piracy Policy." Accessed June 9, 2013. www
.mastercard.com/us/wce/PDF/MasterCard_Anti-Piracy_Policy.pdf.

Matthews, Duncan. 2002. *Globalizing Intellectual Property Rights: The TRIPs Agreements.* New York: Routledge.

Mayer-Schönberger, Viktor. 2008. "Demystifying Lessig." *Wisconsin Law Review* 4:713–746.

McCoy, Damon, Hitesh Dharmdasani, Christian Kreibich, Geoffrey M. Voelker, and Stefan Savage. 2012. "Priceless: The Role of Payments in Abuse-Advertised Goods." In *Proceedings of the 2012 ACM Conference on Computer and Communications Security.* New York: ACM. http://dl.acm.org/citation
.cfm?id=2382285.

McCullagh, Declan. 2012. "Protect IP, SOPA Protests Knock Senate Websites Offline." *C/net,* January 19. www.cnet.com/news/protect-ip-sopa-protests-knock-senate-web-sites-offline/.

McIntyre, T. J. 2010. "Home Office Terrorist Material Report Site—Some Thoughts." IT Law in Ireland, February 9. www.tjmcintyre.com/2010/02
/home-office-terrorist-material.html.

McNamee, Joe. 2011. "The Slide from 'Self-Regulation' to Corporate Censorship." European Digital Rights Initiative. www.edri.org/files/EDRI_selfreg
_final_20110124.pdf.

Mertha, Andrew C. 2007. *The Politics of Piracy: Intellectual Property in Contemporary China.* Ithaca, NY: Cornell University Press.

Millward, Steven. 2013. "By 2016, China Will Have 423 Million E-Commerce Shoppers Spending $457 Billion." *TechinAsia,* February 12. www.techinasia
.com/china-ecommerce-shoppers-in-2016/.

Mitchell, Russ. 2010. "As a CEO, Meg Whitman Has Had Her Ups and Downs." *Bay Citizen,* July 5. https://groups.yahoo.com/neo/groups
/QueerCaliforniaState/conversations/topics/855.

Moncau, Luiz Fernando, and Pedro Nicoletti Mizukami. 2014. "Brazilian Chamber of Deputies Approves Marco Civil Bill." InfoJustice.org, March 25. http://infojustice.org/archives/32527.

Montanaro, Kristina. 2012. "IACC Payment Processor Portal Training Workshop." Presentation by the associate counsel and director of special programs, IACC, at the International Anti-Counterfeiting Coalition Spring Conference, Grand Hyatt Hotel, Washington, DC, May 2–4.

Motion Picture Association. 2012. "Motion Picture Association and Taobao Marketplace Sign Joint Initiative to Address Online Sale of Infringing Content." Motion Picture Association News Release, September 7.

Motion Picture Association of America. 2013. "Understanding the Role of Search in Online Piracy." September 18. www.mpaa.org/?s=Understanding
+the+Role+of+Search+in+Online+Piracy.

Mueller, Milton L. 2010. *Networks and States: The Global Politics of Internet Governance.* Cambridge, MA: MIT Press.

———. 2015. "The IANA Transition and the Role of Governments in Internet Governance." *IP Justice Journal,* September 15. www.ipjustice.org/internet-governance/ip-justice-journal-the-iana-transition-and-the-role-of-governments-in-internet-governance-by-milton-mueller/.

Mueller, Milton, Andreas Kuehn, and Stephanie Michelle Santoso. 2012. "Policing the Network: Using DPI for Copyright Enforcement." *Surveillance and Society* 9 (4): 348–364.

Mügge, Daniel. 2006. Private-Public Puzzles: Inter-firm Competition and Transnational Private Regulation. *New Political Economy* 11 (2): 177–200.

Murray, Andrew. 2011. "Nodes and Gravity in Virtual Space." *Legisprudence* 5:195–221.

Nilson Report. 2015. "Purchase Transactions Worldwide." *Nilson Report* www.nilsonreport.com/publication_chart_and_graphs_archive.php?1=1 &year=2015.

O'Brien, Dick. 2012. "Rooting Out Rogue Merchants I: Online Advertising's Response to Counterfeiting." Presentation by the executive vice president and director of government relations, American Association of Advertising Associations, at the International Anti-Counterfeiting Coalition Spring Conference, Grand Hyatt Hotel, Washington, DC, May 2–4.

Odell, John S., and Susan K. Sell. 2006. "Reframing the Issue: The WTO Coalition on Intellectual Property and Public Health, 2001." In *Negotiating Trade: Developing Countries in the WTO and NAFTA,* edited by J. S. Odell, 85–114. Cambridge: Cambridge University Press.

Office for Harmonization in the Internal Market. 2013. *The European Citizens and Intellectual Property: Perception, Awareness and Behaviour.* Programme of the European Observatory on Infringements of Intellectual Property Rights. https://oami.europa.eu/ohimportal/en/web/observatory/ip_perception.

O'Malley, Pat. 2010. "Simulated Justice: Risk, Money and Telemetric Policing." *British Journal of Criminology* 50:795–807.

O'Reilly, Conor. 2011. "'From Kidnaps to Contagious Diseases': Elite Rescue and the Strategic Expansion of the Transnational Security Consultancy Industry." *International Political Sociology* 5:178–197.

O'Reilly, Tim. 2013. "Open Data and Algorithmic Regulation." In *Beyond Transparency: Open Data and the Future of Civic Innovation,* edited by Brett Goldstein and Lauren Dyson, 3–12. San Francisco, CA: Code for America Press. www.codeforamerica.org/blog/2013/10/14/beyondtransparency _launch/.

Organization for Economic Cooperation and Development. 2011. "OECD Council Recommendations on Principles for Internet Policymaking." December 13. www.oecd.org/internet/ieconomy/49258588.pdf.

———. 2016. *Trade in Counterfeit and Pirate Goods: Mapping the Economic Impact.* Paris: OECD Publishing. www.keepeek.com/Digital-Asset-Management /oecd/governance/trade-in-counterfeit-and-pirated-goods_9789264252653- en#page2

Osawa, Juro. 2014. "Alibaba: A Mix of Amazon, eBay, PayPal with a Dash of Google." *Wall Street Journal,* March 15. www.wsj.com/articles/SB10001424 05270230354620457944047295445o720.

Outdoor Industry Association. 2011. "Court Ruling Helps the North Face Recover Costs of Fighting Rogue Websites." September 8. https://outdoorindustry.org /article/court-ruling-helps-the-north-face-recover-costs-of-fighting-rogue-websites/.

Out-Law. 2014. "Digital Economy Act Copyright Regime Shelved by UK Government." July 24. www.out-law.com/en/articles/2014/july/digital-economy-act-copyright-regime-shelved-by-uk-government/.

Oyama, Katherine. 2011. "Testimony of Katherine Oyama, Copyright Counsel, Google Inc." Hearing on H.R. 3261, the "Stop Online Piracy Act." Before the Committee of the Judiciary, U.S. House of Representatives, 112th Congress, November 16, 2011. Washington, DC.

Pasquale, Frank. 2010. "Beyond Innovation and Competition: The Need for Qualified Transparency in Internet Intermediaries." *Northwestern University Law Review* 104 (10): 105–173.

———. 2015. *Black Box Society: The Secret Algorithms That Control Money and Information.* Cambridge, MA: Harvard University Press.

PayPal. 2015. "PayPal User Agreement." Last modified May 1. www.paypal .com/us/webapps/mpp/ua/useragreement-full#10.

———. 2016. *Annual Report 2015.* February 8. https://investor.paypal-corp. com/secfiling.cfm?filingID=1633917-16-113&CIK=1633917.

PEW Research Center. 2015. "Digital News—Revenue: Fact Sheet." April 29. www.journalism.org/2015/04/29/digital-news-revenue-fact-sheet/.

Piscitello, Dave. 2012. "Thought Paper on Domain Seizures and Takedowns." *ICANN Blog.* www.icann.org/news/blog/thought-paper-on-domain-seizures-and-takedowns.

Powers, Shawn, and Michael Jablonski. 2015. *The Real Cyber War: The Political Economy of Internet Freedom.* Chicago: University of Illinois Press.

Press Association. 2012. "Julian Assange Expresses Surprise over EU WikiLeaks Decision." *The Guardian.* November 27. www.theguardian.com/media /2012/nov/27/julian-assange-eu-wikileaks-decision.

PR Newswire. 2012. "International Anti-Counterfeiting Coalition Announces Collaborations with Taobao, DHgate to Fight Counterfeiting Online." September 20. www.prnewswire.com/news-releases/international-anticounterfeiting-coalition-announces-collaborations-with-taobao-dhgate-to-fight-counterfeiting-online-170518046.html.

———. 2013. "LegitScript Shuts Down 6,700 Rogue Internet Pharmacies." June 28. www.prnewswire.com/news-releases/legitscript-shuts-down-6700-rogue-internet-pharmacies-213544321.html.

Raustiala, Kal, and Christopher Sprigman. 2012. *The Knockoff Economy: How Imitation Sparks Innovation.* Oxford: Oxford University Press.

Reidenberg, Joel R. 1998. "Lex Informatica: The Formulation of Information Policy Rules through Technology." *Texas Law Review* 76:553–593.

Rhodes, Rod A.W. 2012. "Waves of Governance." In *The Oxford Handbook of Governance,* edited by David Levi-Faur, 32–48. Oxford: Oxford University Press.

Ricketson, Sam. 1994. *Intellectual Property: Cases, Materials and Commentary*. Sydney: Butterworths.

Rimmer, Matthew. 2011. "'Breakfast at Tiffany's': eBay Inc., Trade Mark Law and Counterfeiting." *Journal of Law, Information and Science* 21:128–166.

Rothacher, Albrecht. 2004. *Corporate Cultures and Global Brands*. London: World Scientific Publishing.

Rutter, Jason, and Jo Bryce. 2008. "The Consumption of Counterfeit Goods: 'Here Be Pirates?'" *Sociology* 42:1146–1164.

Samuels, Julie, and Mitch Stoltz. 2012. "Google's Opaque New Policy Lets Rightsholders Dictate Search Results." Electronic Frontier Foundation, August 10. www.eff.org/deeplinks/2012/08/googles-opaque-new-policy-lets-rightsholders-dictate-search-results.

Sandoval, Greg. 2011. "Lawmakers Ask Advertisers for Web-Piracy Crackdown." *C/net*, October 11. www.cnet.com/news/lawmakers-ask-advertisers-for-web-piracy-crackdown/.

Sarbanes, Paul S. 2006. "Combating Child Pornography by Eliminating Pornographers' Access to the Financial Payment System." Hearing before the Committee on Banking, Housing and Urban Affairs, U.S. Senate, 109th Congress, September 19.

Schmidt, Eric. 2013. "We've Listened—and Here's How We'll Half This Depravity." *Daily Mail*, November 18. www.dailymail.co.uk/news/article-2509044/Google-chief-Eric-Schmidt-explains-block-child-porn.html.

Schneier, Bruce. 2013. "Surveillance as a Business Model." *Schneier on Security* (blog), November 25. www.schneier.com/blog/archives/2013/11/surveillance_as_1.html.

Scott, Mark. 2014. "French Official Campaigns to Make 'Right to Be Forgotten' Global." *New York Times,* December 3. http://bits.blogs.nytimes.com/2014/12/03/french-official-campaigns-to-make-right-to-be-forgotten-global/.

Sell, Susan K. 2003. *Private Power, Public Law: The Globalization of Intellectual Property Rights*. Cambridge: Cambridge University Press.

———. 2010. "The Global IP Upward Ratchet, Anti-Counterfeiting and Piracy Enforcement Efforts: The State of Play." PIJIP Research Paper no. 15. American University Washington College of Law, Washington, DC. http://digitalcommons.wcl.american.edu/research/15/.

———. 2011. "TRIPS Was Never Enough: Vertical Forum Shifting, FTAs, ACTA, and TPP." *Journal of Intellectual Property Law* 18:447–478.

———. 2013. "Revenge of the 'Nerds': Collective Action against Intellectual Property Maximalism in the Global Information Age." *International Studies Review* 15 (1): 67–85.

Seng, Daniel. 2014. "The State of the Discordant Union: An Empirical Analysis of DMCA Takedown Notices." *Virginia Journal of Law and Technology* 18 (3): 370–473.

Sheffner, Benjamin. 2013. "Comments of the Motion Picture Association of America, Inc." Comments Regarding USPTO's Joint Strategic Plan for Intellectual Property Enforcement Voluntary Best Practices Study. USPTO. www

.uspto.gov/learning-and-resources/ip-policy/enforcement/comments-regarding-usptos-joint-strategic-plan.

Singhal, Amit. 2012. "An Update to Our Search Algorithms." *Google Inside Search: The Official Google Search Blog,* October 8. http://insidesearch .blogspot.com/2012/08/an-update-to-our-search-algorithms.html.

Smith, Brad. 2014. "Unfinished Business on Government Surveillance Reform." *Microsoft on the Issues: The Official Microsoft Blog,* June 4. http://blogs .microsoft.com/on-the-issues/2014/06/04/unfinished-business-on-government-surveillance-reform/.

Spelich, John W. 2012. "Comments by Taobao for Special 301 Review (2012 Special 301 Review)." *Tech Law Journal,* February 10. www.techlawjournal .com/topstories/2013/20130920.asp.

Spink, Amanda, Bernard J. Jansen, Chris Blakely, and Sherry Koshman. 2006. "A Study of Results Overlap and Uniqueness among Major Web Search Engines." *Information Processing and Management* 42:1379–1391.

Staake, T., Thiesse, F., and Fleisch E. 2009. "The Emergence of Counterfeit Trade: A Literature Review." *European Journal of Marketing* 43 (3–4): 320–349.

Sterling, Greg. 2015. "Bing Reaches 20 Percent Search Market Share Milestone in US." Search Engine Land, April 16. http://searchengineland.com/bing-reaches-20-percent-search-milestone-in-us-market-218574.

Stuart, Keith. 2013. "Xbox One DRM Restrictions Dropped after Gamer Outcry." *The Guardian,* June 20. www.theguardian.com/technology/2013/jun /19/xbox-one-drm-second-hand-restrictions-abandoned.

Taobao. N.d. "How to Submit an IPR Infringement Complaint." Accessed August 9, 2013. http://qinquan.taobao.com/?_localeChangeRedirectToken=.

Thompson, Derek. 2010. "Google's CEO: 'The Laws Are Written by Lobbyists.'" *The Atlantic,* October 1. www.theatlantic.com/technology/archive /2010/10/googles-ceo-the-laws-are-written-by-lobbyists/63908/.

Timm, Trevor. 2012. "How PIPA and SOPA Violate White House Principles Supporting Free Speech and Innovation." Electronic Frontier Foundation, January 16. www.eff.org/deeplinks/2012/01/how-pipa-and-sopa-violate-white -house-principles-supporting-free-speech.

Tusikov, Natasha. 2006. *Counterfeit Pharmaceuticals in Canada.* Produced for Criminal Intelligence Service Canada. www.publicsafety.gc.ca/lbrr/archives /cn36429-eng.pdf.

Underhill, Geoffrey R. D. 2003. "States, Markets and Governance for Emerging Market Economies: Private Interests, the Public Good and the Legitimacy of the Development Process." *International Affairs* 79:755–781.

Urban, Jennifer M., Joe Karaganis, and Brianna L. Schofield. 2016. *Notice and Takedown in Everyday Practice.* UC Berkeley Public Law Research Paper no. 2755628. Social Science Research Network. http://ssrn.com/abstract=2755628.

U.S. Department of Commerce. 2012. *Intellectual Property and the U.S. Economy: Industries in Focus.* Prepared by the Economics and Statistics Administration and the United States Patent and Trademark Office. www.uspto .gov/news/publications/IP_Report_March_2012.pdf.

van Eijk, Nico. 2012. "Search Engines, the New Bottleneck for Content Access." Amsterdam Law School Legal Studies Research Paper no. 2012–21. Institute for Information Law Research Paper no. 2012–18. http://ssrn.com/abstract =1609850.

Visa. 2013. Visa International Operating Regulations. October 15. https://usa .visa.com/dam/VCOM/download/merchants/visa-international-operating-regulations-main.pdf.

———. 2016. *Annual Report 2015*. February 3. http://investor.visa.com /annual-report-meeting/.

Walker, Kent. 2010. "Making Copyright Work Better Online." *Google Public Policy Blog,* December 2. http://googlepublicpolicy.blogspot.com/2010/12 /making-copyright-work-better-online.html.

———. 2011. "Testimony of Kent Walker, Senior Vice President and General Counsel Google Inc." Hearing on "Promoting Investment and Protecting Commerce Online: Legitimate Sites v. Parasites, Part II." House Judiciary Subcommittee on Intellectual Property, Competition, and the Internet. Washington, DC.

Wang, Helen H. 2010. "How eBay Failed in China." *Forbes,* September 12. www.forbes.com/sites/china/2010/09/12/how-ebay-failed-in-china/.

Watters, Paul A. 2013. "Measuring Online Advertising Transparency in Singapore: An Investigation of Threats to Users." http://dx.doi.org/10.2139/ssrn .2362626.

———. 2014. "The Prevalence of High-Risk and Mainstream Advertisements Targeting Canadians on Rogue Websites." http://dx.doi.org/10.2139/ssrn .2389850.

Whetstone, Rachel. 2007. "Free Expression and Controversial Content on the Web." *Google Official Blog,* November 14. http://googleblog.blogspot.com .au/2007/11/free-expression-and-controversial.html.

———. 2010. "Controversial Content and free Expression on the Web: A Refresher." *Google Official Blog,* April 19. https://googleblog.blogspot .ca/2010/04/controversial-content-and-free.html.

White House. 2012. "Camp David Declaration." Office of the Press Secretary, White House, May 18–19. www.whitehouse.gov/the-press-office/2012/05/19 /camp-david-declaration.

Wishart, Peter. 2014. "Debate over the Intellectual Property Bill." House of Commons Hansard Debates for January 20, 2014. U.K. House of Commons. www.publications.parliament.uk/pa/cm201314/cmhansrd/cm140120 /debtext/140120-0002.htm.

Woo, Elaine Lee Hee. 2010. "Online Auction Sites and Inconsistencies: A Case Study of France, China, and the United States." *American University Intellectual Property Brief* 1:50–57.

Yee, Denise. 2011. "Testimony of Denise Yee, Senior Trademark Counsel, Visa Inc." Targeting Websites Dedicated to Stealing American Intellectual Property, Hearing before the Committee on the Judiciary, United States Senate, 112th Congress, February 16, 2011. Washington, DC.

Zetter, Kim. 2011. "PayPal Freezes Account of Group Raising Money for Bradley Manning." *Wired,* February 24. www.wired.com/2011/02/paypal-manning-freeze/.

Ziewitz, Malte, and Ian Brown. 2013. "A Prehistory of Internet Governance." In *Research Handbook on Governance of the Internet,* edited by Ian Brown, 3–26. Cheltenham, U.K.: Edward Elgar.

Zittrain, Jonathan. 2006. "A History of Online Gatekeeping." *Harvard Journal of Law and Technology* 20 (1): 253–298.

Index

Milton Keynes UK
Ingram Content Group UK Ltd.
UKHW012212080923
428326UK00006B/737